CAN ANIMALS BE PERSONS?

# Can Animals Be Persons?

Mark Rowlands

OXFORD
UNIVERSITY PRESS

Oxford University Press is a department of the University of Oxford. It furthers
the University's objective of excellence in research, scholarship, and education
by publishing worldwide. Oxford is a registered trade mark of Oxford University
Press in the UK and certain other countries.

Published in the United States of America by Oxford University Press
198 Madison Avenue, New York, NY 10016, United States of America.

CIP data is on file at the Library of Congress
ISBN 978-0-19-084603-9

9 8 7 6 5 4 3 2 1

Printed by Sheridan Books, Inc., United States of America

*For Emma*

# Contents

# Preface and Acknowledgments

ANIMALS, CLAUDE LEVI-STRAUSS once suggested, are both good to eat and good to think. I assume he had nonhuman animals in mind, and I shall adopt the common practice of using the word *animal* to refer to the entire swathe of living, non-sprouting, nonhuman forms of life. Some find the idea of categorizing such a large segment of the earth's biota solely in terms of their not being humans to be a little egotistical on the part of humanity. They may well have a point. Moreover, it can be the source of various logical confusions. Descartes once argued that animals could not have immortal souls because if we granted that one species of animal possessed such a thing, we would have to grant souls to all species—the humble sponge was the animal he cited as a *reductio* of this idea. I assume there is no need to point out how ridiculous is this argument. "Animal" does not pick out a natural biological kind—any more than "living things that have been in my kitchen" would pick out such a kind. However, as conceived, logically pernicious, and biologically gerrymandered as it may be, I cannot think of any other label that will get through the sheer amount of work as the word *animal*. Thus, in this book, I shall use *animal* in the way explained above.

I agree with Levi-Strauss: the living, nonhuman and non-sprouting segment of the natural world can be both good to eat and good to think. The former pleasures have long been denied me: essentially by myself—a protracted, occasionally unsuccessful exercise in self-denial. In reality, I have little choice. You write a book or two defending the idea of animal rights, and no one is going to let you forget it, believe me. Thus, I have to console myself with the other use of animals—tools for thinking, *food for thought*. I think it might have been Hugo—canine, co-father, cosmopolitan, world-traveler, someone I was fortunate to know for almost all of his life—who first got me started thinking about this question of animal person-hood. You see, not only was I convinced he was a person, but I was pretty sure he was a better person than I.

There is an inconvenient principle that seems to have sunk its claws into me over the years, one by which my thought has slowly become tainted: all things being equal, brute, lived reality should always trump philosophical theory. Such reality should, at the very least, always be given the *benefit of the doubt*. I spent a lifetime with this dog, Hugo, and I came to know that he is a person—a unified subject of a mental life. I say I *knew* this, but what I mean is that I could not doubt it. Not in my life. My attitude toward him was, as Wittgenstein once put it, an atti-tude toward a *soul*. On the other hand, I see theories of personhood that tell me he cannot be a person. I can only conclude—as a preliminary operating assumption, an assumption that may, of course, ultimately prove to be mistaken—that per-haps, just perhaps, these theories need a little looking at. That is what I have done. I know, I know: the foregoing tenses are all messed up—*is/was/know/knew*. Hugo died when I was writing this book. He now lives on only in memories and dreams. And maybe, just a little, in the book too.

As with all of my books about animals, this is as much as book about humans. Indeed, it may even be more of a book about humans than animals. The four cen-tral pillars of the book are consciousness, rationality, self-awareness, and other-awareness. These, I shall argue, are core constituents of the person: a person is something in which these four features coalesce. The ostensible question is whether animals have each of these features. But discussion of the question, in turn, highlights what each of these things are and what it means for humans to have them.

The title of this book is a riff on an earlier book of mine, also published by OUP-NY a few years ago: *Can Animals Be Moral?* The present title is not entirely adequate. Of course, animals *can* be persons—if they satisfy the appropriate conditions of personhood. The real question is whether any—nonhuman—animals *are* persons. I am going to argue that, in all likelihood, many are. I am enough of a realist to know that, in many circles, this conclusion will not be unduly popular. The depths of my anticipated unpopularity, however, may not be plumbed by the book's cen-tral contention alone. I can imagine even those who might be sympathetic to this contention being displeased with certain other facets of the book. For example, those of you engaged in the scientific study of animal minds—many of you I am proud to call my friends—the last thing you probably want to hear is: "What you need is more Kant!" Who, a few masochists aside, would want to hear that? Nevertheless, it is what it is. If this book is correct, some level of acquaintance with the *Critique of Pure Reason* might be beneficial for anyone engaged in the scientific study of animal minds. Life can be cruel sometimes.

I'm also surprised by the sheer amount of phenomenology that found its way into the final drafts of this book. Perhaps I shouldn't have been surprised. This sort of stuff has been progressively encroaching on my work over the years, and I don't seem to be able to do a damned thing about it. But, more than that, perhaps it is natural and appropriate. Phenomenology is the study of lived experience and the structures of consciousness that make such experience possible. It is very difficult, these days, to doubt that animals have conscious experience. A few decades ago it was easier, I'm told. But now, forget it. The more cognitively sophisticated mental activity becomes, the more people are tempted to deny it of animals. But experience—that's near the bottom of the sophistication scale, or so many think, and so therefore one of the easier things to suppose animals have. Thus, it is natural that a science—and that is how phenomenology presented itself—of lived (lived, not dead) conscious experience should play a significant role in this book.

I would like to thank Kristin Andrews and David DeGrazia, readers for OUP, whose feedback helped make this book much better than it would otherwise have been. The shortcomings that remain are, of course, entirely my fault. An earlier incarnation of the arguments developed in Chapters 6–8 appeared as a target article in the journal *Animal Sentience*. I am grateful to all who responded to this article. I inflicted many of the ideas of this book on students—sufficiently misguided to enroll in a graduate seminar I taught in the spring of 2017 and sufficiently kind to supply some very helpful comments. My thanks to Henry Arrowood, Elizabeth Cantalamessa, Lou Enos, Justin Hill, Dogan Kazakli, Arturo Leyva, John Odito, and Vedant Singh.

My greatest thanks are, as always, to my family. To my wife, Emma. And to my sons, Brenin and Macsen, who are a constant inspiration. It's all over for me, of course, but I am going to enjoy living vicariously through you for a while. No pressure.

CAN ANIMALS BE PERSONS?

# 1

## ANIMALS AS PERSONS

### The Very Idea

The idea that any nonhuman animal (henceforth, adopting a common if contentious practice, "animal") could be a *person* appears—*prima facie*—to be utterly confused. A quick perusal of my *Merriam-Webster* seems to confirm this. It defines persons in three different ways. First, a person is "a character or part in or as if in a play." This definition, I have to say, does not seem obviously relevant to the claims of animals—and I say this with all due deference to an impressive lineage of animal actors, from Rin Tin Tin the dog to Trigger the horse to Tommy the chimp. There will be more about Tommy later. Second, a person is "one of the three modes of being in the Trinitarian Godhead as understood by Christians" or, alternatively, "the unitary personality of Christ that unites the divine and human natures." Again, with respect to the guiding question of this book, this conception of person seems neither here nor there. Third, a person is "a human being." So, that's it then: game over. A person must be one of these three things: a part in a play, an aspect of God, or a human. An animal is none of these three things. Therefore, no animal can be a person. I can stop writing now.

On the other hand, we philosophers are not supposed to slavishly adhere to dictionary diktat. If we did, we would all be out of a job. Think of all the philosophical problems that could be put to bed by teatime. I used to worry about things. For example: What makes something mental? What sorts of things qualify as mental? A misspent youth, perhaps, but there was a time when questions such as this used to vex me. But, perhaps, I need only have consulted my *Merriam-Webster*. Something is *mental*, it tells me, if it is:

a. *of or relating to the mind; specifically: of or relating to the total emotional and intellectual response of an individual to external reality.*

The first clause is, perhaps, not very helpful. But the second has substantial philosophical bite. *Mental* relates to "total emotional and intellectual response." So, the emotions get in as well as the intellect. Descartes was wrong (and Aristotle was right): the mind is not a purely thinking thing. Even better—much better: "response to external reality." So, there is an external reality! The existence of the mind proves it. Kant claimed it was the "scandal of philosophy" that no satisfactory proof of the external world had ever been devised. Too bad the *Merriam-Webster* wasn't around in 1781.[1]

b. *of or relating to intellectual as contrasted with emotional activity.*

Now, I have to admit, I am confused. Didn't (a) claim that emotions were in?

c. *of, relating to, or being intellectual as contrasted with overt physical activity.*

Bugger! Overt physical is out. So much for 4E—embodied, embedded, enacted, and extended—cognition. That's thirty years of my life down the toilet.

d. *occurring or experienced in the mind: inner.*

So, it has to be inner then. In your face, Wittgenstein!

I could go on, of course. In fact, I'd like to go on: I'm having an enormous amount of fun. (I particularly like condition (f) that proves dualism is true.) But I assume the absurdity of thinking we can settle philosophical disputes by appealing to the *Merriam-Webster* is evident to all. The question of whether animals are persons is

---

[1] The *Merriam-Webster*, at this point, is very reminiscent of Sartre's (1943/1957) "ontological proof" of non-mental reality, conducted in Section V of the Introduction to *Being and Nothingness*. Consciousness (mental reality) can exist only as directedness toward things it is not. The existence of consciousness is, therefore, sufficient to prove the existence of non-mental reality. Sartre characterized his position, reasonably enough, as a "radical reversal of idealism." Is this an indication of the radical existentialist/externalist leanings of the *Merriam-Webster*? Probably not: see definition (d).

not one that can be dismissed by simply looking in a dictionary and noting that *person* is defined as "a human being" or as something else animals are not.

Nevertheless, if we cannot dismiss the question simply by appealing to linguistic fiat, perhaps we might instead appeal to common sense? There is something deeply counterintuitive—something that runs profoundly against common sense—to the idea that animals can be persons. Or so I am frequently told. But, actually, I think this assertion of common-sense contrariness is simply false. Common sense is a lot more equivocal than one might think. In fact, common sense, aided by a little imagination, effortlessly distinguishes between the category of human being and that of the person. This is, to a considerable extent, because of a diet of top-quality science fiction films and TV series with which most of us have grown up. Spock is not human, but he is certainly a person. But he's half human, you say. Okay then: Worf is not a human—he is entirely Klingon—but he is still a person. Switching *Stars* from *Trek* to *Wars*: Yoda is not human but is still a person. Jabba the Hutt is a person. Even the supremely annoying (and-in-some-circles-rumored-Sith-lord) Jar Jar Binks is a person. But these figures, if not human, are all at least vaguely *humanoid*, one might reply. You can't be a person unless you are vaguely humanoid. Okay, I shall up the ante a little: *The Secret Life of Pets*. If there were—presumably there are not, but *if* there were—dogs, cats, hamsters, birds, snakes, and so on that had mental lives as portrayed in this film, then we would be hard pushed to deny them the status of persons. The thing is: as far as their mental lives are concerned, they are *just like us*—animated by the same thoughts, dreams, hopes, fears, and foibles as we. And if we are persons, how could they not also be persons? This idea—that whether or not something is a person is a matter of its mental life rather than its physical appearance—is as much a part of common sense as anything captured in the *Merriam-Webster*. We might think of these fictional cases as a kind of *proof of concept*: a demonstration of the *possibility* of persons who are not humans. Once we grant the possibility, the only question that remains is one of actuality. There *might* be nonhuman persons, but are there, *actually*, nonhuman persons? This book will argue that there are. There are, in all likelihood, plenty of them.

The thing about common sense is that it is eminently vulnerable to infection by the (no doubt) insalubrious activities of philosophers. These fictional cases, in fact, merely reinforce a distinction made by seventeenth-century English philosopher John Locke. Locke also distinguished the category of the human being from that of the person. The category of human being is a *biological* category: what makes an individual a human being is the possession of a certain genotype and therefore, typically, the possession also of a resulting phenotype (although Locke, preceding Gregor Mendel by nearly two hundred years, did not put the idea in quite this way). The category of a person, on the other hand, Locke defined (a definition of which, I predict, you will be heartily sick by the end of this book) as: "a thinking intelligent being, that has reason and reflection, and can consider itself the same thinking thing, in different times and places, which it does only by that consciousness which is inseparable from thinking and seems to me to be essential, to it; it being impossible to perceive without perceiving that he does perceive."[2] The category of a human being is a biological one, but the category of a person is a *psychological* one that involves consciousness, thought, intelligence, reason, reflection, and the ability to "consider" oneself the same thinking thing in different times and places. Most humans are also persons in this sense: most, but not all. Some humans with serious and permanent brain damage, for example, would not qualify. And, as we know from *Star Trek*, *Star Wars*, and *The Secret Life of Pets*, not all persons need, *necessarily*, be humans (even if, as a matter of contingent fact, all actual persons *are* humans).

Locke's definition is, as we shall see, far from perfect. I shall revisit it many times during the course of this book, clarifying it, refining it, extending it, and slowly making it more plausible. Refinements aside, the general neo-Lockean conception of the person as a psychological entity provides a guiding assumption of, and an organizing theme for, this book; and the arguments I develop will be developed in the context of this assumption. This will not please everyone. Opposed to Locke, there is a tradition of thinking of persons in bodily rather than psychological terms. According to what is known as *animalism*, for example, each one of us is not a psychological entity but a human animal, an organism of the species *Homo sapiens*.[3] I shall ignore non-psychological conceptions of the person for two reasons. First, animalism—the most influential recent version of the non-psychological conception of persons—is not an account of what persons are in general. It claims that we humans are animals, with the persistence conditions of animals. But animalism is perfectly compatible with the existence of nonhuman persons. If a nonhuman person were to exist, it would be an organism of its particular species—*Pan troglodytes*, *Canis familiaris*, or whatever. Animalists, in general, show no interest in such matters. Second, bodily conceptions of persons, such as animalism, seem to be far less hostile to the idea that animals are persons. Animals, after all, have bodies; and if it is the body rather than attendant psychology that is definitive of a person, there is no reason in principle why animals could not be persons. The primary opposition to the idea that animals are persons is going to derive from psychological conceptions of the person. This may seem odd, given that I employed

---

[2] John Locke (1689/1979), Book 2, Chapter 27, p. 188.
[3] See Eric Olson (1997) and Paul Snowdon (2014) for influential statements of this view.

the psychological conception to ground a *proof of concept*: a demonstration of the *possibility* of persons who are not humans. But possibility is one thing, and actuality quite another. Locke's psychological conception provides an exacting series of requirements that any animal would have to meet in order to qualify as a person. And, historically, the near universal consensus has been that no animal meets these requirements. While the (possible) dogs in *The Secret Life of Pets* may meet the psychological conditions required to be persons, most think that no real (i.e., actual) dog does. The strategy of this book is to assume the least convenient conception of a person available—to assume otherwise would smack of cheating—and then argue that animals *still* qualify as persons. The least convenient available conception of a person is the psychological one. I must admit a certain instinctive fondness for the neo-Lockean, psychological conception of persons. But, in this case at least, my neo-Lockean instincts dovetail nicely with dialectical necessity.[4]

## 2. LEGAL PERSONS

The claim that animals are persons—or, indeed, that anything is a person—is multiply ambiguous. In this section I begin whittling away at the ambiguities with a view to properly identifying the claim I am going to defend. The first source of ambiguity lies in the fact that the notion of a person can be understood in at least three ways: *legal*, *moral*, and *metaphysical*. The first task is to disambiguate these three senses of person.

An individual qualifies as a *legal* person if (and only if) his or her status as such is enshrined in law. Whether this is so is not, necessarily, an entirely principled matter. The law accords no overriding authority to logic or consistency. Rather, whether the law is willing, or unwilling, to recognize an individual as a person is partly, but essentially, dependent on the vicissitudes of social and legal history. As the American jurist Oliver Wendell Holmes Jr. put it, in the opening stanza of his *The Common Law*:

> The life of the law has not been logic; it has been experience. The felt necessities of the time, the prevalent moral and political theories, intuitions of public

---

[4] This strategy contrasts with that of Elisa Aaltola (2008), whose goal is to identify which conception of person is most hospitable to the idea that animals can be persons. This she labels the "interactive" conception of personhood. There is, of course, nothing wrong with Aaltola's project. Basically, her strategy is to argue that there is a way of thinking of persons on which some animals may qualify as such. But my approach is rather different. I shall try to show that even on highly unfavorable conceptions of personhood—rationalistic, individualistic, logocentric, please insert your preferred "ic"—animals can still qualify as persons. The type of philosophy pursued by this book will be what we might think of as *philosophy in the worst-case scenario*. I'll talk more about this in the final chapter.

policy, avowed or unconscious, and even the prejudices which judges share with their fellow-men, have had a good deal more to do than syllogism in determining the rules by which men should be governed. The law embodies the story of a nation's development through many centuries, and it cannot be dealt with as if it contained only the axioms and corollaries of a book of mathematics.[5]

All these factors—felt necessities, prevalent moral and political theories, intuitions of public policy, prejudices—will go into determining who and/or what gets to be counted as a legal person. The results are quite striking. While the paradigm case of a legal person is still, perhaps, the normal (whatever that is) adult human being, you need to be neither human nor even alive to qualify as a legal person. It is not uncommon for US courts to extend personhood rights to non-sentient, non-living entities such as corporations, municipalities, and even ships.[6] On the other hand, entities that are clearly both living and human have often had a harder time demonstrating their credentials for personhood. American legal history is replete with disputes over whether slaves, women, children, and Native Americans could be considered legal persons. The life of the law is, indeed, not logic.[7]

Having eventually—with, it has to be acknowledged, an unseemly amount of foot-dragging—come down in favor of slaves, women, children, and Native Americans, the legal debate has now moved on to animals. The reason these sorts of debates are possible, indeed inevitable, is that the law is never simply what is printed in black and white. Statutes always require interpretation, and their implications may go unrecognized. Consider, for example, the case of Tommy (briefly mentioned on page 1). Tommy is a chimpanzee—and quite a famous one at that: he starred alongside Matthew Broderick in the (1987) film *Project X*. In recent years, Tommy has been forced to live, isolated, in a small shed, in a used car lot in Gloversville, New York. In late 2013, the *Nonhuman Rights Project* filed for a writ of *habeas corpus* on behalf of Tommy. A writ of *habeas corpus* is an ancient legal device whose function is to ensure that all "legal persons" be protected from unjust imprisonment. If granted, therefore, the writ of *habeas corpus* would have established Tommy's status as a legal person. In 2015, however, Justice Karen K. Peters of New York's Third Department Appellate court ruled

---

[5] Oliver Wendell Holmes Jr. (1881), p. 1.

[6] When Mitt Romney said, "Corporations are people, my friend," he presumably intended this statement to be taken quite literally. The law, it seems, is on his side even if the 2012 electorate were not.

[7] Compare Sir Edward Coke, "Reason Is the Life of the Law" (1628) p. 97b. It would appear not. I assume Holmes's opening stanza was an allusion to this.

that chimpanzees cannot be legal persons because they "cannot bear any legal duties, submit to societal responsibilities, or be held legally accountable for their actions." To an outsider at least, this ruling appears breathtaking in its naivety. To be a legal person is, fundamentally, to have certain rights—such as the right against unjustified imprisonment—under the law. The Peters ruling, in effect, limits legal personhood to what we might call *legal agents*—individuals that can bear legal duties, accept legal responsibilities, and be held legally accountable for what they do. This entails that large swathes of the human population are not legal persons—including children, the intellectually impaired, the senile, and so on. Individuals of these categories, on the Peters ruling, would not have the legal rights of persons.

There is a corresponding confusion one sometimes finds in the sphere of morality rather than legality. There is a certain meme to which some seem unusually susceptible—one often captured in the slogan "no rights without responsibilities." This meme confuses moral *agents* and moral *patients*. A moral agent is an individual who understands that she has obligations and what those obligations are and can be held responsible if she fails to live up to them. A moral patient, on the other hand, is an individual who is deserving of moral consideration: an individual whom you should, morally speaking, take into account when you do something that might impinge on her welfare. The claim that a person cannot have rights unless she also has responsibilities is, in effect, the claim that a person cannot be a moral patient unless she is also a moral agent. On this view, we would have no moral obligations to children, the intellectually impaired, the senile, and so on. That's a view. But, psychopaths aside, it is doubtful it has many adherents.

The "no rights without responsibilities" meme—one that seems to animate Peters's ruling—is one that has insinuated itself quite widely into popular consciousness in recent decades. It does not, however, survive a moment's serious scrutiny. Unfortunately, the effects of this untenable idea are still being felt. In two subsequent decisions, Manhattan Supreme Court Justice Barbara Jaffe ruled against *habeas corpus* petitions for other captive apes, Hercules, Leo, and Kiko, as well as a second *habeas corpus* petition for Tommy, largely on the grounds that she was bound by the Peters decision.

## 3. MORAL PERSONS

The defining feature of a moral conception of the person is that it defines a person in moral terms. A straightforward—and rather undemanding—version of this idea would simply define a moral person by analogy with the legal person. That is, on this undemanding conception, a moral person is simply an individual who is worthy of a certain kind of moral consideration or treatment. This simple conception seems unsatisfactory, for it fails to explain *why* an individual would be worthy of this sort of consideration. That an individual is worthy of moral consideration does not seem to be a brute fact about that individual but would, rather, be due to its possession of certain other qualities. A more demanding conception of the moral person would tie moral personhood to the possession of some specific morally relevant, or supposedly morally relevant, features of the person. For example, Tom Beauchamp characterizes a moral person as an individual who (1) is capable of making moral judgments about the rightness and wrongness of actions and (2) possesses motives that can be judged morally.[8] To be a moral person requires having both moral motivations and the capacity for moral judgment.

One important implication of Beauchamp's conception of moral personhood is that it drives a wedge between such personhood and what is known as moral *considerability*: the former is not a necessary condition of the latter. Something is morally considerable if it is worthy of moral consideration. But it is implausible to suppose that moral persons, in this sense, are the only things worthy of moral consideration. Young children, for example, are not moral persons in Beauchamp's sense. But it would be strange—and disturbing—to conclude that children do not merit moral consideration: that, in effect, we have no moral obligations to them.[9] Essentially, Beauchamp's definition equates moral persons with moral *agents*, where a moral agent is something that acts for moral reasons and can be morally assessed—praised or blamed, broadly understood—for what it does. We can define moral persons in this way if we like, but we must then be careful not to think that only moral persons are moral *patients*, where the latter is defined as something that is worthy of moral consideration. Thus, Beauchamp's view also drives a further wedge between the undemanding and the demanding conceptions of the moral person. The former equates moral personhood with moral considerability. The demanding conception, of the form endorsed by Beauchamp, equates moral personhood with moral agency. I shall address these issues no further since this moral sense of personhood is not the subject of this book.

---

[8] Beauchamp (1999).

[9] As we have seen, this, in effect, is the moral analogue of the mistake made by Justice Peters, when she tied legal personhood to the possession of social responsibilities. See Section 2.

## 4. METAPHYSICAL PERSONS

Neither the legal nor the moral sense of personhood is the primary subject of this book. That accolade belongs to what I am going to call the *metaphysical* person. Michael Tooley observes: "It seems advisable to treat the term 'person' as a purely descriptive term, rather than as one whose definition involves moral concepts. For this appears to be the way the term 'person' is ordinarily construed."[10] This advice yields the metaphysical concept of the person. This choice of locution is, perhaps, ill advised: the term *metaphysical* may suggest some kind of arcane topic or inquiry, at odds with scientific investigation. Quite the contrary: I use the term *metaphysical* in its standard philosophical use, meaning, roughly, "pertaining to what something is." Beauchamp, from whom I have co-opted the expression *metaphysical person*, captures the general idea very nicely: "As I draw the distinction, metaphysical personhood is comprised entirely of a set of person-distinguishing psychological properties such as intentionality, self-consciousness, free will, language acquisition, pain reception, and emotion. The metaphysical goal is to identify a set of psychological properties possessed by all and only persons."[11] Beauchamp assumes the properties in question will be psychological, and this is a common assumption (although not mandatory). Which psychological properties they may be—and whether only psychological properties are relevant—is, of course, open to dispute. But, at present, I am concerned only with the general idea of the metaphysical person. An individual qualifies as a metaphysical person if and only if he or she (or it) possesses certain non-moral, non-legal features that confer the status of persons upon them. Crucially, the individual in question will possess these features independently of whether he is accorded the status of a person in law and/or regarded as having a certain, distinctive moral status.[12]

In claiming that my focus will be on the metaphysical sense of the person rather than its moral and legal counterparts, I do not wish to give the impression that there are no interesting connections between the three. The three conceptions are distinct but not unrelated. If we were all to agree that some nonhuman individual— Tommy the chimp, for example—is a person in the metaphysical sense, this would (or could) have important moral implications, implications concerning the kind

---

[10] Tooley (1983), p. 51.

[11] Beauchamp (1999), p. 309.

[12] Of course, whether an individual is a moral or legal person also depends on the possession of certain non-moral, non-legal features. But in this case, such features confer the status of moral or legal person on the individual only in conjunction with moral principles or legal statutes and legal interpretation of those statutes. There is no echo of this reliance in the case of the metaphysical person. My thanks to David DeGrazia for allowing me to clarify this point.

of consideration or treatment he is owed. And, within the constraints identified by Holmes, it may also have important legal ramifications. If widely accepted, the metaphysical status of animals as persons may also, eventually, impact on the legal status of animal as persons, this acceptance becoming, as Holmes puts it, among "the felt necessities, intuitions (avowed or unconscious) or prejudices" that shape our legal conception of animals. The metaphysical status of animals as persons may, therefore, certainly have moral and legal implications. But these implications will be *corollaries* of the fact that animals are persons, rather than *constitutive* of what it is for an animal to be a person. The primary focus of this book is the metaphysical conception of the person. I shall argue that at least some—in all likelihood, many—animals are persons in the metaphysical sense.

## 5. CONDITIONS OF (METAPHYSICAL) PERSONHOOD

The focus may have narrowed to the metaphysical person, rather than its moral and legal counterparts. But there is still much tidying up to do. The category of the metaphysical person is as mottled and messy as one could imagine. There are a variety of ingredients that might go into making an individual a person in the metaphysical sense, and the relative importance of each is, to say the least, not immediately clear. I shall begin with a survey of the literature—but as much of this "literature" is also a survey of the literature, it might be better to think of what I am doing as a meta-survey of the literature.

Daniel Dennett has identified six distinct "themes," each of which has, by someone at some time, been advanced as a necessary, sufficient, or necessary and sufficient condition of personhood: a person is (1) a rational being, (2) a being to which states of consciousness are attributed or to which psychological or intentional predicates are ascribed, (3) a being to which a certain sort of attitude or stance is adopted, (4) a being capable of reciprocating—treating other persons as persons, (5) a being capable of verbal communication, (6) a being that is conscious in some special way—typically, self-conscious.[13]

Thomas White, in developing his case for the personhood of dolphins, lists the following as ingredients or elements of persons. This is a list White has culled from the philosophical literature—including Dennett's contribution—and he does not necessarily endorse it but, rather, regards it as useful for getting a sense of the sorts of features many people have in mind when they think of persons. An individual is a person if it has the properties of (1) being alive, (2) being aware, (3) feeling

---

[13] Dennett (1987a).

positive and negative sensations, (4) having emotions, (5) having a sense of self, (6) being able to control its own behavior, (7) being able to recognize other persons and treat them as such, and (8) having a variety of sophisticated cognitive abilities, such as analytical thinking, learning, or complex problem-solving.[14]

Tom Beauchamp identifies the following list of features that have been thought to confer personhood on an individual. He writes: "Cognitive conditions of metaphysical personhood similar to the following have been promoted by several classical and contemporary writers: (1) self-consciousness (of oneself as existing over time); (2) capacity to act on reasons; (3) capacity to communicate with others by command of a language; (4) capacity to act freely; and (5) rationality."[15]

The lists of Dennett, White, and Beauchamp are themselves compiled on the basis of literature review. Historically, the rationality theme is associated with Kant,[16] Aristotle,[17] and more recently Rawls.[18] Peter Strawson defends the conception of persons as subjects of psychological attribution.[19] The idea of personhood being a matter of adoption of a stance is associated with Sellars,[20] Putnam,[21] and Dennett,[22] among others. The reciprocity condition is one that has been emphasized by Rawls[23] and Strawson,[24] among others. The self-consciousness theme is associated with Sartre,[25] Locke,[26] and Frankfurt,[27] among many others. Some writers will accentuate one feature over all others. For example, Michael Tooley writes: "What properties must something have in order to be a person, i.e., to have a serious right to life? The claim I wish to defend is this: an organism possesses a serious right to life only if it possesses the concept of a self as a continuing subject of experiences and other mental states, and believes that it is itself a continuing entity."[28] Others are more inclusive, willing to allow that several features can be important in the making of a person. As we have seen, Locke tells us that a person is "a thinking intelligent being, that has reason and reflection, and

---

[14] White (2007), p. 156.
[15] Beauchamp (1999), p. 310.
[16] Kant (1781/87).
[17] Aristotle (1999), 1. 13.
[18] Rawls (1971).
[19] Strawson (1959), pp. 101–102.
[20] Sellars (1966).
[21] Putnam (1964).
[22] Dennett (1971).
[23] Rawls (1971).
[24] Strawson (1962).
[25] Sartre (1943/1957).
[26] Locke (1689/1979).
[27] Frankfurt (1971).
[28] Tooley (1972), p. 39.

can consider itself the same thinking thing, in different times and places."[29] For Locke, thought, intelligence, reason, reflection, and self-awareness all seem to be ingredients of the person. Dennett's view is also more inclusive, but he does think that the first three of his conditions are logically related—that is, three variants on the same condition.

There is some degree of overlap between the conditions of personhood compiled by the above authors—overlap both between authors and within the lists compiled by each author. Eliminating this overlap, we would arrive at the following list of conditions of (metaphysical) personhood:

An individual, C, qualifies as a (metaphysical) person if C satisfies:

(1) The *consciousness condition*: C is conscious.
(2) The *cognition condition*: C can engage in cognitive processes such as learning, reasoning, and problem-solving.
(3) The *self-awareness condition*: C is self-conscious or self-aware.
(4) The *other-awareness condition*: C is capable of recognizing other persons as such.

These four conditions are offered as *collectively sufficient* for metaphysical person-hood, and each condition is offered as *individually necessary*. That is: if an individual satisfies all of these conditions, that individual is a person; and unless an individual satisfies each condition, that individual cannot be a person. However, the latter necessity claim is tangential to my concerns in this book, and while I shall assume it for ease of exposition, I am not, in fact, committed to it. My central goal is to establish that many animals do, in fact, satisfy all four conditions and, therefore, qualify as persons.

This list might seem somewhat truncated compared to the others I have considered. And, in reducing the number of person-qualifying conditions, I might be accused of unacceptably stacking the deck in my favor. This appearance is, however, misleading. Given the broad way in which I understand each of these conditions, any truncation is apparent rather than real. To see why, let us consider each condition in turn.

According to the *consciousness condition* a person is a conscious being. An individual is conscious if it is the *subject* of conscious mental states. This means that (a) mental states can legitimately be ascribed to this individual and (b) in virtue of having these mental states, there is *something that it is like* to be this

[29] Locke (1689/1979), p. 188.

individual—something that it is like to experience the world in the way in which this individual does. The individual has or undergoes mental states of certain sorts, and when it has or undergoes these states things *seem* or *feel* a certain way to it.[30] Various sorts of mental states can make things seem or feel to those beings that have them, including feelings, sensations, moods, emotions, and experiences. The *consciousness condition*, therefore, subsumes White's conditions (2)–(4). It also incorporates half of Dennett's condition (2)—although, in this condition, Dennett runs together conscious states with intentional states, and I think it is better to treat these separately.

Of the four conditions of personhood, the consciousness condition is perhaps the easiest for animals to satisfy—or, more accurately, for us to show that animals satisfy. Although not so long ago talk of consciousness in animals was anathema, at least in certain circles, the shackles have been thrown off in recent decades. Not only is the idea that many animals are conscious part of common sense, but there is also an already considerable and still growing body of scientific evidence to suggest that animals are conscious in the sense outlined in the previous paragraph. Accordingly, I shall devote only a single chapter to this issue—Chapter 3.

To satisfy condition (2)—the *cognition condition*—an individual must be able to engage in cognitive processes of certain sorts. Perception is (arguably) a cognitive process, but the standards embodied in the cognition condition are far more exacting than merely perceiving the world. To satisfy this condition, an individual must be able to engage in learning, reasoning, and problem-solving. Each of these is, in turn, a rather broad category. Learning, for example, ranges from simple associative learning to far more impressive intellectual achievements. It is important to set the bar neither too high nor too low. The capacity to derive the Schrodinger wave equation is, presumably, too high. But the capacity to form simple associations is, presumably too low since it would include molluscs, insects, plants, and microbes.

In dealing with this issue, I propose to take the concept of reasoning as key. To engage in reasoning, an individual must have two things. First, it must have the sorts of states that can provide *reasons* for its actions. Second, it must act *for* or *on*

---

[30] This is *not* to say that the mental states seem or feel a certain way. That is a common mistake with potentially serious consequences—all of which are irrelevant to the purposes of this book and are, therefore, relegated to this footnote. Rather, it is to say that *things* (the world, broadly construed to encompass all the objects that make it up) seem or feel a certain way *in virtue of* the having or undergoing of mental states. If someone slides a knife between my ribs, I do not feel the pain. I feel the knife. And I feel the knife through the pain it occasions. My pain is not something I feel but the way I feel the knife. See Rowlands (2001) for a defense of this view.

*the basis of* these states.[31] Minimally, satisfying these two conditions will require the individual to have a *pro-attitude* (an affective state, broadly construed) toward some situation or state of affairs plus a cognitive state about how this situation is to be brought about or realized. Belief and desire are the most familiar iterations of this general scheme. An individual has a reason if it has a desire for—a pro-attitude toward—a situation X, coupled with a belief about how X is to be attained. Thus, in order to satisfy the cognition condition, an individual must have beliefs and desires and must be able to act for, or on the basis of, these belief–desire couplings. Beliefs and desires are not the only examples of cognitive and affective states that can provide reasons. And in some states—emotions, for example—cognitive and affective dimensions that supply reasons may be intertwined rather than being allocated to two distinct states. But belief–desire couplings are the most familiar examples of reason-providing states and so provide a useful point of departure for discussion of cognition in animals. I shall discuss the question of whether animals can have beliefs and desires—the raw materials of reasoning—in Chapter 4.

The best way to attain a desired situation may not be at all obvious. In such circumstances, the belief about how this situation may be achieved is not simply something an individual has but something that it must work out or identify. That is, when an individual desires a certain end, and the means to achieve this end are not immediately obvious, the individual must identify these means. To do this, the individual must engage in a process of instrumental *reasoning*. Instrumental reasoning is means–end reasoning. The cognition condition is intended to incorporate this kind of reasoning. The cognition condition, thus, subsumes Dennett's condition (1) and Beauchamp's conditions (2) and (5). It incorporates White's condition (8) since the processes he cites in this condition are ones that will be involved in instrumental reasoning. It also incorporates Locke's idea that a person is a "*thinking intelligent* being that has *reason* and reflection. . . ." I shall discuss the ways in which, and the extent to which, animals can engage in reasoning—both causal and logical—in Chapter 5.

The *self-awareness condition* claims that to qualify as a person an individual must be conscious or aware of itself. This condition subsumes Dennett's condition (6), White's condition (5), and Beauchamp's condition (1).[32] Suitably developed—as it will be in Chapters 6–9—it also incorporates Locke's idea that any person must be able to "consider itself the same thinking thing in different times and places."

---

[31] I intend the use of *or* here to be exclusive. To act *for* a reason is not, it is generally thought, the same as acting *on the basis of* a reason. What, precisely, this difference is and how it pertains to the issue of rationality will be discussed in later chapters.

[32] I shall assume that sense of self can be explained in terms of self-awareness of the right sort.

The *self-awareness condition* is, as we shall see, likely to be far more problematic than the consciousness and cognition conditions. It is widely thought that animals are not self-aware creatures. Sometimes, the failure of an animal to pass the *mirror self-recognition (MSR) test* is cited as evidence of the animal's inability to think thoughts about itself—and therefore as evidence of a lack of self-awareness.[33] I shall discuss this test at length in Chapter 6. It is also common to think that self-awareness requires *metacognition*: the ability to think thoughts about oneself and one's mental states and processes. There are a variety of reasons that have been taken to show that animals do not have this ability, including (but not restricted to) the MSR test. If animals lack metacognitive abilities, it is argued, then they cannot be self-conscious or self-aware creatures. And if the self-awareness condition is correct, if animals are not self-aware, then they cannot be persons.

So important do I regard this question of self-awareness, and so difficult do I regard the issues it raises, that I shall devote several chapters—Chapters 6–9—to the question of self-awareness in animals and its connection with animal personhood. For now, I shall simply note the general flavor of the arguments I shall develop there. There are, I shall argue, two significantly different forms of self-awareness. While the existence of one of these forms in animals is questionable—this is the form that requires metacognitive abilities—there is another form of self-awareness that animals do possess. Moreover, and crucially, it is this other form of self-consciousness—the sort that animals do possess—that is relevant to the issue of whether animals are persons.

The fourth condition is the *other-awareness condition*. This, I understand as incorporating Dennett's condition (4) and White's condition (7). To satisfy this condition, an individual must be able to recognize other persons as such and act appropriately toward them because of this recognition. Communication, as I shall understand it, falls under this condition. Part of what is involved in recognizing another person as a person is the understanding that it is the sort of thing with which one can communicate—or, at least, toward whom the attempt to communicate would be appropriate. Conversely, recognition of something as a non-person involves the understanding that it is not an appropriate object of one's communicative endeavors. Thus, the other-awareness condition, as I shall understand it, incorporates Beauchamp's condition (3)—the communication condition. It also incorporates Dennett's condition (5), given one proviso. Dennett, curiously, stipulates that the communication involved be *verbal* communication. *Verbal*, in this case, presumably means, "expressed in words." But then, of course, it all

---

[33] *Locus classicus*, Gallup (1970).

depends on what is meant by "words," and there is, I think, little temptation to insist on a narrow interpretation of this.

The issue of metacognition also arises with respect to the other-awareness condition. In this case, however, the mental states that are the objects of one's metacognitive activities are not one's own but someone else's. It may be argued that the key to recognizing other individuals as persons, and treating them as such, lies in the ability to attribute mental states to these others and to predict and understand their behavior on the basis of this attribution. If this is correct, then one cannot satisfy the other-awareness condition unless one has metacognitive abilities: the ability to think thoughts about mental states—in this case, the mental states of others. If the existence of metacognition in animals is dubious, then so too will be the case for their personhood.

I shall also treat this problem with the utmost seriousness. However, here, my argument is going to piggyback on the solution to the issue of self-awareness. Just as there is another type of self-awareness that does not involve metacognition, so also, I shall argue, is there another type of awareness of the personhood of another that does not involve or require metacognition. The latter form of awareness of the other as a person is a consequence of the advertised alternative, non-metacognitive, form of self-awareness that I shall identify and defend in Chapters 6–9. I shall discuss the other-awareness condition in Chapter 10.

## 6. ON SOME OMISSIONS AND APPARENT OMISSIONS

Most of the conditions of personhood cited by Dennett, White, Beauchamp, Tooley, and Locke are covered under my conditions (1)–(4): consciousness, cognition, self-awareness, and other-awareness. However, not all are covered. Sometimes the reason is obvious. There is little need to discuss White's condition (1)—the being alive condition—for, even if one decides it is legitimate,[34] animals clearly meet it. Beauchamp's condition (4) cites the ability to act freely. This is, I think, clearly questionable. If it were to turn out, for example, that hard determinism is true and that no human actions, choices, and decisions were ever free, it would be a non sequitur to conclude from this that there are therefore no persons—and never have been any. It would be far more reasonable to conclude that we humans are persons but not free ones. Beauchamp's condition, I suspect, confuses freedom

---

[34] The condition does, of course, rule out the possibility of robots qualifying as persons, no matter what level of psychological complexity they were to develop. This, in the eyes of many, may render this condition questionable.

and *flexibility*. We may be disinclined to judge that the *Sphex* wasp is a person—because of its rigidly inflexible behavior that is grounded in fixed motor patterns alone.[35] Flexibility, and thus intelligence, of behavioral repertoire may be a necessary condition of being a person. But this is covered by the cognition condition (2)—at least as I shall describe this condition. It is unclear why we would want to make something (metaphysical freedom) that we may or may not have be a condition of something (personhood) that we clearly possess.

Dennett's condition (3) is a reflection of his *instrumentalism* about intentional mental states. According to Dennett, states such as beliefs, desires, thoughts, and so on are *abstracta*—idealized theoretical posits. Whether or not an individual has such states depends on whether we are willing to adopt an *intentional stance* toward this individual: essentially, to treat that individual *as if* she were the possessor of beliefs, desires, etc. and explain her behavior on the basis of these sorts of states.[36] On this view, the question of whether animals have a mental life of the sort that might confer on them the status of persons depends on whether we are inclined to treat them as such. Dennett is largely skeptical of this prospect.[37] I, however, do not share this anti-realist view of mental states. Adjudicating between realism and anti-realism about mental states is, obviously, well beyond the remit of this book. Therefore, I shall operate on the assumption that the issue of whether or not an individual has mental states does not simply depend on our decision to treat him as having, or not having, them.

Tooley claims that, to qualify as a person, an individual must have, "the concept of a self as a continuing subject of experiences and other mental states, and believes that it is itself a continuing entity." There is, I think, something very right about this and something very wrong. First, the right: Tooley is correct, I think, that being a person has something to do with the *unity* of a mental life—a person is a *persisting* or *continuing* entity rather than a mere succession of mental states—and right to think that this unity has something to do with *self-awareness*. The idea of unity, I shall argue in Chapter 9, is indeed crucial to the person.[38] At the core of the concept of a person we find the idea of a unified mental life. One might debate whether having a unified mental life is sufficient for being a person.[39] But there is little doubt that it is necessary. A disjointed, disassociated sequence of mental

---

[35] The example is taken from Dennett (1973). Keijzer (2013) has questioned the accuracy of Dennett's account. I take no stand on this issue.

[36] Dennett (1987b).

[37] As Kristin Andrews (2014) has pointed out, however, his skepticism is probably unjustified on this matter.

[38] The notion of persistence is built into the notion of unity, as I shall employ the latter notion. Henceforth, the requirement of persistence will not be explicitly reiterated, on grounds of redundancy.

[39] For example, Parfit (1984) doubts this.

states would not be a person—even if such a sequence were to occur in the same brain or organism. Moreover, I shall also argue, it is plausible to think that the unity of an individual's mental life is a matter of that individual having a certain kind of awareness of that mental life. A unified mental life exists because of a form of self-awareness. In all of this, I agree with Tooley.

However, I shall argue that Tooley is wrong to think that the kind of self-awareness he presupposes—involving a concept of a self and a belief about this self—is the sort of self-awareness that is relevant to the unity of the self. Having a unified, persisting mental life is one thing. Having a concept of oneself as having a unified, persisting mental life is quite another. The latter form of self-awareness is not the sort of thing that could supply unity to a mental life because, I shall argue, it presupposes such unity. Instead, the relevant sort of self-awareness involves neither concepts nor beliefs about mental states. The argument for these claims will be developed in Chapter 9. I have chosen not to list the unity of a mental life as a separate condition because it is satisfied, in effect, through the satisfaction of condition (3)—the self-awareness condition. Its failure to appear as an explicit condition on the list should not, however, detract from the vital importance of unity vis-à-vis personhood.

## 7. WHAT ABOUT LANGUAGE?

The breadth of the scope of the four identified conditions of personhood notwithstanding, some may be puzzled—perhaps perturbed—by my (apparent) silence on the issue of language. Why have I not included this as a condition of personhood? Indeed, why have I not said anything about that? The short answer is that I shall talk about language, and its significance to the question of personhood, in due course. This discussion, however, will be distributed through the book, emerging at various points rather than having one dedicated section or chapter. The reason I have done things in this way is because the question of whether animals possess linguistic abilities is, I shall argue, a thoroughly confused one and is better dealt with in an unsystematic, take-each-confusion-as-it-comes sort of way. Nevertheless, at this juncture, a few general remarks might be helpful.

Not so long ago, it was common, certainly among philosophers, to deny that animals possessed linguistic abilities. This denial was based on a conception of language that was inspired by the model of human language. For anything to qualify as a language it must be the sort of thing that humans have. Specifically, it must have *combinatorial* or *recursive* structure. This structure involves a relatively small number of lexical elements and rules for combining these lexical elements into larger units where, crucially, the meaning of these larger limits was a function of the meaning of the lexical elements coupled with the rules for combining those elements. This proprietary conception of language was then used to support the claim that animals lacked linguistic abilities. For example, the seeming inability of apes to *spontaneously* generate sequences of recursively structured linguistic expressions was cited as evidence for their linguistic poverty.[40]

There are two problems with this argument. First, the justification for assuming this proprietary conception of language is not immediately apparent. Even if we accept that this kind of language is beyond the abilities of any animal—more on that subsequently—it is not entirely clear why this entails that animals lack language more generally. Perhaps, in the thrall of this proprietary conception of language, we might wish to deny that animals lack language. But, if so, we would still have to accept that they are capable of *communication*. But if the guiding question is whether animals are persons, why suppose that the key to personhood is the possession of language in this very narrow, proprietary sense rather than more general abilities to communicate? Why, in order to be a person, must an individual possess a language with recursive or combinatorial structure in the sense explained here?

There are, admittedly, avenues one might explore if one wanted to cling to the importance for personhood of this specific form of language. One might argue, for example, that without such a language, thinking is impossible. Thus, without such a language, animals would be unable to satisfy the second condition of personhood—the cognition condition. This view regards thinking as made possible by a language of thought and regards with skepticism the possibility of having a language of thought without also having a public language with combinatorial structure. I shall examine this argument in depth in Chapter 5.

The second problem with fixation on this specific conception of language is that it is a hostage to empirical fortune. The guiding assumption is that no animals could possess such a language. This assumption, however, is looking increasingly frayed around the edges. The assumption has been fueled by the dominant position of apes in research on animal minds, a dominance fueled by the rather parochial assumption that since they are our closest biological relatives, they must be the next best thing in all respects. But this assumption masks the possibility of other creatures that might be far more innately disposed to use language—even language of a sort that approximates ours. For example, some birds have been shown to have a (let us call it) system of communication made up of lexical

---

[40] See Cheney and Seyfarth (1998).

elements, rules of combination of those elements, where the meaning of larger units is sensitive to the order of combination of the lexical elements. I shall discuss this research further in Chapter 2.

There is another type of confusion—a red herring in effect—that arises in connection with the linguistic abilities of animals. It is well known that vervet monkeys—like many other species—have a system of alarm calls that they use in the presence of predators. Specifically, vervets have three different alarm calls, one for leopards, another for pythons, and a third for eagles.[41] Clearly, it is desirable to have a distinct call for each predator since the type of evasive action required differs for each, and one type of evasive action—climbing a tree, for example— might be positively harmful in the presence of the wrong predator (such as an eagle).

There is a legitimate debate concerning the extent to which alarm calls such as these convey *information*. Michael Owren, Drew Rendall, and colleagues have argued that, when used in the context of animal communication, the notion of information is ill-defined. A better way of thinking about communication in animals, they argue, is to examine the ways in which physical characteristics of signals, such as intensity, duration, and pitch, activate emotion-related or motivational systems in receivers.[42] This claim has been strongly resisted by Seyfarth, Cheney, and colleagues.[43] From the perspective of my concerns, this debate is largely tangential. But it will seem more than that if one makes a further, perhaps tacit, assumption: any behavior that is to qualify as linguistic must involve the conveying of information. It is not difficult to see just how problematic is this assumption. Human language, of course, does not only convey information: that is but one of its many uses. It also expresses emotion, and sometimes this expression of emotion is designed to elicit emotions or cognate states in others. Moreover, and rather crucially, there is no necessary incompatibility between a vocalization expressing an emotion, eliciting emotion in others, and having the function of designating some environmental condition, such as the presence of a predator of a certain sort. It may be, for example, that the origin of the vervet monkey's alarm call consists in the expression of an emotion in the presence of a leopard, and this expression has a certain pitch, intensity, and duration. This pitch, intensity, and duration, perhaps via an evolved mirror neuron mechanism, elicits emotion in other vervets. However, the function of the call is not a matter of its origin but why the particular call exists today. A call that originated in the expression and eliciting

---

[41] Seyfarth, Cheney, and Marler (1980).
[42] Rendall and Owren (2002), Owren, Rendall, and Ryan (2010).
[43] Seyfarth et al. (2010).

of emotions can be co-opted for other uses—such as registering the presence of a predator. And if this co-opting explains why the alarm call is extant today, then the call has come to acquire the function of registering the presence of the predator, its origin notwithstanding.[44] These debates about what alarm calls do—express emotions, elicit emotions, represent predators—are all tangential to the question of whether such calls constitute a language. A language can do all of these things. But we should be wary of any claim—not made by Owren and Rendall I hasten to add—that if a system of vocalization works by expressing or eliciting emotions, then it is not worthy of the designation "language."

## 8. REDUCTION AND THE LEGITIMATION OF "PERSON"

The four conditions I have listed—*consciousness, cognition, self-awareness*, and *other-awareness*—are intended to provide a *reduction* of the concept of a person. The category of a person is not basic or sui generis but reduces to, and is explicable in terms of, these conditions. This has one clear and important consequence: *there is nothing that can be said using the language of personhood that can't be said without it*. For some, this may call into question the utility of the term *person*—and this is not an unreasonable position.[45]

Nevertheless, I am going to retain the language of personhood. In part, this is because of expository issues. Without it, the title of this book would be something like *Are Animals Conscious, Cognitive, Self-Aware, and Other-Aware Creatures?* This title has, to say the least, no obvious aura of bestseller. Worse, while the first three terms/expressions may be familiar, the fourth is a little recondite and probably needs explaining. *Other-awareness* denotes the ability to recognize another as a person. But I can't use the fugitive term *person* in the title. Thus, the eventual title would probably have to be something like *Are Animals Conscious, Rational, Self-Aware and Do They Recognize Each Other as Such?* It's a bit of a mouthful. And that's just the title—imagine how things would look when we get to the meat of the book if I were unable to use the term *person*.

There are other reasons besides ease of exposition for retaining the language of personhood. Some features of the world are what we might call, for lack of a better word, *interesting*. Perhaps this is a partly subjective matter but consciousness, cognition, self-awareness, and other-awareness are—for me at least—interesting.

---

[44] Here, I am drawing on the work of Ruth Millikan (1984, 1993).
[45] David DeGrazia (1997), p. 210, writes: "In animal ethics and perhaps generally, there is nothing you can do with the concept of personhood that you cannot do better with clearer concepts."

But sometimes interest attaches not just to individual features but also to the confluence or convergence of (individually interesting) features. And this interest that attaches to convergence of certain features does not reduce to the interest of the individual features that thus converge. That these four features should converge at a single locus, in a single individual, is interesting. They converge in humans. If these features should converge in other things too, that is also interesting. The term *person*, therefore, is also a way of recording an interesting convergence of features.

It is important to remember that a reduction of a property or feature to more basic features is a *legitimation* of that property. A reduction of X to Y is not an elimination of X. The reduction of personhood to the convergence of consciousness, cognition, self-awareness, and other-awareness does not undermine the notion of a person but legitimizes it. To reduce personhood to the convergence of consciousness, rationality, self-awareness, and other-awareness is not to claim that there are no such things as persons. On the contrary, it is to affirm the existence of persons: persons exist, and this is what they are—a convergence of these four features.[46]

There is another important feature of property reductions. While a reduction of one property to another, more basic property (or collection of properties) is a legitimation of that property, it is also true that this reduction may be combined with elements of elimination. The motivation for a reduction may be some question mark about the entity to be reduced. John's prestige is enormous—to borrow an example from Blackburn who uses it to make precisely this point.[47] Being unsure what prestige is, we might be puzzled—perhaps imagining it as a kind of invisible, intangible aura that surrounds John. The reduction solves our problem. John's enormous prestige reduces to the fact that other people admire John—enormously. Our temptation to think of prestige as a kind of invisible aura has been removed. Our original idea of prestige had a certain illegitimate content—or, at least, connotation—and this illegitimate content or connotation has now been excised by our reduction. So, reduction can certainly involve elimination: elimination of some spurious vector of content or connotation is often what provides the motivation for a reduction. Nevertheless, our reduction of John's prestige to other people's admiration of John is not an elimination of prestige but an explanation of what prestige is.

---

[46] Compare: To claim that lightning reduces to an electrical discharge to earth from a cloud of ionized water particles is not to deny the existence of lightning. It is to confirm the existence of lightning and say what lighting is.

[47] Blackburn (1984).

The same kinds of features arise in the reduction of a person to the convergence of consciousness, cognition, self-awareness, and other-awareness. It is sometimes complained that the notion of a person is an unacceptably vague concept. As the term *person* is commonly used, this may indeed be true. Different people may have very different ideas of what a person is, and the resulting vagueness will inevitably be reflected in the efforts of august bodies such as the editorial board of the *Merriam-Webster Dictionary*. The advantage of the proposed reduction is that it eliminates this kind of vagueness. A person is an individual in which the properties of consciousness, rationality, self-awareness, and other-awareness converge. That is all there is to being a person: any other features that we might be tempted to read into personhood can be ignored. The idea that the concept of a person is too vague to be useful can, therefore, be rejected.

## 9. WHEN THE GOING GETS MESSY

Nevertheless, while I think that talk of persons is ultimately legitimate and useful, one should not be blind to the potential pitfalls of its use. The worry is that a certain amount of vagueness will creep in another way: via the elements themselves rather than via other connotations that have been excised in the reduction. The question of whether animals are persons breaks down into four:

(1) Are animals conscious?
(2) Do animals engage in reasoning?
(3) Are animals self-aware?
(4) Do animals recognize others as persons?

In a perfect world, we might be able to answer each of these questions with a simple "yes" or "no." However, things are not that simple. Ludwig Wittgenstein cautioned both philosophers and scientists against a "craving for generality" to which both groups are constitutionally susceptible.[48] Sometimes questions such as "Is X the same thing as Y?" or "Does X require Y?" or "Can X be Y?" have no single, clear answer because X or Y, or both, break down into a multiplicity of distinct things. This is certainly the case with these four questions.

While the notion of consciousness is relatively straightforward, the ideas of reasoning, self-awareness, and reciprocity can each be interpreted in a variety of ways, with none of the resulting candidates standing out as obviously the correct

---

[48] This was in *The Blue Book*. See Wittgenstein (1958), p. 17.

one. Reasoning can be subdivided into causal and logical reasoning and further divided into practical and theoretical variants. Self-awareness, I shall argue, breaks down into two crucially different forms—one of which animals clearly have and one that, arguably, they lack. As a result of this, the idea of other-awareness breaks down into two crucially distinct forms, one of which many animals have and the other which they probably lack. Instead of answers to our four guiding questions, it would seem the best we can do is provide a series of answer *profiles* or *matrices* of the form: if by reasoning/self-awareness/other-awareness you mean . . . then . . . but if you, instead, mean . . . then. . . . At this point in logical space, there are two basic attitudes one might adopt.

The first is simply to chillax. We merely accept that this is generally how things are in philosophy. Instead of a single answer to a question, there exist a number of conditional answers, depending on how the questions are understood. Does cognition require representation? Someone might have spent an unhealthy portion of his or her life trying to answer that. But the idea of representation breaks down into various other notions, and these, in turn, break down into further notions; and in the end the best you can aim for is not an answer but a vast answer matrix.[49] There is nothing wrong with this—unless, of course, you were hoping for more. But it is this hope—this craving for generality—that is illegitimate, and not the answer matrix you eventually identify.

Perhaps this will turn out to be the case with regard to the title of this book: *Can Animals Be Persons?* If so, then this book is most profitably regarded as a book about what animals can do—the ways in which they can be conscious, rational, self-aware, and other-aware. This amounts to a description of the various ways in which they are, or might be, persons—even if those are not all the ways in which one might be a person. There is nothing wrong with this. In many cases, this is all philosophy can do anyway.

Actually, however, in the present context I find myself a little more sanguine than this. I think that in the case of this book's titular question, there are, perhaps, unusual reasons for optimism. Yes, rationality does break down into more than one form. Yes, self-awareness breaks down into two, crucially distinct forms and so too, therefore, does the notion of other-awareness. Nevertheless, a strong case can be made for the idea that, with respect to the issue of personhood, some of these forms are clearly more relevant and more important than others. For example, many animals are, I shall argue, clearly self-aware in one sense. And in the other main sense of self-awareness, perhaps most are not self-aware at all. Nevertheless, a clear case can be made for the claim that the first sense of self-awareness—the

---

[49] For this sort of approach—and to see me at my most chilled—see Rowlands (2015a).

sense in which animals are self-aware—is far more important to the question of personhood than the other sense.

Anyway, this book is what it is. Perhaps it's an exploration of the various ways in which animals can be persons—even if these are not all the ways in which something might be a person. Or perhaps it's an extended argument for the claim that animals can be persons, on the most defensible version of the concept of a person. I am just going to do what I do. What exactly that is, I shall leave up to you.

# 2

## THE GHOST OF CLEVER HANS

The ghost of Clever Hans haunts contemporary discussion of animal minds. Hans was a horse—an Orlov Trotter—who lived in the early part of the twentieth century. Owned by a high school mathematics teacher and amateur horse trainer, Wilhelm von Osten, Hans was believed to be able to do mathematics, among other things. Specifically, Hans could add, subtract, multiply, divide, work with fractions, tell time, keep track of the calendar, differentiate musical tones, and read, spell, and understand German—or, at least, so it seemed. The questions presented to Hans could come in a variety of forms: What is 9 + 7? What is the square root of 16? If the seventh day of the month comes on a Monday, what is the date of the following Wednesday? The questions could be spoken or written, it made no difference. And each time Hans would respond—usually correctly—by tapping out the answer with his hoof.

Hans, as we all now know, could not do mathematics. Nor could he read German. Hans's cruel and public debunking occurred at the hands of psychologist Oskar Pfungst. Pfungst set a series of tests for Hans—tests devised with the goal of separating Hans from anyone who knew the answers to the problems he was set. Either blinds were put up between Hans and the questioner or it was ensured that the questioner did not know the answer to the question Hans was being set. It didn't matter whether the questioner was von Osten—Hans would still answer correctly even when someone else asked the questions. But, in general, Hans answered correctly only when the questioner—whether von Osten or a third party—knew the answer and Hans could see the questioner. When Hans could see a questioner who knew the answer, Hans would answer correctly around 90 percent of the time. But when the questioner was hidden from Hans or when the questioner was ignorant of the correct answer, Hans's success rate would drop to around 6 percent. Hans was not doing mathematics but, rather, picking up on subliminal clues offered by the questioner. As Hans's tapping approached the correct answer, the questioner's posture and facial expression changed, indicating an increase in tension. This tension was released when Hans gave the final, correct, tap of his hoof. This release in tension provided Hans with a cue to stop tapping.

Hans may not have been an equine mathematician but, when you think about it, his abilities are still very impressive. Hans was able to detect very subtle changes in the behavior of a member of another species. The changes were so subtle that most humans would have failed to notice them, even if they were paying very close attention. The sort of difficulty this involves would be on a par with humans detecting subtle changes in the behavior of dogs—something at which even experienced dog owners are, often, not very good.

We can accept that Hans wasn't great at mathematics. But let's face it, why would he be? When his ancestors were galloping around the plains of Europe or Asia, there was no evolutionary pressure on them to become good at that sort of thing. Breeding opportunities, for example, were not going to depend on it. But social communication skills are a different matter altogether. And the communication systems of horses depend, in part, on detection of minute changes in posture. Mess up there, and it can get you killed. That Hans would be good at behavior reading is not unexpected given his evolutionary history. That he would be able to extend these abilities across species—applying them to hairless, bipedal apes that weren't part of his ancestral home—is truly impressive: at least as impressive, in its way, as knowing the square root of 16. Nevertheless, it is not Hans's extraordinary successes that we remember but his failures. Today, we hold up Hans (no pun intended) as a cautionary tale for students of animal minds: Fool me once, clever Hans, shame on you. Fool me twice, shame on me.

Only humans, on this planet at least, can calculate the square root of 16. To suppose that Hans could do this is to commit what is, in the scientific study of animals, a cardinal sin: anthropomorphism. *Anthropomorphism* is the attribution of qualities *only* humans can have to animals. Note: it is not simply the attribution of qualities humans have to animals—for it may be that humans and animals can share certain qualities and, if so, the attribution of this quality to an animal would be correct. Rather, anthropomorphism is, by definition, a *mistake*: the attribution of a quality to an animal that it cannot have because *only* a human can possess this quality.

When charges of anthropomorphism are made against someone, the qualities in question—the qualities that have, allegedly, been wrongly attributed to an animal—are typically psychological ones: consciousness, thoughts, beliefs, desires, memories, emotions, and so on. Attributing such states is felt by some to be especially questionable because we have no direct access to the minds of animals. We might be able to observe their bodies and their behavior, but their minds are shut off from us. Any claims about their psychology must proceed by way of inference from behavior, and that, some argue, is unacceptably suspect in the case of animals: the sort of procedure that will tend to engender anthropomorphic conclusions. Let us call this the *problem of other animal minds*.

Those who raise this problem for animals often seem to forget that there is also a *problem of other human minds*. In fact, the traditional problem of other minds is directed at other human minds. The problem is typically expressed in terms of the distinction between *direct* and *indirect* awareness. I am *often* (not always, not necessarily, but often) directly aware that I am in a given mental state (e.g., happy, sad, thinking about what to have for dinner, etc.). But I am *never* directly aware that someone else is in a given mental state. I can be directly aware of what another human is doing—her behavior. But I can never be directly aware of why she is doing it—her mind. Any information I have about the latter I must, necessarily, acquire indirectly. The distinction between direct and indirect is, in this context, equivalent to the distinction between *experience* and *inference*. I can see (and hear, etc.) what another is doing, but I can only infer what she is thinking and feeling. And I can be justified in my views about what she is thinking and feeling only if my inference from her behavior is a justified inference.[1]

The respective problems of other human and animal minds are grounded in the same kind of reasoning: direct, experiential access to behavior but only indirect, inferential access to the minds of others, whether human or animals. Therefore, if one is impressed by the problem of other animal minds but not by the problem of other human minds, this can only be because one regards the inference involved in the former case to be especially suspect in a way that it is not in the latter case. The inference to what is going on in the mind of the other is, one must assume, more secure or justified in the case of humans than it is in the case of animals. This assumption is widespread but surprisingly difficult to support. Generally speaking,

---

[1] At present, I am merely outlining the reasoning that leads to the problem of other human minds. I am not endorsing it. Indeed, later I shall sharply criticize this reasoning.

as we shall see, one frequently finds discussion of animal minds permeated by double standards: we hold other animal minds up to standards such that, were we to consistently apply them, they would force us to conclude that no human has a mind.

The ultimate goal of this chapter is to make the problem of other animal minds go away. I do not intend to *solve* the problem as such. The problem of other animal minds, like the problem of other human minds, is what is known as a skeptical problem. *Skepticism* is the view that it is impossible to have knowledge or justification in some particular area of inquiry. The area of our inquiry is other animal minds, and the problem we face is one of explaining how we can be justified in our beliefs about the minds of animals. The thing about skeptical problems—and the history of philosophical attempts to deal with skepticism indicates this very strongly—is that they are often extraordinarily difficult to solve or refute. Attempts to meet them head on by definitively solving them tend to not go so well. But sometimes you don't have to meet a problem head on. Sometimes you can sort of sneak around the back of the problem and punch it in the kidneys. That is the strategy I shall adopt here. That is, while I shall not show how to solve the problem of other animal minds, I shall try to show why it is impossible for us to take this problem seriously. In developing this case, I shall exploit some of the parallels between the problem of other animal minds and the corresponding problem of other human minds.

## 2. INFERENTIALIST SOLUTIONS

The attitude of most scientists toward the problem of other animal minds is grounded in an unacknowledged philosophical assumption.[2] The assumption is that a solution to the problem must be an *inferentialist* solution. I am going to argue against this assumption. But first, I need to explain what it is, and I shall do this, initially, in the context of the problem of other human minds.

The problem of other human minds is based on a crucial assumption: the minds of others are hidden from us. We cannot perceive, or in any other way directly detect, the mind or mental states of another human. There is a broad division in the problem of other human minds between those who accept this assumption and those who reject it. Once you accept this assumption, any solution you offer to the problem of other minds will inevitably have to be an inferentialist one. Since we cannot perceive or otherwise directly detect the mind of another human, any

---

[2] See, for example, Harnad (2016).

information we have of this mind must be based on inference. The problem, then, is finding out how to make this inference *justified*.

At this point in logical space, inferentialist views diverge—a divergence based on the kind of inference thought to be required. One version sees this inference as *analogical* in character, yielding the *analogical inference* solution to the problem of other human minds. In adopting the analogical inference solution, I begin with my own case and reason as follows: I know that I have a mind. Therefore, since others seem pretty much like me, I can infer that they have minds too. If correct, this strategy would provide a rationale for thinking the problem of animal minds is a more serious problem than the problem of other minds. Animals are not like me—certainly not as much like me as other humans.

This analogical inference solution, however, would justify thinking that the problem of other animal minds is more serious than the problem of other human minds only if it solves the problem of other human minds. And it is generally recognized to be a non-starter. The type of inference employed in this attempted solution is inductive: I generalize from my own case to make a claim about all, or certainly most, humans. But the strength or legitimacy of an inductive inference depends on the size of the sample class relative to the generalized conclusion. And this is as small as it can get: one case, one person—me. And the conclusion derived from this is a general one about all (or, at least, most) humans. The resulting inductive inference is about as weak as an inductive inference can get. The analogical inference solution is off the table. Therefore, it cannot provide a reason for thinking that the problem of other animal minds is more intractable than the problem of other human minds. If the analogical inference answer to the problem of other minds doesn't work in the case of humans, we can hardly use it as a stick with which to beat the minds of animals.

The other common inferentialist solution to the problem of other human minds is based on the idea of *inference to the best explanation*. This removes the element of analogy present in the analogical inference solution. According to this solution, I can legitimately infer the presence of mental states in other humans because this provides the best explanation of their behavior. Why is Smith walking down the street? Because he wants a coffee and believes there is a Starbucks at the end of the street. Beliefs, desires—minds—are explanatory posits, justified to the extent they make sense of the behavior of another.

Suppose, for a moment, we decide to accept this inference to the best explanation solution to the problem of other human minds. In fact, I don't think we should accept this, and I'll explain why shortly. But, just for the sake of argument, assume it works. Then, an obvious question arises: if it works for the problem of other human minds, is there any reason to assume it won't work for the problem of other animal minds? In the case of other human minds, the justification for explaining their behavior by way of mental states is simple: it works! But someone who believes we can explain the behavior of animals in this way is hardly going to believe that this is because it doesn't work. That is why it is so tempting to use the language of mental states in connection with animals: it seems to be enlightening. Nevertheless, it is common to suppose that ascribing mental states to animals is problematic in a way that ascription of these states to humans is not.

A commonly cited reason for this is that other humans can *tell* us what they are thinking and feeling. Other animals cannot. So, it is the possession of a common language that makes inference to the best explanation justified in the case of humans in a way it is not in the case of animals. There are many reasons why this claim is questionable.

First, as we saw in the previous chapter, the claim that animals do not possess language is dubious. Their languages may, often, be very different from ours, but the claim that they lack language can only be supported by setting very stringent demands on anything that is to count as a language—demands that are inspired by human languages. Human languages have combinatorial structure: they comprise a relatively small number of lexical elements (i.e., words) together with grammatical rules that specify how these lexical elements may be combined together. The resulting combinations (i.e., sentences) have meaning, and this is a function of the meaning of lexical elements plus the grammatical combinatorial structure. If is often claimed that the "languages" of animals do not have this sort of structure and, therefore, are not "real" languages. Even this claim, predicated on a highly specific conception of what a language must be, is of doubtful veracity, for at least some animals do seem to employ languages with combinatorial structure.

The Japanese tit, for example, employs what's known as a "mobbing call" when a predator is in the vicinity. This call has the sequence WXY-Z. The WXY part of the call signifies danger. The Z part of the call, however, functions as something like a "recruitment call." This functions as a call to assembly for members of the flock. Thus, when the sequence WXY-Z is produced, Japanese tits flock together to mob the intruder. However, crucially, the recruitment call is not restricted to contexts of predator threat. It can be used, for example, to attract flock members when there is something to share, such as food. This would not count as combinatorial structure if the resulting behavior were indifferent to the order to the combined elements—if the birds reacted in the same way to Z-WXY as they did to WXY-Z. "Jesus wept" does not mean the same thing as "wept Jesus." In proper lexical or combinatorial structure, the order of lexical elements is important. Thus, to test the hypothesis that lexical ordering mattered for the Japanese tit, Suzuki, Wheatcroft, and Griesser presented Japanese tits with a novel song—an artificial sequence made up of the Japanese tit's WXY alarm call followed by the recruitment call of the related willow tit.[3] Let us represent this as "a." When Japanese tits heard the WXY-a call—it was broadcast via a loudspeaker—they swiveled their heads looking for a predator. But when the novel sequence was reversed—a-WXY—the birds did not react. This shows that the Japanese tits do not perceive their WXY-Z song as an undifferentiated message but rather a message that has two components: *alert* and *approach*. This sequence has meaning only if its constituent elements are produced in the right order: *approach* and *alert* makes no sense to the Japanese tit—as "wept Jesus" makes no sense to us. Combinatorial, syntactic, structure was often held up as the sacred cow of human language, decisively distinguishing our linguistic capabilities from those of animals. This idea is becoming increasingly difficult to defend.

In the face of these empirical difficulties, we might temper the original bald assertion that animals lack language. According to a more moderate position, the problem is not that animals lack language but that we do not understand their language, and this makes explaining their behavior via the ascription of mental states problematic in a way it is not in the case of humans. Here, two claims should be distinguished: (a) animals possess languages we *do not* understand and (b) animals possess languages we *cannot* understand. Let us consider each of these in turn.

The first is too weak to do the work required of it. There are roughly 6,500 extant human languages—almost all of which I do not understand. The failure to understand most human languages is not an insuperable obstacle to attributing mental states to those humans who speak them. The claim that animals possess languages that we *cannot* understand, on the other hand, is both curious and, arguably, question-begging. It is curious because at least animals do a very good impression of being able to learn at least parts of our language: one need only think of Alex the parrot, Koko the gorilla, Washoe the chimpanzee, and so on. If they can learn our language, we would have to be relatively dimwitted if we were unable to learn theirs. Thus, if anything, the claim that we cannot understand the languages of animals makes us their intellectual inferiors and so actually strengthens the case for other animal minds. The claim that we cannot understand their languages also seems to be question-begging. The project of understanding the language of another involves explaining his or her behavior—specifically, verbal behavior—by attributing to him or her mental states. A language can be impossible to understand, in principle, only if we cannot attribute mental states to the language user. But whether we can do this is precisely what is at issue.

---

[3] Suzuki, Wheatcroft, and Griesser (2017).

Another implicit assumption involved in the idea that presence or absence of language is what is decisive in the case of other minds is the idea that language is a smoothly *cooperative* endeavor. This assumption is dubious. Language need not be an intrinsically cooperative affair; it can just as often be *competitive*.[4] Those with language can deceive with much greater facility. And even where explicit deception does not occur, it is common, in conversational contexts, for both speaker and hearer to conceal or elide certain information. Moreover, even when language is being used cooperatively, the simpler needs of animals often compensate for their lack of language.

The most important strike against the idea that language is of decisive importance in the question of other animal minds, however, is obvious: *ultimately, language is just another form of behavior*. No one would (or should) think that it is possible to solve the problem of other human minds simply by noting that others can speak: "Oh, you can speak—you do have a mind after all!" It really wouldn't be much of a problem if that were so. But if the possession of language by the other cannot solve the problem of other human minds, why should we regard it as a decisive point of difference between the problem of other human minds and the problem of other animal minds—something that renders other animal minds problematic in a way the problem of other human minds is not? This seems to be another clear case of double standards.

There are other reasons—ones not directly based on language—that are cited for thinking the problem of other animal minds is a greater problem than that of other human minds. Some claim that concepts of mental states are learned in the case of humans and extended to animals only by analogy. There are at least two problems with this argument. First, even if true, extension of concepts beyond the contexts in which they are acquired is both common and often legitimate. We need to be given reasons for thinking that the extension in the case of animals is illegitimate. Second, the argument is based on an utterly contingent claim about how concepts are *acquired*, and no implications can be drawn from this about how they are to be *applied*. Thus, it might easily be the case that some humans learn some of their mental concepts in connection with the family dog or cat and then analogically extend these to other humans.[5]

I suspect that these arguments are all, ultimately, moot. Neither version of inferentialism provides a satisfactory response to the problem of other human

---

[4] "Everything is fine!" says your significant other but in the sort of detached, wistful way that suggests everything is not fine at all. You persist: "Really?" And the other continues on in the same manner, etc., etc. The thing is: if you have to be told, you have failed. You must be able to work it out on your own.

[5] Raymond Gaita (2003) makes this point.

minds. Therefore, neither version can be used to justify the claim that the problem of other animal minds is more serious than the problem of other human minds. Both forms of inferentialism share a common flaw. No inference—whether analogical or to the best explanation—can underwrite what we take ourselves to have regarding our knowledge of the minds of other humans. An inference to unobservable entities is only ever *probable* and thus cannot capture the certainty with which I invest the minds of others.[6] I do not, for example, think it is, 75 percent likely that my wife and sons have minds. I do not even think it is 95 percent likely. I am *certain* they have minds. I am not, as Wittgenstein (more or less) put it, of the *opinion* that they have minds.[7] I am certain they have minds—as certain as I could ever be of anything—and it is difficult to see how inference of either form could provide such certainty.

The advocate of inferentialism may try to answer this objection by appealing to the distinction between *logic* and *psychology*. On the one hand, there is a *psychological* question: to what extent are we *certain* that other humans have minds (or, conversely, to what extent can we *doubt* they have minds). Certainty and doubt are psychological states, and this is accordingly a psychological question concerning, in effect, our degree of credence. But, on the other hand, there is a *logical* question, which concerns the *justification* of our belief that others have minds. Whether analogical or to the best explanation, inference, they might argue, concerns the justification for our belief in other minds, rather than our confidence or degree of credence. It might be that while we take ourselves to be certain that other humans have minds, the justification we have for this belief does not warrant this certainty.

The problem with this response is that we cannot insulate the logical question from its psychological counterpart in the way the response assumes. Once I become familiar with a lack of justification for a given claim, I must, if I am rational, adjust my psychology accordingly. Suppose I am certain that the sun revolves around the earth. Then, I am introduced to the empirical evidence that, in fact, the reverse is true. I must, if I am rational, adjust my beliefs. If I adopt an inferentialist account of other minds and then it is pointed out to me that inferences are only ever probable and never certain, then I am rationally obligated to adjust my level of credence in other minds. I cannot, if I am a rational being, accept that it is certain that my wife and sons have minds, while at the same time adopting an inferentialist view of other minds.

---

[6] Sartre (1943/1957, pp. 304–305) makes this point.
[7] "My attitude towards him is an attitude toward a soul. I am not of the opinion that he has a soul." Wittgenstein (1953), p. 178.

The inferentialist solution to the problem of other human minds, therefore, puts me in this situation. When I go home in the evening and hang out with my family, I can't be sure they have minds. I'm not sure what the numerical value is, but my justification has a value that, put in Bayesian terms, is less than 1. I should, to some numerical value or other, be guarded in my belief that the spouse I have known for nearly twenty years and the children I have watched grow from birth actually have minds.

## 3. DIRECT PERCEPTION AND OTHER MINDS

The guiding assumption that motivates both the problem of other human minds and the inferentialist attempts to answer it is that the minds of others are hidden from us. We cannot, in any way, see or otherwise experience what is going on in the mind of another. Direct perception views reject this assumption. According to such views, we can, in some cases at least, see, or otherwise directly access, what is going on in the mind of another. Therefore, we do not need to infer these goings-on from the other's behavior. Beyond this common core, however, direct perception views can take numerous forms.

*Classical behaviorism*, at least on one interpretation, is an example of a direct perception solution to the problem of other human minds. One can think of behaviorism as an *eliminativist* position or as a *reductionist* position. Understood as an eliminativist position, behaviorism is the view that there are no such things as mental states. There is just behavior. That is not so much a solution to the problem of other minds but a *dissolution*—a denial that there ever was such a problem. Understood as a reductionist position, on the other hand, behaviorism is the view that mental states exist and they are simply—one and the same thing as—behavior. That, if true, would be a solution to the problem of other minds: we can see the minds of others simply by seeing their behavior—for minds are simply nothing more than behavior. This solution is as plausible as the premise that mental states and processes are identical with behavior. At one time popular, time has not been kind to this view, and I shall discuss it no further.

Another view is based on an account not of what mental states are but of how we come to learn the meaning of mental words—*pain, belief, happy, sad*, and the like. This view is influenced by Wittgenstein's attack on the possibility of a logically private language: a language that can, in principle, be learned only by one person. There can be no such language, Wittgenstein argued, because, in such a language, there would be no standards of correctness: standards governing how words are correctly applied. A language where terms referred to inner, private states of a person would be a logically private language. Since such a language cannot exist, mental terms cannot get their meaning in this way.[8]

Wittgenstein's alternative account of how mental words acquire their meaning accentuates the public, social character of language acquisition. You learn the meanings of mental words in the same way you learn the meanings of any other word: trial, error, and correction from competent speakers of your linguistic community. When you start to learn the meaning of the word *pain*, you apply this word—both to yourself and others—and your application will be confirmed or corrected by others. For example, when you apply to a person who is behaving erratically you might say, "He is in pain." You are corrected: "No, he is not in pain. He is happy." This is the kind of process whereby you learn the meaning of the words *pain* and *happy*, and it has nothing to do with applying this word to inner, private sensations.

This idea can be applied to the problem of other minds. You see someone acting in a certain way in a certain context. He has dropped a bowling ball on his foot and is hopping up and down, yelling profanities. He seems to be in pain. But, given the problem of other minds, is this judgment justified? On the view of language acquisition just canvassed it is, for, very roughly, this is just what it means to say someone is in pain.

This view might justify more skepticism about the problem of other animal minds. We learn to apply mental words to humans, not animals. But, in part, as I mentioned in Section 2 this is a contingent matter concerning how one learns mental words. For some people, animals might have been woven into this story of language acquisition: the meaning of mental words was learned, in part, by application to the family dog or cat, followed by subsequent correction or confirmation from a competent speaker of the language—a parent or other caregiver, for example. But the question of whether we can apply this account to the case of animals is neither here nor there since the account will not allow us to solve the problem of other human minds anyway. This attempted solution confuses the issue of the *meaning* of mental words with the issue of the *correctness* of their application.[9]

Consider, for example, the case of witches. People used to believe in them, and the word *witch* was acquired in the usual way. You were supposed to apply it to people who exhibited certain characteristics: elderly, female, has no friends, has a black cat, etc. When learning the word, if you applied it to people without the usual characteristics you would likely have been corrected. In this way, the word *witch*

---

[8] Wittgenstein (1953), Sections 244–71.
[9] Aune (1986) makes this point.

came to acquire a clear and relatively consistent meaning. But, still, there are no witches. Is old mother so-and-so a witch? Well, of course she is: she's old, female, a bit weird, lives on her own, and has a black cat. This is just what it means to be a witch. But she is, in fact, not a witch. The same might be true of mental words: indeed, this possibility is one way of expressing the problem of other minds. The man in front of you has recently dropped a bowling ball on his foot and is now hopping up and down and screaming profanities. This is just what it means to be in pain, you say. Maybe: but he may still not be in pain—just as old mother so-and-so is not a witch. On the one hand, there is the issue of how mental words acquire meaning. On the other, there is the issue of whether they are correctly applied. We cannot derive an answer to the latter from an answer to the former.

Another direct perception approach to other minds is inspired by *enactivist* accounts of visual perception.[10] Such accounts begin with the idea that, at any given time, we never see objects in their entirety but merely the surfaces that presented to us. Nevertheless, it would be misguided to say that we never see objects but only surfaces. I see a book. But I am in direct visual contact only with the part of the book that is facing me—the front cover, say. Nevertheless, it seems to me that I see a book and not a book part or book façade. The reason is that seeing the front of the book has generated certain expectations or anticipations regarding how my experience will change in given circumstances. I anticipate, for example, that if the book is rotated, I shall see first the spine of the book, followed by its back cover. Seeing it as a book façade, on the other hand, would involve generation of a rather different set of anticipations.

Some think this general account can be applied to other minds.[11] I see other minds in the same way that I see the part of the book that is not facing me. I see behavior, and this generates a certain set of expectations, the result of which is that I also see the mental states that cause or animate the behavior. The problem with this sort of account, however, is that there is a clear disanalogy between the back of the book and the mental states of others. I can always walk around the book and see the side that was hidden from me. That is precisely what I cannot do in the case of the mental states of another person. The back of the book may be hidden from me, but I can always take steps to render it visible. No such similar steps are available in the case of the mental states of another.[12]

---

[10] For an exceptionally clear and compelling statement and defense of this view, see Noë (2004).

[11] These sorts of ideas prove very important later in the book, when I discuss the idea of self-awareness. What they do not give us, however—and this is my present point—is a solution to the problem of other minds.

[12] See Krueger (2012).

Another form of direct perception view may be underwritten by *extended* accounts of mental processes.[13] According to such accounts, some mental processes are, partly, composed of operations occurring outside the head—specifically operations performed by a cognizing organism whereby it (1) manipulates and/or exploits certain structures in its environment, where (2) these structures carry information that is relevant to the cognitive task the organism is trying to perform, and (3) by operating on these structures the organism makes available—to itself or to subsequent processing operations—the information thus contained.[14] If this sort of view is correct, not all mental processes are confined to processes occurring inside the brain. Rather, they are amalgamations of neural processes, wider bodily processes, and certain sorts of actions that organisms perform on environments. In certain circumstances, therefore, seeing what an organism is doing to or with its environment is a way of seeing part of a cognitive process. But to see part of a thing, X, is the same as seeing X. In seeing the part of the book that is facing me, it would be strange to deny that I thereby see the book. To see the part of the book that is oriented toward me is to see the book. Thus, if the thesis of extended cognition is correct, at least some mental processes can be visible.

The thesis of extended cognition is controversial. I'm convinced, obviously: I've spent a significant proportion of my life defending it. But others may demur, even in the face of the devastating arguments developed by we extended-minders. And given that this is so, it is best not to assign too much weight to it here. The approach I am going to develop—a dissolution of, rather than a solution to, the problem of other animal minds—is a version of the direct perception view but a different one from any of those considered thus far. The argument I shall develop comes in three parts. In the first part, I introduce a distinction between *seeing* and *seeing that*. The second part turns on a distinction between *formal* and *functional* descriptions of behavior introduced by Colin Allen and Marc Bekoff. In part three, I shall argue that functional descriptions of behavior are often disguised *psychological* descriptions. Combining these three dialectical components yields the conclusion that we can often see the mental states of animals—or so I shall try to show.

---

[13] See Clark (1997), Rowlands (1999) and (2010).

[14] This is a rather slanted view of what the thesis of extended cognition is—it is my version, the view I defend in Rowlands (1999), (2003), and (2010). Other versions of the extended mind thesis can be rather different. None of this need concern us here.

4. SEEING VERSUS SEEING THAT

Can you see a tornado? Has anyone ever seen a tornado? I'm pretty sure I've seen one or two. In fact, I seem to remember seeing one pass almost directly over my house when I lived in Tuscaloosa, AL. But given that a tornado is a vortex of violently rotating air, and given that air is invisible, it is possible that someone might wish to correct my assumption: I could not have seen a tornado but only its *effects*—the rotating dirt, dust, water vapor that have been caught up in the vortex. No one ever really sees the tornado: we see only its effects. This, I think, is a bad way of thinking about what we see, and I am going to build on this to try to undermine the problem of other animal minds.

There is an element of truth in the idea that you do not see the tornado: you cannot see *that* something is a tornado. That there is a tornado present is something you hypothesize in order to explain the aforementioned effects. *That* a tornado is responsible for these effects is, of course, an *inference to the best explanation*. I see certain effects, and the presence of a tornado is the inference I draw from these effects—a hypothesis that best explains the effects. I cannot see *that* it is a tornado that is producing these effects because the same effects could have, in principle, been produced by something else—for example, a gravity vortex of the sort you might find in a sci-fi film. I could, in principle, see the same effects even if a tornado was not there. Nevertheless, even though I cannot see *that* something is a tornado, it would be strange to deny that I can see a tornado. If the violently rotating dirt, dust, water vapor, and sundry items are, in fact, caused by a tornado, then to see these things is precisely what it is to see a tornado. It is this distinction between (a) seeing X and (b) seeing that something is X that I am going to exploit in trying to dissolve the problem of other animal minds.

5. FORMAL VERSUS FUNCTIONAL DESCRIPTIONS

With the distinction between seeing X and seeing that something is X in mind, consider another distinction, drawn by Allen and Bekoff, between *formal* and *functional* descriptions of behavior.[15] Described formally, behavior consists in a series of bodily movements: changes in the spatial location and orientation of the body, and its various parts, through time. Between time $t_1$ and $t_2$, let us suppose, the Cartesian coordinates of my left index finger might change from coordinate (x, y, z) to coordinate (x\*, y\*, z\*), whereupon the upper portion of the finger rapidly

---

[15] Allen and Bekoff (1997).

oscillates between positions $(x^*, y^*, z^*)$ and $(x^{**}, y^{**}, z^{**})$. Or, as it is more commonly known, I am scratching my nose. Formal descriptions, one might glean from this, can tend to be rather baffling. "Scratching my nose," on the other hand, is a functional description rather than a formal one. A functional description characterizes behavior in terms of its *purpose*. A series of bodily movements and transformations are collected together into a single whole—while other bodily movements are ignored—by way of a description of the purpose of the resulting collectivity. The resulting conglomeration of bodily movements is, thus, individuated by means of a functional kind.

Switching our focus from human to nonhuman animals, consider Allen and Bekoff's example of the *play bow* performed by dogs. There is a certain type of behavior that occurs in dogs prior to their engaging in play. We could describe this behavior formally: there is a lowering of the front end of the dog, a bending of the forelegs, elevation of the rump, including the tail, and so on. However, we could also describe it functionally. The purpose of this behavior is to signal to the other dog that play is about to ensue and that actions that might ordinarily be taken to be threatening—seizing and shaking of the neck, for example—don't mean what they ordinarily mean. This is the function of this behavior, and to describe the behavior as a "play bow" is to allude to this function.

As Allen and Bekoff point out, describing the behavior functionally, as a play bow, can be useful for several reasons. First, the description can highlight important aspects of the behavior that formal descriptions will miss.[16] Second, functional descriptions are powerful because they allow us to individuate behaviors in salient ways. Some play bows are incomplete: some other element of the behavior—understood formally—is missing. Sometimes the dog will not raise its tail to full mast, or the rump is only marginally elevated. If we focused purely on the formal elements of the behavior, we might have to characterize the complete and incomplete play bows as distinct behaviors. Characterizing them functionally, in contrast, allows us to group them together—and if our project is to understand dog behavior, this is far more useful.

In general, functional descriptions tend to be enlightening in ways that formal descriptions often are not. This is not to say that functional descriptions are always to be preferred over formal ones. They have their perils too—notably a tendency toward over-interpretation that we saw in the Clever Hans case. Allen and

---

[16] Nina was a German shepherd/malamute mix. Tess was a wolf dog. They used to engage in seemingly ferocious bouts of play fighting, alternately pinning each other to the ground by the throat, growling, and shaking the neck. This was, often, to the consternation of passersby who didn't realize they were playing. Either not seeing the play bow or not understanding its significance, they focused unduly on the formal aspects of the behavior and, therefore, missed its meaning.

Bekoff argue that whether a formal or functional description is preferable depends on context, our interests, and whether there is sufficient evidence to justify a functional interpretation. This seems sensible. Nothing in my argument requires that functional descriptions are always preferable to formal ones, merely that functional descriptions of behavior are perfectly legitimate and often useful.

With respect to what we see, the play bow has the same kind of status as the tornado. You cannot see *that* something is a play bow. "Play bow" is a *theoretical* description: it is theory-laden. *That* a sequence of behavior is a play bow is not *directly* visible. We might imagine, for example, a poor, old, arthritic dog that, upon meeting another dog, stumbles and accidentally performs exactly the same sequence of movements that would, ordinarily, be a play bow. But the old dog, being rather crotchety, by no means wishes to play. Nevertheless—and this is crucial— although you cannot tell whether a behavior is a play bow simply by looking at it, play bows are perfectly visible. You may not be able to see, directly, *that* a piece of behavior is a play bow. But if it *is, in fact*, a play bow, you can certainly see it. Despite being theoretical in this sense, behavior functionally described is perfectly visible.

## 6. FUNCTIONAL AND PSYCHOLOGICAL DESCRIPTIONS

Few would deny the legitimacy of employing functional descriptions of behavior in attempting to explain the behavior of animals. I am relying on this widespread acceptance. The final stage in the argument is to argue that functional descriptions are not what we think they are. Functional descriptions are, in fact, disguised mental or psychological descriptions. This is not, of course, to claim that *all* functional descriptions are disguised psychological descriptions. Rather, the claim is that the functional descriptions employed to describe and explain behavior of animals are often disguised psychological descriptions. The reason for this ultimately stems from what we might think of as the *intransigence*—the uncooperativeness— of the world. To see how this works, we must recall a philosophical myth, devised by Wilfred Sellars—sometimes called the Myth of Jones or, perhaps more commonly nowadays, the Myth of our Rylean Ancestors.[17]

Our Rylean ancestors are humans who have the language to describe observable objects, events, and processes in their environment but who lack any way to talk about their mental states. With this language, they explain behavior by citing features of the world. Why is Smith walking down the street? He is going to the

---

[17] Sellars (1997).

grocery store, and so on. This is a functional description of Smith's behavior. We describe it not in terms of bodily movements—foot and arm movements, etc.—but in terms of its purpose: going to the grocery store. As such, we cannot see *that* it belongs to this functional kind—Smith might be going somewhere else or just taking a stroll. Nevertheless, the behavior that we thus characterize is perfectly visible behavior. Anyone can see Smith walking down the street in the direction of the grocery store. And if he is, *in fact*, going to the grocery store, then we see Smith walking to the grocery store.

The problem with the explanatory strategy employed by our Rylean ancestors is that it only works when the world is the way said ancestors think it is. Smith is going to the grocery store, and that is why he is walking in that direction down the street. Too bad: the store has been demolished and replaced with a Starbucks. The world is not the way Smith thinks it is. And that is what is crucial for Smith's behavior: not the way the world is but the way Smith takes it to be. Sellars imagines that among our Rylean ancestors is a genius named Jones who realizes this: it is not the way the world is that explains our behavior but the way we take it to be.

How might we describe Smith's behavior? He is not, in fact, going to the store—he can't be because the store no longer exists. But we might say that he is *trying* to go to the store. Or we might say he *intends* to go to the store. He *wishes* or *desires* to go to the store. Or we might say that Smith is going to where he *believes* the store is. In short, Smith is the subject of one or another combination of *affective* and *cognitive* states—pro-attitudes plus beliefs vis-à-vis the store. He desires to go there, or intends to go there, and believes the store is where he is going. We cannot explain his behavior in terms of his going to the store because there is no store. But we can explain it in terms of these affective and cognitive attitudes he has toward the store. Now—by invoking affective and cognitive attitudes—we are in the realm of the mental. The description of Smith we have employed is a psychological one.

With this in mind, consider again the play bow. The purpose of this is to initiate play, and the bow may either prove successful or unsuccessful in achieving this purpose. Consider, first, the case of an unsuccessful play bow. The other dog—the recipient of the bow—turns out to be rather pusillanimous and decides that, all things considered, it would rather fight. Such is the intransigence of the world. In this case, we cannot describe the dog's behavior as initiating play because he is not, in fact, initiating play. The dog is *trying* to initiate play rather than initiating play. He *intends* to initiate play but is not successful. He *desires* to initiate play, but his desire is thwarted. Functional descriptions of behavior are both useful and widely regarded as legitimate. But it would be a mistake to suppose that the functional descriptions that we apply to the behavior of animals are always neutral with regard to the mental. When the purpose of a play bow is not achieved, we cannot describe the dog's behavior as initiating play—because the dog is not, in fact, initiating play—but must fall back on some description that imputes a psychological motive such as trying, intending, or desiring. In this case at least, the functional description we employ is a disguised psychological description.

A play bow performed by a dog is a perfectly visible behavior. There is nothing hidden about a play bow. It is overt rather than covert. I may not be able to tell, from perception alone, *that* what the dog is doing is a play bow—I refer you to the example of the old, arthritic dog. But if it is, in fact, a play bow, then I am certainly able to see it. But in cases where the play bow fails, I do not see a dog initiating play, for the dog does not, in fact, initiate play. What I see is the dog trying or intending or desiring to initiate play. I cannot see *that* the dog is trying or intending or desiring to initiate play. *That* the dog is doing this is an inference I draw on the basis of what I see. But if the dog is, in fact, trying or intending or desiring to initiate play, then this is what I see. The dog's trying or intending or desiring to initiate play is not something hidden behind its behavior. In seeing the behavior, I see the dog trying or intending or desiring to initiate play. The trying, intending, or desiring is part of the behavior, rather than a hidden, inner cause of the behavior.

This conclusion is enough to show that we cannot take the problem of other animal minds seriously. According to this problem, there is no justification for believing that animals are the subjects of psychological states. This is a *blanket* claim. It does not claim that in some situations or circumstances we cannot be justified in thinking that a particular animal has one or another particular mental state. This latter, restricted, claim is both true and anodyne. Of course, there are some circumstances in which we do not, and perhaps cannot, know what an animal is thinking or feeling. That's what Clever Hans is all about. But the problem of other animal minds goes much further than this. To take this problem seriously is to accept that we never, at any time, have any justification for the claim that any animal has, or is the subject of, any mental state. We see now that this claim cannot be sustained. In a case of an unsuccessful play bow, we can see a dog trying or intending or desiring to initiate play. We cannot see *that* the dog is doing this. But we can, nevertheless, see the dog doing this. The only way to avoid this conclusion is to eschew functional descriptions of the dog's behavior. But this will leave us with no workable version of behavior. In short, we must either give up the project of understanding animals or accept that, in some cases at least, we can see—not infer, but see—what they are trying or intending or desiring to do. In some cases at least, we can see the psychological states of animals.

The other case to consider is when the dog's play bow is successful. In such a case, I can say that I see the dog initiating play. Does this mean that my functional description of his behavior is innocent of psychological import? That is a possible option, but it comes with a heavy price. The price is that we would have to categorize successful and unsuccessful play bows as different behaviors.[18] Suppose a dog successfully employs a play bow to initiate play on one occasion, but then on a later occasion, with a different dog, his attempt is unsuccessful. It would be, and I think is, implausible to claim that the dog is doing two completely different things on each occasion—that the behavior in which it engages is of two different kinds in each case. Surely, it is more plausible to suppose that the dog's behavior is of the same kind in both cases but that it is the world—in the form of the other dog—that is different. The behavior is the same, but the world plays ball on one occasion but not on the other.

If this is right, then there is a good case for thinking that, whether successful or unsuccessful, when the dog performs a play bow I see the dog trying or intending or desiring to initiate play. We have established that this is what I see when the play bow is unsuccessful: I cannot see the dog initiating play because play is not, in fact, initiated. I see the dog trying, intending, or desiring to initiate play. If we accept that the behavior involved in the successful play bow is of the same kind as the behavior involved in the unsuccessful play bow, then we seem compelled to accept that I see the dog trying or intending or desiring to initiate play in the successful case as well. The difference between the two cases is simply this: in the successful case, but not in the unsuccessful counterpart, in seeing the dog trying to initiate play, I thereby, in fact, see him initiate play. In both cases, the trying, intending, or desiring is not something hidden behind the behavior. In seeing the behavior, I see the trying, intending, or desiring.

It should be noted that the strong claim—that I see psychological states in the case of successful behavior—is not necessary to undermine the problem of other animal minds. Given the blanket nature of the skeptical problem of other minds, that problem is undermined if we can show that, *in some cases* at least, we can see the mental states of animals. The case of the unsuccessful play bow establishes this claim. As far as the problem of other animal minds goes, the claim that we also see mental states in cases of successful play bows is an optional extra. Nevertheless,

---

[18] There is, in fact, a precedent for this in other areas of philosophy. In the philosophy of perception, there is a view known as *disjunctivism* that regards successful acts of perceiving and unsuccessful acts (e.g., illusions, hallucinations) as distinct kinds of psychological state. This position may or may not be plausible in cases of perception, but the corresponding position holds little appeal in the case of animal behavior.

I think it is plausible to suppose that we do also see this in the case of successful play bows.


## 7. BIDDING ADIEU TO THE PROBLEMS OF OTHER MINDS

In making sense of what animals do, we help ourselves to functional descriptions of their behavior. We have to do this or be left with merely formal descriptions that are, typically, rather unenlightening. Functionally described behavior is perfectly visible. I might not be able to see *that* a behavior is an example of a play bow. But if it is, in fact, an example of a play bow, I can certainly see it. But, in this case, the functional description is a disguised version of a psychological description. When I see the dog performing a play bow what I see is the dog trying or intending to initiate play. This is a simple corollary of the intransigence of the world. If I were to say, "I see the dog initiating play," then few, today, would have any qualms. But given the world we live in, success is never guaranteed. What I, in fact, see is the dog trying or intending to initiate play. If the world plays ball, then I thereby also see the dog initiating play. We have arrived at this conclusion in three steps. First there is the distinction between seeing and seeing *that*. Second, there is the distinction between formal and functional descriptions of behavior and the concomitant idea that functional descriptions are both legitimate and important in our attempts to understand animal behavior. Third, there is the idea that functional descriptions are, often, tacitly psychological descriptions. To see behavior is to see the trying, intending, or desiring that animates it. I cannot see *that* the animal tries or intends or desires to do something. But I can, nevertheless, see the animal trying, intending, or desiring to do it.

It is important to be clear on what this argument does and does not show. It is not, as I have mentioned, a *solution* to the problem of other animal minds. If it were intended as such, it would rely on a question-begging assumption. *If* the rotating pattern of dust, dirt, and water vapor is, in fact, caused by a tornado, I have argued, that in seeing the pattern I see the tornado. But in the context of other minds, the "if" in question is a rather big one. Indeed, it is what the problem of other minds is all about. *If* the raised rump, lowered snout, etc. of the dog is, in fact, caused by the intention, desire, or trying to initiate play, then in seeing this behavior I see the intention, desire, or trying. But that it is caused in this way is precisely what the skeptic about other animal minds will deny. If the argument I have developed were proffered as a solution to the problem of other animal minds, it would, therefore, be question-begging. The argument, however, is not intended to work in this way.

Rather, the argument is intended to *dissolve* the problem of other animal minds. The dissolution has the following form. *Given the descriptions we employ of the behavior of animals*, we cannot take seriously the problem of other animal minds. Many of the functional descriptions of the behavior of animals we employ are tacitly psychological descriptions. To abandon these would mean abandoning functional descriptions and relying only on formal alternatives. But formal alternatives are unenlightening at best, often downright confusing, and would likely make any sort of illuminating scientific study of animals impossible. If we want an illuminating science of animal behavior, then I am afraid we are just going to have to accept that they have minds. Moreover, if we accept this, then we must also accept that in seeing behavior we thereby see the mental states of the animal that engages in it. If we want any sort of illuminating science of animal behavior, we should acknowledge that our primary access to the minds of animals is not through inference but through perception. Of course, we can be wrong in particular cases about what is going on in the mind of an animal—that is what happened in the case of Clever Hans. But what we can rule out is our ever believing in the possibility of widespread, or blanket, error of the sort countenanced by the problem of other animal minds. It is true, we have to suppose, that many animals have minds, for the most useful ways we have of describing their behavior make no sense unless it is true.

It will come as little surprise that I suspect the same general strategy is also applicable to the problem of other human minds. A dissolution of that problem should also focus on the distinction between seeing and seeing that, on the poverty of purely formal descriptions of behavior, and on the tacitly psychological nature of functional descriptions of behavior. As in the case of other animal minds, the result will be dissolution—rather than a solution—of the problem based on the idea that, in some cases at least, we can directly perceive the mental states of others. The only way of resisting this would be to abandon functional descriptions of human behavior in place of purely formal ones, and this would almost certainly leave us with no suitable notion of behavior to provide the target of our explanations. But my interest is in the animal case, the problem of other animal minds. Whether the strategy developed here can be extended to the problem of other human minds lies beyond the concerns of this book.

# 3

## CONSCIOUSNESS IN ANIMALS

In Chapter 1, I identified four conditions, each of which is necessary, and the set of which is collectively sufficient, for a creature to qualify as a person: consciousness, cognition, self-awareness, and other-awareness. This chapter discusses the consciousness condition. After all, I might as well start with the easiest one: today—things were a little different in the not too distant past—the claim that animals are conscious is now widely accepted. There are, as we shall see, very good reasons for this.

The term *consciousness* can mean quite a few different things. The relevant sense of consciousness, for the purposes of this chapter and our first condition of personhood, is what is typically called *phenomenal* consciousness. In his well-known paper "What Is It Like to Be a Bat?" Thomas Nagel characterizes this sort of consciousness as follows:

> [N]o matter how the form [of conscious experience] may vary, the fact that an organism has conscious experience at all means, basically, that there is something that it is like to be that organism. . . . [F]undamentally, an organism has

conscious mental states if and only if there is something that it is like to be that organism—something it is like *for* the organism.[1]

The claim that a creature is phenomenally conscious is, as a first approximation, the claim that *there is something that it is like* to be that creature. This expression involves what's known as an existential quantification: "there is"—and such quantificational expressions can often, and in a variety of contexts, engender confusions. If we are told, for example, that there is something it is like to be a bat, then we immediately face a question over what is known as the *scope* of the quantifier—of what sort of thing the quantifier *ranges over*. There is little need to think, for example, that the quantifier ranges over some experiential quality that pervades all bat experience, such that whenever a bat has an experience it is aware of this distinctive *batty* quality of its experience. Similarly, if we claim there is something that it is like to be human, there is no need to interpret this in terms of some sort of human-y quality that pervades or attaches to all human experience.[2] Instead, talk of there being something it is like to be a bat and something it is like to be human can be interpreted less extravagantly: bats have experiences and humans have experiences, and while there might be some overlap, many of the experiences bats have are experiences humans do not have, and vice versa.

The notion of phenomenal consciousness is also often explained in terms of the notion of things *feeling* or *seeming* a certain way. There is also a potential ambiguity here, involving the idea of what, precisely, it is that seems or feels a certain way. Someone slides a knife into your ribs. Do you feel the pain or do you feel the knife? Both options have their supporters. Personally, I prefer the second. Pain is not what I feel, but the way I feel the knife, or the way I feel the damage caused by the knife. I feel the knife, or the bodily damage, *painfully*. If I drop a bowling ball on my foot, then I feel my crushed toes—painfully. Similarly, if I see a bright red tomato, then it is not my visual experience that seems red—it is the tomato that seems red in virtue of the visual experience I have of it. Phenomenal consciousness, in

---

[1] Nagel (1979), p. 166. Bats, Nagel assumed, are conscious, but what interested him was that this consciousness was likely to be, relative to humans at least, highly idiosyncratic. Many bats use echolocation to navigate, and the form their consciousness takes may be beyond the ability of humans to understand—and this is true even if we knew everything there is to know about the neural and bodily processes by which the bat echolocates. Whether or not Nagel is correct in this contention does not concern us here. What does concern us is the notion of consciousness that Nagel adopts. A slight digression, motivated by nothing more than a mild fascination with bats: not all bats use echolocation. Microbats—which used to be known as Microchiroptera but most of which are now known as Yangochiroptera, use it; but macrobats generally do not. The exception is the Egyptian fruit bat, *Rousettus aegyptiacus*. However, *R. aegyptiacus* uses a different method: clicks are formed using its nasal passages rather than larynx.

[2] See Rowlands (2001), pp. 4–6, for a debunking of this interpretation of the expression "there is something it is like."

general, is not something *of* which I am aware but something *with* which I am aware: something in virtue of which (parts of) the world (my ribs, my toes, the tomato) feels or seems a certain way.[3]

This distinction allows us to understand talk of there being something it is like to be a bat, or something it is like to be a human, in a natural, indeed I think obvious, way. Bats—at least the Yangochiroptera—do not experience tomatoes in the same way humans do. When I look at a tomato, the tomato seems bright and red to me. It does not seem this way to the bat whose engagement with the tomato is underwritten by echolocation rather than vision. That is, all talk of there being something that it is like to be a bat, or human, should be taken to mean: the way things in the world—where the "world" subsumes the body—seem or feel to organisms. You are phenomenally conscious if and only if the world seems or feels a certain way to you.

Phenomenal consciousness is generally accepted to be distinct from self- consciousness. General acceptance is not the same as universal acceptance, however; and there is a history, especially in the sciences, of confusing the two. To take one notable example, in interpreting his famous *mirror self-recognition* (MSR) test,[4] Gallup runs together phenomenal consciousness with self-consciousness. He claims that self-awareness—which he understands as the ability to be able to think about one's own body or mental states—is required for having any conscious states at all. Therefore, animals that fail to exhibit MSR have no conscious mental life. (Indeed, according to Gallup, they have no mental states of any sort—neither conscious nor unconscious. Creatures that fail the MSR test have no minds.[5]) Although some have tried, there is, in fact, no compelling reason for strongly associating phenomenal consciousness and self-consciousness in this way. I shall return to this topic in later sections of this chapter.

## 2. PHENOMENAL CONSCIOUSNESS IN ANIMALS: BEHAVIORAL EVIDENCE

The prospects for proving the existence of phenomenal consciousness in animals are thought, by some, to be bleak. Such consciousness is by definition inner, private, and subjective and, therefore, skeptics argue, is not the kind of thing amenable to the public, objective methods of scientific inquiry. What possible experiment, it

---

[3] I have been refining this view for more years than I care to remember, beginning with Rowlands (2001). See Rowlands (2010), (2015b), and (2015c) for more recent developments of this general theme.
[4] See Chapter 6 for discussion of the MSR test.
[5] Gallup (1982).

might be asked, could establish the existence of phenomenal consciousness in animals? That this assessment is unduly pessimistic can be seen from remembering that exactly the same point applies to humans: phenomenal consciousness is no less inner, private, and subjective when it occurs in humans than when it occurs in animals.

In response to the animal consciousness skeptic—someone who is skeptical about consciousness in animals but not in humans—one can point to three main forms of evidence in favor of the claim that many animals are phenomenally conscious. The first is *evolutionary*. The category *Homo* (human) first emerged, having split from the category *Pan* between 2.5 and 2.8 million years ago. Anatomically modern humans emerged around 200,000 years ago, and evidence of *Homo sapiens*[6] emergence dates back to around 160,000 years ago. On an evolutionary scale—life began approximately 4.1 billion years ago, and eukaryotes emerged 2.1 billion years ago—200,000 years, or 2.5 or 2.8 million years, are merely the very rapid blinks of an eye. How strange it would be, then—how utterly remarkable, in fact—if consciousness has chosen to reside only in in a creature that emerged so recently! Putting aside the problem of other human minds, we know that we humans are conscious. Given what we know about the enormous evolutionary continuity between us and other animals, it would be bizarre, and astonishing, if we turned out to be the only creatures in which the light of phenomenal conscious chose to dawn. This is a familiar argument, vitiated only by our failure to identify a clear evolutionary purpose for phenomenal consciousness.[7] I shall not rely on this argument but, instead, employ two other sources of evidence for the claim that animals are phenomenally conscious.

The first of these is obvious: *behavior*. Many animals certainly behave *as if* they are conscious. I take it this is too obvious to require further elaboration. However, it is common to think that human behavior is more indicative, or revelatory, of the presence of phenomenal consciousness than the behavior of any other animal. This is because—to cut a long story short—we can *talk* about it. In the preceding chapter, I talked about some of the pitfalls of thinking that language makes a decisive difference when dealing with skepticism about other minds. Language is simply another form of behavior. Here, I shall take a different—although complementary—tack: examining the ways in which non-verbal behavior is commonly taken to be indicative of the presence of phenomenal consciousness.

---

[6] In the modern, rather than archaic, form.

[7] A way—not the only way, but a way—of expressing the so-called hard problem of (phenomenal) consciousness is this: why did neural machinery ever give rise to consciousness? What advantage did consciousness bestow on its possessors that could not have also been bestowed by the appropriate, non-conscious, neural processing operations? See Chalmers (1995).

AR—accurate report—is generally taken to be an acceptable behavioral index of phenomenal consciousness in humans. Indeed, more than acceptable, it is now employed as the *standard* behavioral index of such consciousness in humans. Of course, if we took seriously the problem of other human minds it would be no such thing. We cannot solve *that* problem simply by noting the existence of solicited and unsolicited verbal behavior in humans. Verbal behavior is just behavior, and the problem of other human minds arises when we think that behavior is all we have to go on. The fact that we are allowed to take AR as the standard behavioral index of phenomenal consciousness in humans, therefore, indicates that we are now, in this context, refusing to take seriously the problem of other human minds. That is fair enough. In the previous chapter, I gave some reasons for thinking that we cannot take the problem of other minds seriously since it would leave us with no workable notion of behavior. And without a workable notion of behavior, it is not even clear that we can state the problem of other minds. Therefore, as far as I am concerned: hurrah to not taking the problem of other human minds seriously. However, if we do not take the problem of other human minds seriously, then it would be a little unfair to revive it when the focus switches to the minds of animals.

With this in mind, it is important to realize that even in the case of humans, AR is not restricted to verbal reports. It is widely accepted that any appropriate voluntary movement will do. For example, eye movements are commonly taken as instances of AR in cases of paralysis or lucid dreaming. If we accept this broadening of what constitutes AR, then we must also accept that at least some animals are capable of it. For example, behavioral reports—in the form of pressing a key to deliver a comment about a previous discrimination—have become familiar components of experimental protocols in studies of primates and cetaceans.[8] And it has been standard to use AR by matching tasks in studies of vision in rhesus macaques.[9] It is also common to test AR via naming tasks, and this method has been employed in studies of a number of species, including primates, cetaceans, and such birds as African gray parrots and budgerigars.[10] Thus, the situation seems to be as follows. First, AR is taken as the gold standard of behavioral indices of phenomenal consciousness in humans—a practice that clearly requires downgrading the problem of other human minds. Second, several animals exhibit AR. A refusal to accept AR in animals can, it seems, only be because of a determined attempt to

---

[8] See, for example, Cowey and Stoerig (1995) and Stoerig and Cowey (1997).

[9] See Brewer et al. (2002).

[10] See, for example, Herman, Morrel-Samuels, and Pack (1990), Marino (2002), Pepperberg and Wilcox (2000), and Pepperburg and Shive (2001). For a good review, see Griffin and Speck (2004).

revive the problem of other minds when it applies to animals, while ignoring the same problem when applied to humans. In such circumstances, it is difficult to shake the conclusion that the game is rigged.

## 3. NEUROBIOLOGICAL EVIDENCE

A few years ago, a largish group of prominent cognitive neuroscientists, neuropharmacologists, neurophysiologists, neuroanatomists, and computational neuroscientists gathered at a conference at the University of Cambridge. The result of this conference was the "Cambridge Declaration on Consciousness," written by Philip Low and edited by Jaak Panksepp, Diana Reiss, David Edelman, Bruno Van Swinderen, and Christof Koch. The declaration concludes:

> The absence of a neocortex does not appear to preclude an organism from experiencing affective states. Convergent evidence indicates that non-human animals have the neuroanatomical, neurochemical, and neurophysiological substrates of conscious states along with the capacity to exhibit intentional behaviors. Consequently, the weight of evidence indicates that humans are not unique in possessing the neurological substrates that generate consciousness. Non-human animals, including all mammals and birds, and many other creatures, including octopuses, also possess these neurological substrates.

While the existence of the declaration proves nothing—all of these world-leading signatories may, in principle, be mistaken—it is instructive to look at the kinds of evidence they had in mind when putting together the declaration.[11]

This is what we now know about phenomenal consciousness in humans. First, waking consciousness is correlated with *low-level, irregular neural activity*, of a frequency *ranging from roughly 20 to 70 Hz*. On the other hand, it is also known that unconscious states such as deep sleep, states induced by anesthesia, vegetative states, and epileptic seizures display predominantly higher-amplitude and more regular waves at a frequency of less than 4 Hz.

Second, phenomenal consciousness in humans is strongly correlated with activity in the *thalamus* and *cortex*.[12] In contrast, regions such as the hippocampal system and cerebellum can be damaged without loss of consciousness. Damage to the thalamus can eliminate the state of consciousness—rendering the subject

---

[11] For an excellent overview of the evidence, see Baars (2005) and Seth, Baars, and Edelman (2005).
[12] Baars, Banks, and Newman (2003)

unconscious. Local damage in the sensory cortex, on the other hand, typically deletes only specific conscious features—color vision, conscious experiences of objects or faces, visual perception of movement, and so on. Thus, as a rough rule of thumb, thalamic activity is generally taken to be responsible for the global state of consciousness (that is, for a creature being conscious rather than unconscious), while the cortical activity (not on its own, but interacting with the thalamus) is correlated with specific features or *contents* of consciousness.[13]

Third, in humans, phenomenal consciousness is associated with *widespread activation* in the brain.[14] Sensory input triggers activity that spreads rapidly from the sensory cortex to parietal, prefrontal, and medial-temporal regions. Unconscious input, on the other hand, does not exhibit the same sort of profile of spreading activation, being largely restricted to the sensory cortex. Similarly, novel tasks—which tend to be conscious (as judged by AR)—recruit many different regions of the cortex. As these tasks become routine and automatic—the sorts of things that are done without conscious care or attention—the cortical regions they recruit become far more limited.

Therefore, the available evidence seems to indicate that phenomenal consciousness is correlated with "*widespread, relatively fast, low-amplitude* interactions in the *thalamocortical* region of the brain."[15] The case for phenomenal consciousness in animals is, therefore, straightforward: we find precisely the same kind of activity in many other animals including, as the declaration states, "all mammals and birds, and many other creatures, including octopuses." In other words, the neural correlates of phenomenal consciousness in humans are also found in many other species. This strongly suggests animals are phenomenally conscious also.

## 4. BLINDSIGHT AND ACCESS CONSCIOUSNESS

Those who wish to resist this conclusion may try to avail themselves of the phenomenon known as *blindsight*. The cause of blindsight is a lesion, or lesions, in the *striate* cortex (also known as the *primary visual cortex* or *V1*).[16] When this happens, a person might profess—AR—to have no visual consciousness in a part of the visual field, known as a *scotoma* or blind spot. Typically, the scotoma will comprise one half of the visual field. Nevertheless, the person can respond to visual stimuli

---

[13] Seth, Baars, and Edelman (2005), p. 123.
[14] Srinivasan et al. (1999).
[15] Seth, Baars, and Edelman (2005), p. 124. Italics in original.
[16] For a classic study, see Weiskrantz (1998).

that fall within this scotoma. Thus, when asked to guess the type, location, or movement of an object, he can do so at rates greatly above chance. Thus, according to a widespread interpretation of the results, he processes visual information but does so in the absence of conscious visual experience.

Ned Block distinguishes between phenomenal consciousness and what he calls *access consciousness* (in his terminology, A-Consciousness, which is distinct from P-Consciousness).[17] We can usefully frame the phenomenon of blindsight in terms of this distinction. Roughly, an item is access-conscious if it is available for use in reasoning and/or for direct control of action, including speech. A person with blindsight can be access-conscious of information that falls within her scotoma—that is why she is able to respond in ways suggestive of sight—but is not phenomenally conscious of these items. Moreover, according to Block, reportability—the ability to report on the contents of one's mind—is "often the best practical guide to A-consciousness."[18] This raises a more general worry about the use of AR as a guide to phenomenal consciousness: AR need not be indicative of phenomenal consciousness at all but only of access consciousness—of the sort that a blindsighted patient has to the contents of his blind spot.

This is, indeed, always a possibility—it is the sort of possibility that motivates the problem of other minds, human and animal. But there is little reason for thinking it is true in the case of animals. Blindsighted patients behave very differently from those with unimpaired visual consciousness. Crucially, as Jamieson and Bekoff have pointed out, blindsighted patients do not *spontaneously* respond to things presented to their scotomas but must be trained to make responses using a forced-response paradigm.[19] Thus, if we want to draw any conclusions concerning access versus phenomenal consciousness based on the blindsight cases, it seems we should make spontaneous response to objects presented in one's visual field as an operational test of phenomenal consciousness. Animals, of course, do spontaneously respond to objects in their visual fields.

If a Martian were to visit earth with a view to identifying which creatures are, and which are not, phenomenally conscious, she would find the same sorts of evidence in us as in a wide variety of other animals. In both us and many other animals, she would find widespread, relatively fast, low-amplitude, re-entrant activity in the thalamocortical complex. She would find that this activity engages the same anatomical structures and exhibits the same kind of activation profile in us and many other creatures. She would, in addition, find no evidence that either

[17] Block (1995).
[18] Block (1995), p. 249.
[19] Jamieson and Bekoff (1992).

we or these other creatures behave like blindsighted subjects with respect to their visual experiences. In other words, the neurobiological evidence she finds for consciousness in us she would also find in an array of other animals, including, as the Cambridge Declaration puts it, all mammals and birds, and many other creatures.

## 5. CONSCIOUSNESS AND HIGHER-ORDER THOUGHTS

While there are good scientific reasons for thinking that many animals are phenomenally conscious, there, nevertheless, remain specifically philosophical objections. Actually, there is really just one specifically philosophical objection, and it is found in the *higher-order thought* (HOT) model of consciousness. The HOT theory of consciousness is a species of a more general genus: *higher-order representation* (HOR) theories of consciousness. This genus divides into two species: HOT and *higher-order experience* (HOE) theories of consciousness. Common to both versions of HOR is the idea that a mental state is conscious when, and only when, the individual that has it is conscious *of* it. Where HOT and HOE differ is with respect to what is involved in the individual becoming conscious of a mental state. For HOE theories, an individual is aware of a mental state, M, when, and only when, he has an experience—typically, an introspective experience of a quasi-perceptual sort—of it: an experience whose intentional object is M.[20] According to the HOT model, on the other hand, what makes M conscious is the fact that the individual has a thought about M—a thought to the effect that he or she is in M.

I am going to focus mainly on the HOT theory. It is this theory that has been used to argue that animals are not conscious. The idea that animals can have thoughts about their own mental states is thought to be problematic in a way that the claim they can have higher-order quasi-perceptual experiences is not. The general idea is that thoughts require concepts, and so to have thoughts about one's mental states one would have to have concepts of mental states; and this sort of conceptual sophistication is, it is assumed, beyond all or most animals. Therefore, all or most nonhuman animals are unconscious. However, it is worth noting that

---

[20] The notion of an intentional object will become much more prominent in the next chapter, and I shall explain the idea in more depth there. But the basic idea is this. Many mental states are about things. You don't just think, you think something. You don't just believe, you believe something. You don't just see, you see something, and so on. Thoughts, beliefs, and perceptions are examples of what philosophers call *intentional* states: states that are about things. The thing that the state is about is called the *intentional object* of the state. An intentional object can, but need not be, an object in the usual sense. Sometimes this object does not exist. Often—some think always—it is not an object in the colloquial sense but a state of affairs: roughly, an arrangement of objects and properties in the world (when I think, for example, that the cat is on the mat).

many advocates of the HOT model have taken great care to show that their theory does not, in fact, entail that animals lack phenomenal consciousness. They do so because they realize that this sort of implication would be tantamount—or at least very close—to a *reductio ad absurdum* of their preferred theory. However, at least one advocate of the HOT theory—Peter Carruthers—has bitten the bullet and denied consciousness to animals based on the HOT model.[21]

Why, one might think—not unreasonably—would I bother to discuss a theory that (a) might, conceivably, deny consciousness to animals but where (b) most of whose advocates deny that this entailment really holds? The answer is that, here, I have a longer game in mind. My real target is not the HOT theory specifically but HOR theories in general. I shall argue that the general form of explanation HOR models have of what makes a mental state conscious is fatally flawed. To explain the consciousness of mental states, we do not need to appeal to a higher-order state—neither a higher-order thought nor a higher-order experience. The consciousness of mental states is a first-order phenomenon. This is a longer game in the sense that the diagnosis of the general mistake made by HOR models will prove important as this book progresses. In essence, I shall argue that they hold a mistaken conception of the awareness *of* mental states. They think of this "of" as the "of" of intentionality. It is not, at least not typically—or so I shall argue. This paves the way for the discussion of the self-awareness condition in later chapters.

In order to understand HOR models in general, one requires two distinctions. The first is between *creature* and *state* consciousness. Consciousness can be ascribed to both creatures and mental states. A creature can be conscious in the sense that it is awake as opposed to asleep. This is creature consciousness. But a mental state—a desire, to take an obvious Freudian example—can also be conscious or unconscious. This is state consciousness. The second distinction is between *transitive* and *intransitive* consciousness. Transitive consciousness is consciousness *of* something. If I (consciously) think that the cat is on the mat, then I am transitively conscious of this state of affairs—I am conscious of the cat being on the mat. Creatures are transitively conscious of things; mental states are not. My thought that the cat is on the mat is not conscious *of* anything. Rather, I am conscious of the cat being on the mat in virtue of having this (conscious) thought. My thought that the cat is on the mat, on the other hand, is intransitively conscious when I am (consciously) thinking it. Based on these distinctions, we can express the guiding idea behind all versions of the HOR theory as follows: *intransitive state consciousness is to be explained in terms of transitive creature consciousness.*

---

[21] Carruthers (1989). He reiterated this claim and identified what he thought of as some of the moral consequences of it in Carruthers (1992).

A mental state is intransitively conscious if and only if the creature that has it is transitively conscious of it.

The HOE and HOT species of the HOR theory differ with respect to what they take to be the basis of transitive creature consciousness. According to the HOE model, a creature is transitively conscious of a mental state (thereby making that state intransitively conscious) if, and only if, it has a higher-order, broadly introspective, experience of the mental state. According to the HOT model, transitive creature consciousness is secured by way of a higher-order thought rather than experience. A creature is transitively conscious of a mental state (thereby making that state intransitively conscious) if, and only if, the creature has a higher-order thought about the state—a thought to the effect that it is in this mental state.

This may be a little abstract, so let's consider an example. Suppose I am in pain. All versions of the HOR model agree that this pain is not, in itself, intransitively conscious: I could, in principle, spend my entire life in unrelenting pain without being aware of it. My pain becomes intransitively conscious only when I become transitively conscious of it. This transitive consciousness is, on the HOE account, secured by my having an (introspective, quasi-perceptual) experience *of* it. On the HOT account, on the other hand, my transitive consciousness of my pain is secured by my having a thought about my pain—specifically, a thought to the effect that I am in pain. On both accounts, the intransitive consciousness of a pain is something added to that pain by an act of awareness that is distinct from the pain itself: my transitive consciousness of this pain. It is this general picture of where the intransitive consciousness of a mental state comes from—an act of transitive consciousness directed toward that state—that is the principal target of the arguments I am going to develop in the remainder of this chapter. I shall develop these arguments, initially, in connection with the HOT model.

There is one, final, preliminary point. The HOT model itself divides into two sorts. On the one hand, there are *actualist* versions of the HOT model—and this is the version captured by the preceding characterization of the HOT model. According to the actualist version, for a mental state of mine to be intransitively conscious, I must (actually) have an occurrent thought to the effect that I am in pain. There is, however, also a dispositionalist version of the theory—and this is, in fact, the version adopted by Carruthers.[22] According to this version, for a mental state of mine to be intransitively conscious, I do not (actually) need to have an occurrent thought to the effect that I am in this state. It is enough for me to be *disposed* to have this thought: a mere tendency to have this thought is enough to make my mental state intransitively conscious. I shall discuss the actualist version

---

[22] Carruthers (1992).

first and argue that there are serious problems with it. The problems with the dispositionalist version of HOT are, if anything, even worse.


## 6. A DILEMMA

The HOT theory of consciousness, I shall argue, falls foul of a dilemma. Proponents of the theory are generally well aware of one horn of the dilemma and take pains to avoid it. But they are far less familiar with the other horn. Together, these two horns are, I shall argue, fatal to the HOT theory. Here is the dilemma:

(1) The higher-order thought that makes the subject conscious of a mental state, M, and thereby makes M intransitively conscious, is either intransitively conscious or not.

(2) If the higher-order thought *is* intransitively conscious, then the HOT theory does not explain intransitive state consciousness but presupposes it.

(3) If the higher-order thought is *not* intransitively conscious, then it cannot make the subject transitively conscious of its mental state, M. And since M's intransitive consciousness is supposed to be explained by the subject's transitive consciousness of M, this means that the HOT theory cannot explain the intransitive consciousness of M.

Premise (1) is clearly true. Proponents of HOT theories are well aware of the dangers of (2). If the higher-order thought is intransitively conscious, we are quickly presented with a regress. According to the HOT account, it is having a higher-order thought about a mental state that makes that state intransitively conscious. If the higher-order thought is, itself, intransitively conscious, then we will have to introduce another thought—a third-order, or higher-higher-order, thought—in order to make the higher-order thought conscious. But then the same question arises for the third-order thought: is it or is it not intransitively conscious? And then, we are well on our way to an infinite regress.

Of course, it is possible to stop the regress at any time by denying that the higher-order (or third-order, fourth-order, etc.) thought is conscious. But this brings us to premise (3). If we grasp the second horn of the dilemma—described in premise (3)—then we need to be able to explain how an intransitively unconscious mental state (the higher-order thought) can make its subject aware of the object of that thought (a first-order mental state). This is problematic, to say the least, because intransitively unconscious thoughts do not make their subjects transitively conscious of what those thoughts are about. Indeed, and rather crucially, *that is precisely what it is for them to be intransitively unconscious.*

Most of the beliefs we have are, most of the time, unconscious. My belief that Ouagadougou is the capital of Burkina Faso is a long-standing belief but one that only rarely appears on the conscious stage. When it becomes conscious, it does something that it does not do in its unconscious form: it makes me aware of the fact that Ouagadougou is the capital of Burkina Faso. Not making me aware of this fact is precisely what it is for this belief to be unconscious, and making me aware of it is precisely what it is for the belief to be conscious.

The same is true of thoughts as well as beliefs. Suppose, for example, I think unconsciously—perhaps due to various mechanisms of repression—that someone very close to me is seriously ill. What would this mean? We might explain it in terms of various unexplained feelings of melancholy that assail me when I am talking to them or a vague sense of foreboding that I can't quite pin down. However, what the thought cannot do, in its unconscious form, is make me aware of the fact that the person is seriously ill. Because as soon as it does that it becomes, by definition, a conscious thought. To become aware of the fact that my friend is seriously ill is to consciously think that my friend is seriously ill. The thought has, thus, become intransitively conscious. If a thought is intransitively unconscious, then it does not make me aware of the fact or state of affairs it is about: that is precisely what it means for thought to be intransitively unconscious. Conversely, as soon as it does make me aware of what it is about, it becomes an intransitively conscious thought—because making me aware of what it is about is precisely what it is for the thought to be intransitively conscious.

The HOT theory either is committed to an infinite regress or faces the seemingly impossible task of explaining how an intransitively unconscious thought can make its subject aware of what this thought is about—for that is precisely what intransitively unconscious thoughts do not do. Either way, the HOT model of consciousness should be rejected.

This objection has been directed at the actualist version of the HOT theory. But it applies, *a fortiori*, to the dispositionalist version. If an actual, occurrent but unconscious, higher-order thought does not make me transitively conscious of the mental state that thought is about—if its not doing this is precisely what it is for the thought to be unconscious—then a disposition to have an intransitively unconscious thought does not have hope of doing this. And if one responds that the disposition is to have a conscious higher-order thought, then one immediately faces the problem that intransitive state consciousness is being presupposed and not explained. There are further problems with the dispositionalist version of the HOT model. First, one must appreciate how deeply counterintuitive the theory is. It is very difficult to see how phenomenal consciousness could be a disposition. Indeed, it is almost as difficult to see how such consciousness could simply consist in dispositions to think certain things as it is to see how it could consist in dispositions to behave in various ways. Consciousness certainly seems to be a categorical phenomenon: you have it or you don't, and the attempt to explain it in terms of tendencies or dispositions seems woefully off target.

The dispositionalist version of HOT is also too weak to be useful. Indeed, it undermines the sorts of examples Carruthers uses to motivate his theory. For example, Carruthers employs the example of driving at night—when one suddenly "comes to" and realizes one has no recollection of the past fifteen miles or so one has driven. There are lots of ways to interpret this phenomenon, but Carruthers fastens on one: it is an example of unconscious experience. Therefore, he concludes, unconscious experience is a possibility, and it might be that the experience of animals is like this. Unfortunately for Carruthers, however, his own dispositionalist account seems to rule out this case as counting as a case of unconscious experience. After all, if you are driving along in the sort of fugue state Carruthers presupposes, you still have a disposition or tendency to have thoughts about your experiences. If your passenger asks you what you see on the road ahead, for example, then you will "wake up" and be able to reply. So, you do have a disposition to have thoughts about your experiences after all, and they, therefore, do not qualify as unconscious experiences.

## 7. CONSCIOUSNESS AS A FIRST-ORDER PHENOMENON

The HOT theory, therefore, can—though if many of its proponents are correct need not—be used as a way of denying consciousness to animals. This should not worry us unduly because the HOT theory does not seem to be tenable. What I am far more interested in, however, are not the various tribulations of the HOT theory itself but the mistake that led to the idea that it was a viable candidate. This final section will try to diagnose the mistake.

The second horn of the dilemma we leveled against the HOT theory strongly suggests another way of thinking about consciousness that has important ramifications both for HOT theories specifically and for HOR models more generally. According to the HOT model, and HOR models more generally, a mental state had by an individual is (intransitively) conscious if and only if that individual is (transitively) conscious of it. At this point, I think, a short remark of Ludwig

Wittgenstein is entirely apposite: "The decisive movement in the conjuring trick has been made, and it was the very one we thought quite innocent."[23]

The fundamental assumption of all higher-order theories of consciousness is this: a mental state of an organism is conscious in virtue of that organism being conscious of it. This is assumption is widespread and may seem unavoidable. It is even endorsed by some officially opposed to higher-order theories. For example, Uriah Kriegel, in developing his own "self-representational" account of consciousness, writes: "[T]he general motivation for this premise is the thought that it is somehow essential to a conscious state that its subject be aware of it. . . . The thought under consideration is that inner awareness is somehow essential to phenomenal consciousness."[24] In a similar vein, William Lycan, an HOE theorist, develops a—short and rapid—argument for a HOR account of consciousness, based on premises that he seems to regard as too obvious to require any real defense.[25] He argues thus:

(1) A conscious state is a mental state whose subject is aware of being in it (definition).
(2) The "of" in (1) is the "of" of intentionality; what one is aware of is the intentional object of the awareness.
(3) Intentionality is a representation; a state has a thing as an intentional object only if it represents that thing.
(4) Awareness of a mental state is a representation of that state (2, 3).
(5) A conscious state is a state that is itself represented by another of the subject's mental states (1, 4).

I think this argument fails on several counts, but for present purposes we can simply note that the combination of premises (1) and (2) is, in this case, the decisive movement in the conjuring trick.

Despite its seeming obvious and unavoidable to some, there is absolutely no reason to accept the claim that a mental state is (intransitively) conscious in virtue of the subject of that state being (transitively) aware of it. Accepting this claim leads inexorably to the dilemma described in the previous section. This supplies a pretty good reason for revising this initial assumption, and the above reflections on the second horn of the dilemma suggest how to do so. We can make the revisions using exactly the same conceptual apparatus as employed in HOR theories, merely with a little bit of, let us call it, *rewiring*. A mental state of mine—at least, an

---

[23] Wittgenstein (1953), Section 308.
[24] Kriegel (2011), p. 16.
[25] Lycan (2001), pp. 3–4.

*intentional* mental state of mine—is intransitively conscious not because I am transitively conscious of it but because it makes me transitively conscious of *something else*—what it is about. My thought that my friend is seriously ill becomes an intransitively conscious thought when, and only when, it makes me transitively conscious of the fact that my friend is seriously ill. If it does not do this, it is, by definition, unconscious.

Compare this with the case of belief. At any given time, the vast majority of a person's beliefs are unconscious—existing in dispositional rather than occurrent form. Only occasionally does my belief that Ouagadougou is the capital of Burkina Faso become a conscious one. What is the difference between the belief in unconscious and conscious forms? HOR theories tell us the difference is this: the belief is conscious when I am conscious of it and unconscious when I am not. Here is the alternative: the belief is conscious when it makes me conscious of what it is about—of the fact that Ouagadougou is the capital of Burkina Faso. It is unconscious when it does not make me aware of this.

In other words, the problem with HOR accounts is that they put transitive creature consciousness in the wrong place. They regard transitive creature consciousness as being inwardly directed—onto a mental state. But the inward directedness of transitive creature consciousness is not what makes a mental state intransitively conscious. It is the outer directedness of transitive creature consciousness that does this. A mental state is intransitively conscious when, and only when, it makes me, the designated creature in this case, transitively conscious of what it—the state—is about. A mental state is intransitively conscious when it makes its subject transitively conscious of the world—and not when its subject is transitively conscious of the state.

From this perspective, HOR accounts are based on a confusion of two different things: they conflate consciousness *of* and consciousness *with*.[26] I can, of course, be conscious of my belief that Ouagadougou is the capital of Burkina Faso. But the circumstances in which I am thus conscious of it are relatively unusual. Certainly, I do not need to be conscious of it in order for it to be an intransitively conscious belief. For that, all that is required is that I be conscious *with* it: that is, it makes me conscious of what it is about—the fact that Ouagadougou is the capital of Burkina Faso.

The confusion of consciousness of and consciousness with is certainly part of the story of why HOR models of consciousness are ultimately untenable. However, underlying this is, I suspect, a deeper confusion. This is a *vehicle-content* confusion.[27] A vehicle of content is something that has content. A mental state, such as a

---

[26] See Dretske (1982).
[27] For the general idea of a vehicle-content confusion, see Hurley (1998).

thought, would, thus, qualify as a vehicle of content. Therefore, HOR accounts assume that intransitive state consciousness consists in transitive consciousness of a *vehicle* of content. This is the crucial error. Intransitive state consciousness arises when I, the subject, am transitively conscious not of the state itself (the vehicle) but of the *content* of the state. Intransitive state consciousness arises through awareness of the content of the state, not awareness of the state itself.

## 7. CONCLUSION

To show that animals are persons, I have argued, requires showing that they satisfy four conditions: consciousness, cognition, self-awareness, and other-awareness. The consciousness condition is almost certainly the easiest on this list. Scientific evidence strongly supports the attribution of phenomenal consciousness to many other animals. The main philosophical objection, based on the HOT account of consciousness, is unconvincing. Therefore, it is likely that many animals satisfy the first condition on personhood, the consciousness condition.

That's pretty much all I have to say about phenomenal consciousness in animals. Next up, the focus switches to the cognition condition of personhood. I shall begin with what I take to be an essential prerequisite of this condition: *belief*. No animal that lacks beliefs has a chance of engaging in cognition—certainly not in the sort of reasoning I have identified as central to this condition. The idea that animals can have beliefs has seemed problematic to some—mainly, but not exclusively, philosophers. The next chapter explores these issues.

# 4

## TRACKING BELIEF

### 1. MALCOLM'S DOG

A certain chicken, we are asked to accept, crossed the road because it wanted to get to the other side. Of course, this would be only a partial explanation of its behavior. The chicken wanted to get to the other side, granted. But it must also have believed that crossing this road would be a good way of getting there. A very obvious, and tacit, belief, admittedly—but presumably the chicken must have had it. It presumably also lacked any countervailing beliefs that would have overridden this belief—concerning, for example, the likelihood of being squashed by oncoming motor vehicles, and so on. Pro-attitudes (wants, desires, etc.) in combination with cognitive attitudes (beliefs, thoughts, etc.): we use these when we explain the chicken's behavior via beliefs and desires. In explaining the chicken's behavior thus, we are employing what is known as *folk psychology*.

There is a good reason why, in our quest to understand human behavior, we use these folk psychological, belief–desire explanations: they work! In general, we humans manage to coordinate our behavior astonishingly well. There are open and interesting questions about the precise form belief–desire explanation takes, whether it is used in the same way for prediction and for explanation, and so on. There are also questions about the precise relation between belief–desire explanations and other, possible or actual, ways of explaining human behavior—for example, neurophysiological explanations. One can acknowledge that belief–desire explanations are far from perfect, but—the efforts of a few skeptics aside[1]—it is difficult to deny that, in general, they work rather well.

At first glance, one might expect belief–desire explanations to work just as well for nonhumans. Consider an example provided by Norman Malcolm.[2] A dog chases a squirrel. The squirrel runs up a tree, then jumps to the next tree and the next, and eventually disappears. The dog does not see this, and sits at the foot of the tree barking. It seems natural—and, indeed, enlightening—to explain the dog's behavior in the belief–desire terms of folk psychology. First, the dog wants—desires— to catch the squirrel: that is why he was chasing it, and his subsequent barking can be understood as frustration-behavior stemming from the non-satisfaction of this desire. Second, the dog believes the squirrel is in the tree: that's why his barking is taking place at the foot of the tree specifically. After all, he cannot *see* that the squirrel is in the tree because the squirrel is not, in fact, there.[3]

In some respects, the use of beliefs and desires in the explanation of animal behavior has met with less resistance than the attribution of phenomenal consciousness.[4] Nevertheless, there remain objections to the legitimacy of belief–desire explanations of animal behavior. These objections coalesce around the notion of *content*. Beliefs and desires are states that have intentional content. The same is true of many other states too: thoughts, hopes, fears, expectations, (semantic) memories, and so on. These sorts of states are known as *propositional attitudes*. When we ascribe these states to a human or animal, we use a certain sort of linguistic construction known as a *that*-clause. We say that Malcolm's dog believes *that* the squirrel is in the tree. What follows the "that" is a complete sentence, "The squirrel is in the tree." Sentences such as these have meaning. And the content

---

[1] The 1980s were the heyday for skepticism about beliefs and folk psychology more generally. For good examples of this skepticism, see Churchland (1981) and Stich (1983).

[2] Malcolm (1972). Malcolm actually talks about a cat rather than a squirrel.

[3] Perhaps one does not like imaginary examples. If not, here is a real one. Tess was a wolf dog of ours, who grew very attached to another wolf dog she would meet in the summers, and other holidays, in a village in France where we had a house. The other wolf dog—an ancient wolf-collie mix—belonged to an elegant, older, Parisian lady. One day, after we had just arrived back in the village for the Easter break, we were out walking Tess (and our other dog, Nina), when the Parisian lady appeared from around a corner across the other side of the road. Tess shot across the road and disappeared around the corner. This was very uncharacteristic behavior for Tess as she was trained and almost always well behaved. It is tempting—that is not to say it is correct—to explain her behavior by way of a belief: having seen the Parisian lady, Tess believed the wolf dog would be close (and desired to see the wolf dog, etc., and inferred that, since she could not see him, he must be around the corner). But could she not have smelled (thus, perceived) his presence around the corner? This is unlikely. It turned out that the old wolf-collie had died some six months before—shortly after we had departed the village in September, in fact.

[4] For example, Carruthers (2004), who we saw in the preceding chapter was unwilling to accept that any animals are phenomenally conscious, is quite happy to accept that even insects can have beliefs. Carruthers, however, does think that possession of belief is a matter of degree rather than an all-or-nothing affair.

of a belief (that the squirrel is in the tree; that the wolf dog is around the corner) is taken to be identical with—the same thing as—the meaning of the sentence contained within the scope of "that."

Beliefs, desires, and other propositional attitudes do not just *have* content. They are *individuated* by this content. The belief that the squirrel is in the tree is distinguished from the belief that the rabbit is in the hole by their differences in content. Therefore, if we are unable to identify the content of a belief or desire, then we cannot individuate it: we cannot say what this belief is, and we cannot, therefore, differentiate it from other beliefs and desires. And there are considerations that seem to militate against the possibility of identifying the content of the belief and desires of animals such as Malcolm's dog.

This general worry about content can be developed in two ways. One is *epistemological*: in many cases, perhaps most, we might not be able to *know* which content should be ascribed to animals, and we are therefore unable to know which beliefs and desires they have. The second is *ontological*: in many cases at least, it seems likely that contents we are tempted to ascribe to animals are, for one reason or another, contents that they cannot entertain.[5] Therefore, the beliefs and desires we are tempted to impute to them are ones they cannot, in fact, have. The goal of this chapter is to rescue belief–desire explanations of animal behavior from these two kinds of problem.

## 2. THE ANCHORING ARGUMENT

Donald Davidson and Stephen Stich have, independently, raised the same kind of objection to belief–desire explanations of animal behavior. Davidson states the problem argument as follows:

> Can the dog believe of an object that it is a tree? This would seem impossible unless we suppose that the dog has many general beliefs about trees: that

---

[5] I employ the term *entertain* here in a semi-technical philosophical sense. As such, it is used as a generic marker for whatever is the relation in which a subject stands to content. If you think that the sky is blue, you are entertaining the content THE SKY IS BLUE in this sense. If you hope that it is blue, doubt that it is blue, and so on, you are also entertaining this content. As a matter of fact, there are almost certainly differences between the idea of entertaining a proposition in the colloquial sense and other relations, such as believing it. Colloquially, I can entertain a proposition without believing it. But here I am employing the notion of entertaining in the semi-technical sense that renders it a placeholder for any specific type of content-involving mental act. I shall try not to use this locution—using instead more specific relations such as believing or desiring. Sometimes, however, it is unavoidable. When I do use it, however, please bear in mind its status as generic marker.

they are growing things, that they need soil and water, that they have leaves or needles, that they burn. There is no fixed list of things someone with the concept of a tree must believe, but without many general beliefs there would be no reason to identify a belief as a belief about a tree, much less an oak tree. Similar considerations apply to the dog's supposed thinking about the cat.[6]

The more general moral of these considerations, according to Davidson, is:

> We identify thoughts, distinguish between them, describe them for what they are, only as they can be located within a dense network of related beliefs. If we really can intelligibly ascribe single beliefs to a dog, we must be able to imagine how we would decide whether the dog has many other beliefs of the kind necessary for making sense of the first.[7]

Stich makes a similar point about a dog's belief that there is a bone buried in the yard:

> It surely cannot be quite right to say that Fido believes there is a meaty bone buried in the yard. After all, Fido does not even have the concept of a bone, much less the concept of a meaty bone or a yard. He may be able to recognize bones tolerably well. . . . But this is hardly enough to establish that he has the concept of a bone or any beliefs or desires about bones. For Fido does not, it seems safe to assume, have any beliefs about the origin and general anatomical function of bones. Nor would he recognize or exhibit any interest in chewing atypical bones—the bones of the middle ear, for example, or the collarbone of a blue whale. Worse yet, Fido does not know the difference between real bones and a variety of actual or imaginable ersatz bones (made of realistic looking plastic, perhaps, and partially covered with textured soy protein suitably flavored). Nor is there anything that would count as explaining the difference between real and fake bones to the dog. Fido is incapable of understanding that distinction. But given Fido's conceptual and cognitive poverty in matters concerned with bones, it is surely wrong to ascribe to him any belief about a bone.[8]

---

[6] Davidson (1982), p. 320.
[7] Davidson (1982), p. 320–21.
[8] Stich (1979), p. 18.

Davidson focuses on the tree, and Stich on a bone. I'll focus on the squirrel of Malcolm's example. Does the dog—let us call him Hugo—believe that the squirrel is a mammal, that it is warm-blooded, that it has a skeleton, and so on? All these beliefs, Davidson (and Stich) would claim, are part of our concept of a squirrel, and so without them Hugo cannot share our concept. Therefore, the attribution to Hugo of the belief that there is a squirrel in the tree is problematic. The attribution to Hugo of a belief about the squirrel depends on his possession of the concept of squirrel. However, possession of a concept depends on possession of a network of related beliefs, and Hugo does not possess the requisite network of beliefs.

We might call this the *anchoring* argument. My concept of a squirrel is anchored to me—in virtue of a set of beliefs I have about squirrels—and this renders problematic my using this concept to attribute content to Hugo. In a little more detail[9]:

(1) I have a concept of a squirrel.
(2) The content of this concept is constituted by *my* possession of a network of related beliefs about squirrels. A different network of beliefs would yield a different concept.
(3) The concept is, thus, *anchored* to me.
(4) Hugo does not possess the network of related beliefs that constitute my concept of a squirrel.
(5) Therefore, I cannot ascribe to Hugo the belief that the squirrel is in the tree. To do so would inevitably require using *my* concept of a squirrel, and this is a concept Hugo does not possess.

There are two distinguishable components of this argument. First, there is the idea of anchoring in general. Second, there is a specific account of the basis of this relation—in what this anchoring relation consists. For Davidson and Stich, the basis of the anchoring relation is a network of related beliefs that collectively delineate the content of a given concept and thus restrict the possession of the propositional attitude involving this concept to only individuals that possess this specific network. But the idea of anchoring can be understood more generally than this. Understood in more general terms:

---

[9] This formulation of the argument is truer to Stich's version than Davidson's. Davidson would not like the "concept" formulation. For our purposes, this does not matter. What is important is the general form of the argument rather than the specific details of its implementation. We could make the argument truer to Davidson's version by replacing talk of the content of concepts with the content of beliefs.

Anchoring: A content, *p*, is anchored to X if and only if there is some feature F such that (a) X has F, and (b) F is a necessary condition of the entertaining of *p*.

The notion of *entertaining*, as mentioned in note 5, is a generic marker for more specific relations such as believing, desiring, thinking, etc. To entertain content is to believe it, desire it, think it, hope it, fear it, remember it, and so on. X can range over individuals or collections of individuals. Content *p* is anchored to an individual—Jones—if Jones has F and F is necessary for entertaining *p*. But, typically, X will pick out a collection of individuals. Perhaps, for example, this collection might be the human race—or the majority of it. Perhaps it will be normal, adult speakers of a given language. This will vary, depending on the specific content—the specific version of *p*—that is entertained. Put in these general terms, the anchoring argument against the possibility of attributing content to animals is this: content entertained (believed, desired, thought, etc.) by humans is anchored to humans because of some or other (content-determining) feature, F, that humans possess and nonhuman animals do not. Such content cannot, therefore, be used to explain the behavior of anything that is not human.

## 3. DE-ANCHORING CONTENT: TWIN EARTH

The Davidson–Stich objection to explaining animal behavior in terms of beliefs and desires is, therefore, grounded in the general idea of anchoring plus a specific account of the basis of this anchoring. The content that we want to attribute to animals in order to explain their behavior is, in fact, content that is anchored to humans. And the basis of this anchoring is a network of beliefs that only humans can have. I shall argue that if this anchoring of content to humans is the problem for attributing beliefs and desires to animals, then there is a method of *de-anchoring* content. This method is based on the idea of what I shall call *tracking*. The idea of tracking, in turn, fragments into two further ideas: (1) *narrow content* and (2) *truth-preservation*.

Consider, first, a standard twin earth thought experiment, made famous by Hilary Putnam.[10] Twin earth is exactly like earth in almost every respect. On twin earth, there is a twin you, currently reading a twin edition of this book, which was written by a twin me and published by a twin Oxford University Press. Your twin, a molecule-for-molecule duplicate of you, has led what seems to be exactly the same life as you—experiencing the same events in the same order and reacting in the same way to

---

[10] Putnam (1975).

them. And so on and so forth—you can fill in the details if you are thus inclined. The only difference between earth and twin earth: on the latter planet, there is no water. Instead, there is a substance that looks, tastes, and so on exactly like water, but is not made of hydrogen and oxygen at all. We might call this substance "retaw." Your twin, however, doesn't call it that: he or she is a speaker of twin English, and so calls it "water." She may use the same syntactic/phonetic form, but she is, nevertheless, referring to a substance distinct from the one that you label "water."

Suppose I explain my twin's water-drinking behavior by positing that he (1) desires to quench his thirst and (2) believes that water is thirst-quenching. Strictly speaking, my explanation is incorrect. My twin lives on twin earth. Therefore, if Putnam is correct—and, simply for the sake of exposition, I shall assume he is—my twin cannot have water-beliefs.[11] His beliefs are about an entirely different substance—retaw not water (even though he calls retaw "water"). Therefore, my explanation of his behavior cannot be correct because it attributes to him a belief that he cannot have.

However, even if my explanation is not, strictly, correct, there is something about it that is *not so very far off the mark*. It is not as if, for example, I explained his behavior by postulating a desire to commit suicide coupled with the belief that the liquid in his glass was poison. That explanation is also incorrect (my twin has no suicidal tendencies since, as far as I know, I have none). But it is, intuitively, far *more* incorrect than my explanation. And it is incorrect in a quite different way than my explanation. My explanation—that appeals to the desire to quench thirst coupled with the belief that water will do the trick—is, I think it is plausible to say, not so far off the mark. Indeed, there is a sense—one that I shall try to make precise in the upcoming pages—in which it is legitimate to explain my twin's behavior using my content, even though this is content my twin cannot entertain. My explanation is not *exactly* true, but it is, nevertheless, in the *vicinity* of truth. This talk of being "in the vicinity of truth" can be explained using the ideas of narrow content and truth-preservation.

## 4. TRACKING 1: TRUTH-PRESERVATION

Let us consider, first, the idea of *truth-preservation*. Consider the relation between the content of my belief and that of my twin. The content of my belief is that water

---

[11] Putnam's concern was actually meaning rather than belief content. So, his arguments were restricted to the meaning of sentences rather than the content of beliefs. But, as others pointed out subsequently, the same arguments apply to the contents of beliefs and other propositional attitudes.

is thirst-quenching. I would express this content by way of the sentence "Water is thirst-quenching." My twin would express the content of his corresponding belief using the same sentence: "Water is thirst-quenching."[12] However, the content of his belief is that retaw is thirst-quenching. Therefore, since beliefs are individuated by their content, my belief and my twin's belief are distinct.

Nevertheless, while they are different beliefs, the truth of my belief *guarantees* the truth of my twin's belief. If my belief that water is thirst-quenching is true, then my twin's corresponding belief about retaw will also be true. This truth-guaranteeing or truth-preserving relationship between our beliefs holds in virtue of the contents of these beliefs: if water is thirst-quenching, then retaw will also be thirst-quenching.

In this specific case, the truth of my belief guarantees the truth of the corresponding belief of my twin simply because of the way the twin earth thought experiment is set up. The thought experiment is designed in such a way that water and retaw share all non-molecular properties. Thus, if any non-molecular claim about water is true, the corresponding claim about retaw will also be true. Moreover, in this specific case, truth-preservation runs both ways: if my twin's belief that *retaw* is thirst-quenching is true, then my corresponding belief about water must also be true. This is because if retaw is thirst-quenching, then water will be thirst-quenching also. This is a peculiarity of the twin earth thought experiment, where every (non-molecular) property of water is also possessed by retaw *and vice versa*. This sort of situation—in which truth-preservation runs in both directions—is relatively unusual. It is more common, certainly in the case of animals, for truth-preservation to run in only one direction: the truth of a belief that $p$ guarantees the truth of a belief that $q$, but not vice versa. This sort of unidirectional truth-preservation is both more prevalent and more important for our purposes.

## 5. TRACKING 2: NARROW CONTENT

I first introduced the idea of tracking in a book that was published a few years ago.[13] There, tracking consisted not simply in truth-preservation but truth-preservation *by a reliable route*. In the twin earth case, the truth-preserving relationship between my belief and that of my twin (and vice versa) holds because

---

[12] Whether it is the same sentence, in fact, depends on how you individuate sentences. Individuated syntactically, they are the same sentence. Individuated semantically, they are different sentences that merely appear to be the same. For my purposes, this complication is irrelevant. For expository purposes, I am supposing that sentences are individuated syntactically.

[13] Rowlands (2012a), Chapter 2.

of a reliable connection between the properties of water and retaw. With the exception of molecular properties, any property possessed by water will also be possessed by retaw (and vice versa—and that's why the tracking runs both ways in this case). Therefore, if water is thirst-quenching, then retaw will also be thirst-quenching. We can capture the reliability of the connection between the properties of water and retaw by way of conditionals of the form, "If water has (non-molecular) property P then retaw has P also (and, in this case, vice versa)." Or, perhaps our tastes run more to the counterfactual: "If water did not have (non-molecular) property P, then retaw would not have it either (and, again in this case, vice versa)."

I am not, by any means, abandoning the idea of a reliable connection, or the idea of truth-preservation by way of a reliable route. I have come to think, however, that this idea can be captured by way of a more basic, and more illuminating, idea: the idea of *narrow content*. The idea of narrow content arises because of certain fairly obvious considerations. My behavior with respect to water is, in a sense that is intuitive but surprisingly difficult to pin down precisely, the same as my twin's behavior vis-à-vis retaw. Roughly: whatever I do with water he does with retaw and vice versa. Therefore, since the function of beliefs and desires is, at least in part, to explain behavior, this gave rise to the idea that my beliefs (and desires) and those of my twin must have something in common. This something in common that they were assumed to have was labeled "narrow content."

Why is it that whatever I do with water my twin does with retaw and vice versa? The reason is that they share all non-molecular properties. This led to the idea that we can explain narrow content in terms of such properties. The narrow content of my belief that water is thirst-quenching would be something like, "The colorless, odorless, transparent, potable . . . liquid is thirst-quenching." But this would also be the narrow content of my twin's belief that retaw is thirst-quenching. This content is, therefore, content that we both share.

There are problems with this way of thinking about narrow content, which are familiar to many philosophers and probably not of much interest to anyone else—and so I shall relegate them to a footnote.[14] These problems all ultimately converge

---

[14] First, the above specification involves items that are, arguably, subject to twin earth cases. On earth, for example, a liquid is something with a certain kind of molecular structure. But we could set up a twin earth case that involves something that looks and tastes and feels, etc., exactly like a liquid but, in fact, has a radically different structure, involving perhaps radically different elements of a sort not exhibited or present on earth. Therefore, we need to purge these sorts of terms for the specification of narrow content. But once we have done this, the worry is that there won't be enough specificity remaining to supply a plausible version of narrow content. Attempts to solve this problem by way of a causal constraint—"The colorless, odorless, transparent . . . stuff that is *causing* this visual experience is thirst-quenching"—suffer a similar fate: we merely need to imagine a world in which a Humean view of causality is true and another world where there is such a thing as natural necessity.

on the idea that the narrow content of a belief is *inexpressible*. This idea provided the basis of an excellent idea developed by the late Jerry Fodor.[15] Let us grant that the narrow content of a belief is not something that can be expressed—because to express it would require concepts that are anchored to one context or another and therefore cannot capture what beliefs that straddle two contexts (e.g., earth and twin earth) have in common. Nevertheless, Fodor argued, we can still make sense of the idea of narrow content because we can supply a *criterion of identity* for such content.

The idea underlying such a criterion is that narrow contents are *functions from contexts to contents*. My belief that water is thirst-quenching and my twin's corresponding belief share narrow content in this sense: there is something, $p^n$, such that when $p^n$ is plugged into my earthly context it yields the content that water is thirst-quenching, but when plugged into a twin earthly context it yields the content that retaw is thirst-quenching (content that my twin would express with the sentence, "Water is thirst-quenching," of course). The narrow content I share with my twin is that which, when anchored to me (i.e., my context) yields the content that water is thirst-quenching, and when anchored to my twin yields the content that retaw is thirst-quenching. That is, narrow content, $p^n$, plus context, W, yields ordinary, anchored, content, $p$. Understood in this way, narrow content is not a *component* of content—in the sense of an expressible form of content that forms a separable part of ordinary content. Rather, it is a *vector* of ordinary, expressible content.

According to the tracking hypothesis, it is legitimate—and enlightening—to explain my twin's behavior by way of content that I, but not he, can entertain—as long as my content tracks his. Understood in isolation, however, this would be a curious claim: how, and why, can one explain a person's behavior by employing content that he or she cannot entertain? Crucially, mere truth-preservation cannot underwrite this claim. A content, $p$, might guarantee the truth of another content, $p^*$, because, for example, $p$ entails $p^*$. But this fact alone cannot establish that it is legitimate to explain an individual's behavior by way of $p$ instead of $p^*$, or $p^*$ instead of $p$, because the individual might not realize that the entailment holds.[16] The answer—and missing ingredient—is that there is a common vector possessed both by my twin's content and by mine. This is narrow content. It is

---

[15] Fodor (1986), Chapter 2.

[16] A footnote for philosophers: more generally, truth-preservation will only get you extensional equivalence. If you believe that $p$, then the truth of $p$ guarantees the truth of a claim extensionally equivalent to it. But this will not safeguard the opacity or intentionality of belief attributions. Ensuring the latter claim is precisely the function of narrow content—a task that narrow content, when it was introduced in other contexts, was more or less explicitly designed to do.

not possible to say what this content is: narrow content is inexpressible. Only anchored content can be expressed. Nevertheless, as we have seen, it is possible to provide an extensional criterion of identity for narrow contents based on the idea that narrow content is a function from contexts to (ordinary, wide) content.

Two important ideas emerge from the discussion of narrow content and truth-preservation. The reason I can legitimately explain my twin's behavior by way of content that he cannot entertain is (1) his content and mine have a component in common—they share *narrow content*—and (2) the truth of my belief with this (anchored to me) content that I use to explain my twin's behavior guarantees the truth of the belief with the (anchored to him) content he, in fact, entertains. When the truth-preservation and narrow content conditions are met—when the belief that $p$ guarantees the truth of a belief that $p^*$ and $p$ and $p^*$ share narrow content— then I shall say that the belief that $p$ *tracks* the belief that $p^*$. It is the idea of tracking, understood in this way, that I shall bring to bear on the question of the legitimacy of belief–desire explanations of animal behavior.

## 6. EXPLAINING ANIMAL BEHAVIOR

There is nothing in the anchoring argument per se that precludes the possibility of a dog, such as Hugo, possessing some or other belief about the squirrel. The anchoring argument, at most, would show only that I am unable to *attribute* beliefs about squirrels to Hugo because to do so would require the employment of concepts that I possess but Hugo does not. Any attribution of belief, that is, involves contents that are anchored to me. The argument does not show that Hugo lacks beliefs. Rather it shows that we humans are not able to attribute beliefs to him. And if we are unable to attribute beliefs to Hugo, then, it seems, we are also unable to explain his behavior in belief–desire terms. Using the de-anchoring strategy developed in the previous section, I shall now try to show how this ex-planatory problem can be circumvented. The key to the strategy involves drawing a clear distinction between (1) the attribution of beliefs to an individual and (2) the explanation of an individual's behavior in terms of beliefs.

The anchoring problem is compatible with Hugo having some or other repre-sentation of the squirrel. I do not need to take any stand on what this manner of representation is, but purely for purposes of exposition, let's make an ini-tial assumption. I shall indicate how we can rid ourselves of the assumption in due course. Let's assume that Hugo represents the squirrel in affordance-based terms. I am tempted to ascribe to him the belief that the squirrel is in the tree, but, let us suppose, the content of his belief is actually this: *the chase-able thing is up there*. Let us call the belief I am tempted to ascribe to Hugo *my belief*. It is my belief not in the sense that I must actually have it—I may, for example, realize the squirrel has disappeared—but in the sense that it involves concepts that I have but, we are supposing, Hugo does not. It is, thus, the sort of belief that I *can* have—whether or not I actually have it. If the de-anchoring strategy described in the previous section is correct, then I can legitimately explain Hugo's behavior via the ascription to him of my belief, then, as long as (1) my belief and his share narrow content and (2) the truth of my belief guarantees the truth of Hugo's belief.

For clarity, to make it clear that I am talking about the content of beliefs rather than beliefs or the sentences used to ascribe beliefs, I shall adopt the relatively common (for philosophers at least) convention of capitalizing content. The content of my belief is: THE SQUIRREL IS IN THE TREE. The content of Hugo's belief, I am supposing for the sake of argument, is: THE CHASE-ABLE THING IS UP THERE. Given certain, not unreasonable, qualifications, the truth of THE SQUIRREL IS IN THE TREE guarantees the truth of THE CHASE-ABLE THING IS UP THERE. [17] The most obvious qualification is that squirrels are, for Hugo, reliably chase-able. This may not be true for all dogs. Hugo is a German shepherd, and what is chase-able for him may not be for, for example, a chihuahua. But if we assume that squirrels are reliably chase-able for Hugo, and he regards them as such, then the truth of THE SQUIRREL IS IN THE TREE guarantees the truth of THE CHASE-ABLE THING IS UP THERE.

This general idea can be put in more formal terms. Truth-preservation is a relation that holds between *anchored* contents. My belief has the content THE SQUIRREL IS IN THE TREE. This content is anchored to me: it involves at least one concept that, we are supposing, I have but Hugo does not: the concept of a squirrel, where this is determined by a network of beliefs that I have but Hugo does not. Let us represent this as:

(1) [M: THE SQUIRREL IS IN THE TREE]

---

[17] Talk of the "truth" of content will no doubt justifiably grate on the ears of philosophers. I employ this as a shorthand for talk of the truth of a belief with a given content. Truth attaches to vehicles of content, such as beliefs or sentences, and not to content itself. I should really talk of the *obtaining* of content: the obtaining of one content guarantees the obtaining of another, and the *truth* of one belief that has this content, thereby, guarantees the truth of the other. Contents obtain or not, and the vehicles of these contents (such as beliefs) are, as a result, true or not. I beg your indulgence. Considerations of exposition, in this case, trumped those of accuracy. Later on, I'll be a little more accurate—and that, as you will see, is annoying in its own way.

"M:" is an anchoring operator: its function is to indicate that the content that follows it is anchored to me (M). Hugo's belief, we have assumed, has the content THE CHASE-ABLE THING IS UP THERE. Let us represent this as:

(2) [H: THE CHASE-ABLE THING IS UP THERE]

"H:" anchors this content to Hugo. Then, the first condition on tracking is this:

(3) If [M: THE SQUIRREL IS IN THE TREE] is true, then
    [H: THE CHASE-ABLE THING IS UP THERE] is also true.

If the anchored (to me) content THE SQUIRREL IS IN THE TREE is true, then the anchored (to Hugo) content THE CHASE-ABLE THING IS UP THERE is also true.

For tracking to occur, these anchored contents that stand in this truth-preserving relation share narrow content. Narrow content is a function from contexts to contents. That is, narrow content is the sort of thing that when plugged in—anchored—to a particular context yields a normal, *broad* content. The narrow content condition is satisfied, therefore, if the content I believe, THE SQUIRREL IS IN THE TREE, and the content Hugo believes, THE CHASE-ABLE THING IS UP THERE, share this narrow vector of content. That is, they share a vector of content such that when this vector is anchored to my context, it yields the content THE SQUIRREL IS IN THE TREE. And when anchored to Hugo's somewhat different context—a context composed of very different cognitive, conceptual, experiential, and emotional capacities—it yields the content THE CHASE-ABLE THING IS UP THERE.

There are good reasons for supposing that my belief and Hugo's share this narrow content. The idea of narrow content is closely tied to the notion of motivation and explanation of behavior. In terms of the role it plays in motivating/explaining behavior, my belief that water is thirst-quenching is identical with my twin's corresponding belief about retaw. If we are both thirsty, then my belief plays the same role in motivating/explaining my water-drinking behavior as the corresponding belief of my twin. That is the principal motivation for thinking that our beliefs share narrow content, for narrow content is simply the causal-explanatory component of ordinary content.

Of course, to fill in the details of this account, we would need to insert a judicious "all things being equal" clause at an appropriate juncture. I, for example, have little interest in chasing squirrels. But if I did, then my belief that the squirrel is in the tree would, all things being equal, have the same kind of effects on my behavior as Hugo's belief that the chase-able thing is up there. This is the sort of thing that would be covered by the "all things being equal" clause. Moreover—hopefully—I would deal with frustration better than Hugo, and would not stand at the foot of the tree shouting. But the "all things being equal" clause is introduced to accommodate this sort of difference also. All things are not equal between Hugo and me. What is important, for the idea of narrow content, is how things would be *if* they were.

Suppose, for example, I was a rather different sort of man—a far more Hugo-like man, as it were. This other me is utterly obsessed with chasing squirrels and is generally unable to contain his emotions when he suspects a squirrel is ensconced just out of reach. But I do, nevertheless, possess a fairly typical set of beliefs about squirrels: warm-blooded, mammals, skeletons, etc. This is the sort of thing I have in mind by the "all things being equal clause." With such a clause in place, the idea that the (anchored to me) content THE SQUIRREL IS IN THE TREE and the (anchored to Hugo) content THE CHASE-ABLE THING IS UP THERE share a common component of content—narrow content—would be well motivated: arguably as well motivated in the case of Hugo as it is in the case of my twin. In both cases, the idea that we share a vector of content is motivated by the role this content-vector plays in causing or explaining our behavior—whether this be water drinking behavior or squirrel-chasing behavior.

## 7. REFINEMENTS OF THE DE-ANCHORING MODEL

When the narrow content and truth-preservation conditions are met, it is legitimate to explain Hugo's behavior by way of content that he does not, indeed cannot, entertain—in the same way, and for the same reasons, that it is legitimate to explain my twin's behavior by way of content he cannot entertain. However, in developing this idea, I have helped myself to an assumption to which, one might think, I had no right. I assumed, for expository purposes, that I knew the content of Hugo's belief: THE CHASE-ABLE THING IS UP THERE. The point of the anchoring objection is, in effect, that we can never attribute content to animals because doing so would require us to use concepts that only we have. Therefore how, one might think, can I make this assumption—even if only for purposes of exposition?

Very well: it is time to kick away the ladder. The beauty of the de-anchoring strategy is that it does not require us to know the content of Hugo's belief. Nor does it require us to be able to express that content. To see why, let us return, briefly, to twin earth. There may be an uncountable number of twin earths—each with a different substance filling its oceans, lakes, and rivers. I need never know the underlying nature of these substances, and so never know the content of my various twins' beliefs. My ignorance matters not one bit. As long as it is true that whatever content my twin entertains shares narrow content with the content I entertain, and as long as the content I entertain guarantees the truth of the content my twin entertains—whatever that is—I can still use my content, hence my beliefs, in the explanation of my twin's behavior.

Precisely the same points apply to my explanation of Hugo's behavior using a belief he cannot have. I can legitimately employ my content, hence my belief, in the explanation of Hugo's behavior, even if I never know which content Hugo believes. Suppose, for example, that the above assumption about the content of his belief did not give Hugo enough credit. Hugo, let us suppose, does have an affordance-based system of categories, but one that is far more discriminating. Perhaps bitter experience and the necessity of adjusting chasing strategies have forced him to distinguish chase-able things that go up (squirrels, as we know them) from chase-able things that go down (or rabbits as they are more commonly known to humans).

In these circumstances, the content of Hugo's belief would be: THE CHASE-ABLE THING THAT GOES UP IS UP THERE. Or perhaps the way Hugo represents squirrels is entirely different: a manner of representation that is beyond our ken. There may be an indefinite number of candidates for the way in which Hugo represents squirrels, some of which we might be able to understand and some of which we might not. As long as it is true that (1) whatever content he entertains shares narrow content with our belief and (2) the content of our belief guarantees the truth of the content of his, then we can explain Hugo's behavior by employing content—*our* content—that he does not and cannot entertain.

When we explain an animal's behavior by way of content that is anchored to us we are, in effect, placing a *bet*. The bet is this: (1) there is *some* content that the animal entertains, (2) the content we use and the content the animal entertains share narrow content, and (3) the truth of the (belief with the) content we entertain guarantees the truth of the (belief with the) content the animal entertains. It may be that we can never be certain that our bet is a winning one because we can never properly identify the content of the animal's belief. Any bet can go awry, and sometimes, of course, it will. Nevertheless, sometimes we can be reasonably confident in the bet we have made. The best evidence that we have made a good bet is, of course, the reward: belief–desire explanations of the behavior of many animals actually work—and work very well.

## 8. A TWIST IN THE TAIL: DE-ANCHORING BEGINS AT HOME

The preceding arguments may, perhaps, leave one with a residual sense of dissatisfaction. Perhaps it is sometimes legitimate, one might accept, to explain the behavior of animals by way of content they cannot entertain. Nevertheless, one might insist, this sort of explanation has a decidedly inferior look to it. Belief–desire explanations of human behavior are superior because they invoke content that humans actually do entertain, rather than content that merely shares a component with, and guarantees the truth of, content that they actually entertain. In short, while belief–desire explanations of animal behavior are possible and—in some sense—legitimate, they have a distinctly second-class status compared to belief–desire explanations of human behavior. In response, I shall argue for a final twist in the de-anchoring strategy: *de-anchoring is required in order to explain human behavior*. If the arguments of Davidson and Stich are correct, then explaining human behavior by appeal to content that the human in question cannot, in fact, entertain is not just common: it is so common it verges on the norm.

The argument for this idea that de-anchoring begins at home is, perhaps, best introduced by the case of other cultures. One of the common objections to Davidson–Stich-style arguments against attributing beliefs to animals—an indication that somehow, somewhere along the line, these arguments have gone awry—is that the same objection applies to certain other human beings. We might, for example, imagine an exotic culture whose members harbor very different beliefs about such things as squirrels. Perhaps they believe squirrels are woodland demons; perhaps they believe squirrels are the spirits of their ancestors. Perhaps they believe something else altogether. This culture, we might further suppose, knows nothing of what it is to be a mammal, or warm-blooded. They have a very different concept of squirrels than we do. Nevertheless, it certainly seems appropriate, and perhaps necessary, after suitable empirical investigation, to explain their behavior by postulating that they have certain beliefs about squirrels. If members of the culture run screaming from every squirrel they see, or if they build shrines to them, this (to us) strange behavior seems to call out for an explanation in terms of beliefs they hold about squirrels.

At this point, the Davidson–Stich argument kicks in: the possibility of attributing the beliefs about squirrels to members of this culture falls foul of the fact that the content in such an attribution is anchored to us—via a network of beliefs we hold about squirrels. If this is a good argument against attributing beliefs to animals, it seems equally good an argument against attributing beliefs to members of radically alien cultures of this sort. This would come as something of a shock to social and cultural anthropologists, whose entire raison d'être has just been called into question—just as the application of the Davidson–Stich argument to animals called into question the discipline of cognitive ethology. But, fear not, we can salvage anthropology in the same way: we de-anchor contents. It is legitimate to explain the behavior of members of an exotic or alien culture—where this judgment of exoticism is made relative to our lights, of course—using content that is anchored to us as long as two conditions are met: (1) the truth of (beliefs with) our content guarantees the truth of (beliefs with) theirs and (2) our contents and theirs share narrow content. If the de-anchoring strategy applies to animals, then it also applies, equally and for the same reasons, to alien cultures. However, matters do not stop there.

Young children are, in certain respects at least, akin to radically different cultures. When my younger son was around two years old, he had a fascination with the squirrels that populated our back garden. Every sighting of a squirrel was greeted with great excitement, manifesting itself as both gesticulation and an utterance that sounded something like "Squirrel!" (but might just as easily been "Gavagai!" I suppose).[18] Nothing took precedence over squirrels. Any and every activity would be immediately interrupted on the appearance of a squirrel. (Yes: my son was the human equivalent of Dug the talking dog.[19]) My son, therefore, certainly seemed to have beliefs about squirrels—at least rudimentary ones such as "Squirrel, there!"

On the other hand, at that time he would have had no idea that squirrels are mammals, that they are warm-blooded, that they have skeletons, and so on. He may have been unable to distinguish squirrels from faux squirrels or robot squirrels, and even been unable to grasp that there is a difference between the two. I am tempted to explain his behavior by saying that he believed there was a squirrel over there. But what, precisely, does he believe? The content I use in characterizing his belief is, if the Davidson–Stich argument is correct, anchored to me. Therefore, if their argument is correct, I am guilty of explaining his behavior by attributing to him content that he cannot, at the time of these squirrel-based episodes, entertain. If we do want to explain the behavior of my son in terms of squirrel-content, then we must, once again, employ the de-anchoring strategy. Explaining the behavior of my son by way of content that he cannot entertain is legitimate as long as (1) the truth of the (belief with the) content I use in the explanation guarantees the truth of the (belief with the) content he, in fact, entertains and (2) the content I use in the explanation shares narrow content with whatever

---

[18] Philosophers, but probably no one else, will get that one.
[19] As featured in the Disney Pixar film *Up*.

content he entertains.[20] When I explain my son's behavior in terms of mental states with squirrel content I am, in effect, betting that these conditions do, in fact, obtain.

Once we accept that the de-anchoring strategy must be applied to children, however, then the floodgates well and truly open. *We were all children once, and can remember our earlier lives.* Thus, we might run a Malcolm-style scenario for my son: he spots a squirrel, chases it, watches it disappear up a tree, and stands at the foot of the tree articulating and gesticulating, while the squirrel, unbeknownst to him, has long since vacated the area. Many years later, thinking back on this event, he muses: I must have believed the squirrel was in the tree. However, as an adult, he has a very different concept of squirrel. As an adult, he knows all about mammals, warm-bloodedness, skeletons, and so on, and can effortlessly distinguish real and faux squirrels. Thus, the anchoring problem arises *within* a person as well as *between* persons. How can my future adult son explain the behavior of his earlier self if the content he uses in this explanation is anchored to his adult self, and so is not content he could have entertained at the time to which this explanation is directed? The content used in the explanation is anchored to the person of now. But the person whose behavior is to be explained—the person of an earlier time—would not have been able to entertain this content. The content my imagined adult son uses to explain the behavior of his earlier self is anchored to his current self and so cannot be attributed to his earlier self.

The solution is the same: we must de-anchor the current content. My son can legitimately explain his past behavior using content he could not have entertained at the time if (1) the content that he now uses shares narrow content with the content he entertained at the time and (2) the truth of the (belief with the) content he now uses in the explanation guarantees the truth of the (belief with the) content he entertained at the earlier time. When we explain the behavior of our earlier selves by way of content these earlier selves could not have entertained, we are, in effect, making a bet that (1) and (2) are satisfied. We can make this bet even if we do not know what content our earlier selves did, in fact, entertain and, more importantly, even if we can no longer attribute the correct content to our earlier selves. What reasons have we for supposing that this bet is successful? Only this: these explanations of the behavior of our earlier selves prove to be enlightening.

---

[20] You see how annoying the parenthesized "(belief with the)"s are? As predicted in footnote 17, in fact. I am just being a little more accurate now since I am in the process of summing up rather than developing a case. Truth-preservation is properly understood as a relation between beliefs in virtue of their contents rather than a relation between contents. Accurate can sometimes be as irritating as inaccurate is grating.

The problem of anchoring, therefore, arises *within* a single person and not just *between* different persons.[21] If one is committed to the Davidson–Stich holistic model of concept-possession, then one is also committed to the idea that possession of a concept of an object X (such as a squirrel) is a function of the beliefs one has about X. But the beliefs one has about an object X can vary quite dramatically through the course of a lifetime—and such variations can continue throughout adulthood. If this is correct, de-anchoring of content is going to be necessary to even ascribe to oneself beliefs through time. There may never be stable contents that are available to an individual through time. Rather, the contents an individual entertains are always shifting, depending on the vicissitudes of the surrounding doxastic environment—that is, the surrounding network of beliefs. If so, then de-anchoring is not a peculiar strategy we must apply only to alien entities—animals, exotic cultures, and the like. Rather, it is something that begins truly at home—in the efforts at self-understanding of each and every one of us. In our attempts at self-understanding, we are all alien to ourselves. Belief–desire explanations of animal behavior are, therefore, not poor relations of belief–desire explanations of human behavior. De-anchoring lies at the heart of, and underwrites the possibility of, all such explanation. That is, de-anchoring, like radical translation, *begins at home*.

## 9. GOOD TO THINK

The purpose of this chapter has not been to prove that animals have beliefs (and desires and other states with content). That was never really at issue. The best reason for thinking that many animals have beliefs, desires, and other content-involving states is that explanations of their behavior that appeal to such states work. Although we might be led astray in certain cases—Clever Hans cases, for example—in general such explanations are, or certainly seem to be, enlightening. Nothing in the Davidson–Stich kind of anchoring objection can show that animals do not have beliefs and desires. Rather, the objection is that the content we use is inevitably anchored to us and so is not content that can be attributed to animals.

To undermine the anchoring argument, I have outlined a de-anchoring strategy, grounded in the ideas of *tracking*—understood as the conjunction of

---

[21] Colin Allen (2013), I think, also recognizes this problem. When we ascribe mental states to ourselves, our words, Allen argues, only approximate our thoughts. He asks us to consider the thought, "I like bicycling" in two different contexts: the first when sat at a dinner table, and the second while struggling up a steep hill. The content of the thought is only approximately the same in each case.

truth-preservation and narrow content. If correct, this shows that we can continue to explain the behavior of many animals in belief–desire terms, even if we can never know the specific content of their beliefs and desires—indeed, and more significantly, even if the content we use in the explanation is content they cannot, in fact, entertain. In effect, I inserted a wedge between attributing content to animals and explaining the behavior of animals. We can legitimately understand animals—explain their behavior—using content they cannot entertain as long as this content stands in a certain relation to content they do entertain. When we use beliefs and desires to explain the behavior of animals, we are, in effect, betting that our content stands in this relation to theirs.

The discussion of belief in this chapter provides a very good illustration of Levi-Strauss' claim that animals are *good to think*. The argument eventually turns away from animals toward us. Suppose you buy some version of the anchoring argument. Content is anchored through some or other feature—perhaps by a doxastic network, as in the Davidson–Stich argument; perhaps by environmental factors, as in the Putnam twin earth case; perhaps by linguistic community, as in accounts inspired by Wittgenstein[22]; or perhaps by something else entirely. Then, a question immediately arises: how stable is the basis of the anchoring relation? In particular: (1) Does it hold across different people? (2) Does it hold for a single person through time?

On the holistic model endorsed by Davidson and Stich, it seems the answer to both these questions must be "no." Many regard this as an objection to the holistic model: the instability of the anchoring relation both at a time (i.e., between people) and through time (between people and within a single person) seems to undermine the possibility of communication. There is, it seems no stable content that can be transmitted from one person to another, or even from a single person at one time to that same person at a later time. Whatever virtues or vices one's account of content has, one might think, it had better not preclude the possibility of communication—that would be a *reductio* of the account.

The ideas that have emerged in this chapter show how we can reconcile a holistic account of concept-possession—and similarly unstable versions of the anchoring relation more generally—with the possibility of communication. The general model of communication that emerges is not based on a picture of stable, shared content being transmitted from one person to another, or from one time to another, but on a rather different picture. In communication, essentially, *we do enough to get by*. It is not that there are stable, shared contents that persist across persons and through time but, rather, that in communication, both at and

---

[22] Wittgenstein (1953). See also Burge (1979).

through time, the contents entertained are similar enough: one content tracks another—the truth of (a belief with) one content guarantees the truth of (a belief with) the other, and the two contents share a vector of content, understood as a function from contexts to contents.

Interestingly, the relative instability of contents has been a prominent theme in recent neuroscience. The general trend has been to move away from a *storage* model of content to something more *dynamic*.[23] On a storage model, contents are stored, in a manner akin to files, and later retrieved as and when needed. This makes sense when you think of the brain as something akin to a classical computer, but far less sense when you think of it as it actually is—a dynamic arrangement of connected neurons, with electrochemical activity spreading across those neurons, and where the general shape of this activity is determined by a series of connection weights burned into the neuronal ensemble through past experience. In this sort of model, contents are not stored as such, but constructed and reconstructed as needed. As such, they are far more labile and transient—unstable—than the storage model can allow. If we accept this sort of constructivist account—and that certainly seems to be the way the empirical winds are blowing at present—then we are going to need an account of how communication, both between and within persons, is possible. It might be that the idea of tracking will provide a useful way of addressing this issue.

---

[23] See, for example, Nader (2003).

# 5

## RATIONAL ANIMALS

1. CAUSAL REASONING

Beliefs and desires are the raw materials of reasoning. I have placed reasoning at the core of the cognition requirement—the second condition of personhood. In this chapter, the focus switches from the raw materials of reasoning to the process of reasoning itself. In according reasoning a central role in the cognition requirement, I have, in effect, remained faithful to Locke's definition of a person, which identifies "reason" as one of the constitutive elements of personhood. On this requirement of personhood at least, Locke's empiricist successor, David Hume, comes down firmly on the side of animals. In his book *A Treatise of Human Nature*, there is a short section entitled "Of the reason of animals." Hume opens this section with the observation that:

> Next to the ridicule of denying an evident truth, is that of taking much pains to defend it; and no truth appears to me more evident, than that beasts are endowed with thought and reason as well as men. The arguments are in this case so obvious, that they never escape the most stupid and ignorant.[1]

---

[1] Hume (1739/1975), Part III, Section xvi.

I'm inclined to agree. But, while arguments for the claim that animals are rational may or may not escape the most stupid and ignorant, they have certainly escaped some of history's more gifted thinkers—most notably, perhaps, René Descartes, who claimed that reason was the sole preserve of the human soul.

*Reason* can mean quite a few different things. A broad distinction between *causal* and *logical* reasoning is as good a place as any to begin. Causal reasoning involves understanding of the properties of objects and the ability to be able to use this understanding in pursuit of one's goals. For causal reasoning at least, we have, in recent years, amassed a body of evidence that may well have delighted Hume. Corvids are leading the charge. New Caledonian crows (*Corvus moneduloides*) have demonstrated the ability to engage in causal reasoning regarding the properties of liquids and displacement—learning to drop small pebbles into a tube of water that contains a floating peanut in order to raise the level of the water to a point where the peanut can be retrieved. The crows do not drop pebbles into a similar tube containing sand or sawdust instead of water, thus demonstrating causal knowledge of displacement of liquids (but not solids) by objects.[2]

This is an example of tool use—one of the most common forms of causal reasoning in animals. In general, when using or making tools to solve some or other problem, or achieve some or other end, one must understand that certain properties in the world need rearranging or realigning, and how the properties of the tool one is to use can help effect such a realignment. New Caledonian crows are adept in the use of several different kinds of tools. They also, for example, whittle sticks into hooks and use them to extract food from hard-to-reach places. Hawaiian crows make similar use of sticks. Crows in urban Japan use tools made by someone else to achieve their ends. They drop hard-shelled nuts onto roads, wait for them to be run over by a car, and then eat the exposed soft interior.[3]

A team from the University of Auckland set out to investigate these abilities. Seven captured crows were placed in an aviary and presented with a quite complicated problem, comprising: (1) some out-of-reach food, (2) a long tool that could be used to extract the food but which was also out of reach, and (3) a short tool, attached to a piece of string dangling from the crow's perch, that could be used to reach the long tool. The birds, therefore, needed to understand that they could use the short tool to get the long tool and the long tool to get the food.[4]

The birds were split into two groups. The first group—of three birds—was allowed to try out every individual step in the experiment before being presented

---

[2] Jelbert et al. (2014).

[3] This is a widely observed phenomenon. However, for an alternative explanation see Cristol et al. (1997).

[4] Hunt and Gray (2004).

with the multi-step task. Each of the three birds managed to solve the three-stage problem on the first attempt. The second group of birds was not allowed to try out each step before facing the multi-step task. While they were familiar with the properties and affordances of sticks and strings, they had never before faced a situation where a tool was linked to a string or where one tool was needed to collect another. Nevertheless, each bird quickly solved the multi-step task. One bird, named Sam, inspected the apparatus for 110 seconds, before completing each of the steps without error. Another bird, Casper, seemed initially puzzled by the string, but also completed the multi-step task on his first try. The other two birds accomplished the task on their third and fourth attempts.

New Caledonian crows have demonstrated other forms of innovative tool use. Perhaps most famously, one crow—Betty—was observed at Oxford University's Behavioral Ecology Lab consistently bending pieces of wire into hooks, and using the resulting tool to retrieve food from a bucket. This was the first time any animal had been observed making a tool for a specific use in the absence of an extended period of trial and error learning.[5]

Although they are particularly impressive in this respect, tool use in the animal kingdom is by no means restricted to corvids. Chimpanzees have also shown themselves to be adept in the construction and deployment of tools. Jane Goodall observed chimpanzees in the Gombe Stream National Park using grasses and twigs to fish termites out of termite mounds. The chimps would often modify the twigs, by stripping off their leaves, so they could be used in this way—demonstrating, like the New Caledonian crow Betty, a facility for tool construction as well as tool use.[6] Not far away, and around the same time, Kinji Imanishi's team found chimpanzees using rocks to crack nuts.[7] Chimpanzees, in fact, construct and use a range of tools for a variety of purposes. Chimpanzees in Bossou, Guinea, use the leaf petiole of oil-palm trees as a pounding tool to deepen a hole in the oil-palm crown, thus gaining access to the apical meristem of the tree, a prized food.[8] Chimpanzees have been observed manufacturing spears—a four-step process—in order to hunt bush babies.[9] Chimpanzees also construct tools that are designed to be used in a specific order: Goualougo chimpanzees manufacture a perforating tool to enlarge holes in a termite nest and, when that goal has been achieved, insert a fishing stick.[10]

---

[5] Weir and Kacelnik (2006).
[6] Goodall (1986).
[7] Nishida (1990).
[8] Yamakoshi and Sugiyama (1995).
[9] Preutz and Bertolani (2007).
[10] Sanz and Morgan (2007).

The use of tools in the wild extends far beyond corvids and the great apes. It has been discovered across taxa, including invertebrates such as octopuses, many species of bird, fish, amphibians, reptiles, non-primate mammals, and monkeys. Veined octopuses, for example, have been observed to carry coconut shell halves under their bodies, and then later assemble them into shelters—the first observation of tool use in invertebrates.[11] A blackspot tuskfish has been observed smashing a clam on a rock until it breaks open.[12] Alligators have been observed placing twigs on their snouts in order to attract nesting birds.[13]

Tool use is a form of causal reasoning. Certain properties of an object are identified, and these properties are understood to be useful in executing a goal or project of an animal—execution that involves using the properties of the tool to effect a realignment of properties of the world. We have to conclude that at least one form of reasoning is widely distributed in the animal kingdom. Is this reasoning a form of rationality? The answer you get will depend, in part, on whom you ask. On the one hand, it does seem a little contrived to deny that causal reasoning is a species of reasoning, hence a form that rationality might take. There are, however, those who like to reserve the rubric *rationality* for another type of reasoning—supposedly superior to the "mere" causal reasoning of animals. This is logical reasoning. It is to this that we now turn.

## 2. LOGICAL REASONING

The Stoic philosopher Chrysippus once told a story, perhaps apocryphal, of a dog tracking a rabbit. Running nose to the ground, the dog arrives at a three-way branch in the path. The dog quickly sniffs the first two paths, and not finding the scent in either of the first two, immediately runs down the third path, without bothering to sniff first. Chrysippus claims this provides evidence of the dog's ability to execute a logical inference of the form:

(1) Either A or B or C
(2) Not A
(3) Not B
(4) Therefore, C

---

[11] Finn, Tregenza, and Norman (2009).
[12] This behavior was filmed by diver Scott Gardner. See https://www.wired.com/2011/07/fish-tool-use/.
[13] Dinets, Brueggen, and Brueggen (2015).

This is a three-option version of what is known as *disjunctive syllogism* or *modus tollendo ponens*. In its more standard, two-option, form, a disjunctive syllogism looks like this:

(1) Either A or B
(2) Not A
(3) Therefore, B

To reason in such a way is to engage in *logical* reasoning. Very roughly, one engages in such reasoning when the beliefs one forms are constrained by the rules of logic, rather than the causal or mechanical affordances of objects. The capacity to execute disjunctive syllogism has been tested in several species of animal.

In outline, the tests are all variations on the following theme. An animal is presented with two opaque cups, A and B. Both cups are initially empty (and the animal is shown this). The animal then sees an experimenter baiting one of the cups, but precisely which one is hidden from the animal by an opaque barrier. The experimenter then reveals that one cup—say, cup A—is empty. The animal is then allowed to choose a cup. If it is capable of executing a disjunctive syllogism, it should choose cup B.

Several species have succeeded at this task, including great apes,[14] monkeys,[15] ravens,[16] and dogs.[17] The question is: what do these successes show? There are, actually, at least two distinct questions here that are often run together:

(1) Are these animals actually executing a disjunctive syllogism, or is there some other explanation of their behavior?
(2) Are these animals reasoning logically?

These questions should not be confused. Logical reasoning is a far broader category than the execution of deductive inferences. And this is not simply because not all logic is deductive logic.

---

[14] Call and Carpenter (2001), Call (2004).
[15] Grether and Maslow (1937), Petit et al. (2015), Marsh et al. (2015).
[16] Schloegl et al. (2009).
[17] Erdőhegyi et al. (2007). The case of dogs is interesting. They can pass the test, but apparently would rather not—preferring to use cues from the experimenter if at all possible. They pass the test when isolated from humans (as when the cups are manipulated remotely). In this, dogs seem to embody Whitehead's (1911, p. 72) observation that, "Operations of thought are like cavalry charges in a battle— they are strictly limited in number, they require fresh horses, and must only be made at decisive moments."

Let us first consider (1) as this seems to be the question that has most exercised researchers. The animals that pass these tests may do so by executing deductive inferences, but they may also do it by following other algorithms. At least three other algorithms have been proposed:

(1)  *Avoid the Empty Cup*: The animal searches in cup B not because it infers that it contains food but because it sees cup A is empty, has an aversion to empty cups, and cup B is the only alternative hiding place.

(2)  *Maybe A, Maybe B*: The animal initially represents both cups as possible locations of food, but then eliminates cup A when shown to be empty. It does not, however, update its representations of cup B, but instead chooses it simply because it is the only remaining cup. This distinguishes it from disjunctive syllogism, in which a subject would draw a conclusion about the state of cup B.[18]

(3)  *Probabilistic Reasoning*: Animals use cognitive maps to represent the possible locations of objects, assign subjective probabilities to the likelihood of an object being at a given location, and then update these probabilities as experience unfolds. Thus, cups A and B might be initially represented as equally probable locations of food, but when cup A is shown to be empty they raise the probability that the food is in cup B. Contrary to disjunctive syllogism, there is no inference that the cup definitely contains food.[19]

These are all possible alternative explanations of the capacity of these animals to engage in what, *prima facie*, appears to be disjunctive syllogism. The empirical jury is still out on which, if any, of these explanations is the correct one. But each hypothesis is, in principle, testable.[20] My current concern, however, is with logical rather than empirical issues and, in particular, with a series of confusions that might prejudice the conclusions we are tempted to draw in these cases.

The first confusion to avoid is a familiar one: we should not conflate logical reason with *deductive* reason. Any assumption—explicit or implicit—that a creature can be rational, in a logical sense, only if it is capable of executing the laws of specifically deductive logic should be resisted on the grounds it exhibits an unwarranted fetishism for the deductive. Even if one wants to run together reason with logic—itself a questionable conflation—logic can, of course, come in various other

---

[18] Mody and Carey (2016).
[19] Rescorla (2009).
[20] These alternate hypotheses are outlined by Beck (2017). See Beck, also, for a useful examination of possible ways of testing these alternate hypotheses.

forms: inductive (obviously), abductive (maybe). The sort of Bayesian creature hypothesized in (3)—which engages in probabilistic reasoning grounded in mental models plus an updating of subjective probabilities in accordance with Bayes's theorem—certainly seems to be a rational creature. Indeed, it seems to be a logical creature: it is just that the logic it employs is (broadly) inductive rather than deductive. Even employing the kinds of algorithms hypothesized in (1) and (2) does not preclude a creature from qualifying as (logically) rational. For example, in the *Maybe A, Maybe B* hypothesis, a creature initially represents both cups as possible locations of food (a not unreasonable hypothesis), and then (rationally, surely?) eliminates cup A when shown to be empty. The fact that it does not update its representation of B might show that it does not execute a *modus tollendo ponens*, but it does not show that the creature lacks rationality. Indeed, even the *Avoid the Empty Cup* algorithm can be perfectly rational—inductively. The language of "aversion" masks this fact. Let's face it: an animal is not simply going to have an *aversion* to an empty cup. Its aversion will be grounded in experience—experiences, for example, of empty cups not containing food (more generally of food not being the same as nothing, etc.). *Avoid the Empty Cup* is, therefore, an inductively rational algorithm to adopt given certain basic facts of the world.

Therefore, none of these alternate hypotheses, if proved to be true, are incompatible with a creature being rational, in a logical sense. On the contrary, they seem to strongly indicate that the creature is rational. It is easy to see why exclusion reasoning has featured so prominently in experimental studies—it is relatively easy to experimentally test and measure. But to the extent this focus has tempted us to equate rationality with the execution of deductive inferences, this focus is, perhaps, regrettable. In any event, we should resist this equation: reason, and indeed logic, is far broader than the execution of deductive inferences. I take it that once this point is made clear, Hume's claim that the reason of animals is an evident truth is difficult to contest—even if they do not execute deductive inferences.

The rest of this chapter will be concerned with the narrower question of whether animals can execute deductive inferences. This I regard as a Levi-Strauss *good to think* sort of question: interesting in its own right, but also for the wider issues it raises about the human capacity to execute deductive inferences and, indeed, the even more basic question of what it is, precisely, to execute a deductive inference.

## 3. LOGICAL REASONING: SOME MYTHS DISPELLED

There is a way of thinking about deductive reasoning that makes it impossible, or at least very unlikely, that animals can engage in such reasoning. Jose Luis

Bermudez has argued that animals are incapable of logical reasoning—by which he seems to mean deductive reasoning.[21] His argument stems from a particular conception of what such reasoning involves. He writes:

> Consider a conditional thought of the sort that might be expressed in the sentence "if A then B". To entertain such a thought is to understand that two thoughts are related in a certain way—namely, that the second thought cannot be false if the first thought is true. . . . Logical thinking depends upon language, therefore, because it presupposes the capacity for intentional ascent, which in turn depends upon semantic ascent.[22]

"Intentional ascent" is Bermudez's expression for the ability to think higher-order thoughts. To understand an inference of the form "if A then B" is, Bermudez claims, to understand how two *thoughts* (A and B) are related. Therefore, Bermudez argues, no creature incapable of higher-order thoughts can reason logically. And, he also argues, no creature lacking in language ("semantic ascent" in his terminology) is capable of higher-order thoughts. Therefore, no animal is capable of logical reasoning.

Bermudez's argument is only as strong as its initial premise: when we think a conditional of the form "if A then B," what we are thinking is that two *thoughts* are related in a certain way: we are thinking that if the first thought is true, then the second thought must also be true. Similarly, if we think "either A or B"—the basis of any disjunctive syllogism—then what we are thinking is this: either thought A is true or thought B is true. More generally, when we grasp a logical rule we grasp a certain relation between *thoughts*: broadly speaking, we understand that the truth-value of one thought has a certain impact on the truth-value of another thought. And to do this, we not only need concepts of truth and falsity but also need to be able to think thoughts about thoughts. That is, we must have a capacity for higher-order thought. If we assume that animals lack such a capacity—and Bermudez thinks they lack this capacity because they lack language—then we must also accept that animals cannot reason deductively.

Bermudez's assumption—that to understand a logical rule is to understand a relation between thoughts—is, however, unwarranted. There is no reason to suppose that the understanding of a logical rule *must* consist in understanding relations between thoughts. The understanding of a logical rule can take this form, but it need not. Bermudez's explanation of the understanding of a logical rule is

---

[21] Bermudez (2003, 2007).
[22] Bermudez (2007), p. 331.

an explanation in what is known as the *formal mode*. There is nothing wrong with formal mode explanations of deductive inference—this is the way such inference is typically explained to undergraduate students learning formal logic for the first time (although, here, logical rules are typically explained in terms of sentences and their truth-values, rather than thoughts). However, anything that can be said in the formal mode can also, and equally, be said in what is called the *material mode*. An explanation of our understanding of logical rules in the material mode would appeal not to thoughts and their truth or falsity but to different ways the world is or might be, and relations between these ways the world might be.

To see the difference between formal and material mode explanations, consider the sort of exclusion reasoning we encountered in Section 2, studied in chimpanzees, monkeys, ravens, and dogs. In such cases, if an animal does execute a disjunctive syllogism, the animal in question would reason as follows:

> Either the toy is under cup A or cup B. It is not under A. Therefore, it is under B.

On Bermudez's way of glossing this, the ability to reason in this way requires the ability to understand the following:

(1) The thought EITHER IT IS UNDER CUP A OR IT IS UNDER CUP B is true, and (2) the thought IT IS UNDER A is false and so (3) the thought IT IS UNDER CUP B must be true.

But there is no reason to explain the ability to execute a disjunctive syllogism in this way. The alternative is clear: to have this ability, I must understand that if the world is one way, then it must be another way. That is, I understand that the world has to be such that:

(1a) EITHER THE TOY IS UNDER CUP A OR IT IS UNDER B

But I also know that:

(2a) IT IS NOT UNDER CUP A

So, then I know the world must be arranged another way:

(3a) THE TOY IS UNDER CUP B

To execute an inference of this sort, I do not need to be able to think *about* thoughts at all. I merely need to be able to think about ways the world is, or might be, and understand relations between these ways. Neither higher-order thoughts nor the concepts of truth and falsity are required for the ability to reason deductively. Deductive reasoning does, in fact, not require thinking about thinking.

In effect, Bermudez is guilty of the sort of *vehicle-content* confusion we encountered in Chapter 3—in our discussion of the higher-order thought theory of consciousness. This is unsurprising since Bermudez is essentially offering a higher-order theory of the grasping of a logical rule. On the one hand, there is a thought. A thought is about something—it *has* content. A thought, therefore, is a *vehicle* of content: something that has content. On the other hand, there is the *content* that this thought has—something not to be confused with the thought itself. On the one hand, there is, for example, my thought that grass is green. On the other hand, there is the content of my thought, what my thought is about: grass is green. But the content of a thought, therefore, is simply a way that the world might be—grass being green is one way the world might be (and it is, of course, in fact that way). Therefore, in confusing thoughts and the ways the world might be—a confusion that is evident in his account of understanding a logical rule—Bermudez is confusing vehicles and contents, thoughts and what they are about. Bermudez assumes that understanding a logical rule requires understanding the relations between thoughts. But all it requires, in fact, is understanding the relations between the *contents* of thoughts.

Bermudez also argues that while animals cannot reason logically, they can reason causally. However, his distinction between logical and causal reasoning is vitiated by his mistaken conception of logical reasoning. Causal reasoning, Bermudez accepts, involves only awareness of ways the world is or might be:

> One might expect on both experimental, observational, and evolutionary grounds that some capacity for causal cognition is very widespread among animals and available at a very early stage in human development. The ability to detect certain types of causal regularity and to distinguish genuine causal relations from accidental conjunctions has obvious survival value. Causal dependence relations are directly observable, highly salient and pragmatically significant in a way that no other dependence relations are. How might causality be understood by non-linguistic animals? It seems plausible that the core of the understanding of causation at the non-linguistic level is sensitivity to regularities in the distal environment.[23]

---

[23] Bermudez (2007), p. 333.

Bermudez's contention is that while logical reasoning involves understanding re-lations between thoughts, causal reasoning only requires understanding relations between different ways the world is or might be. This is misguided. There is, of course, a difference between causal and logical reasoning. But the difference is not that we are thinking about different things in each case—thinking about the world when we reason causally but thinking about our thoughts when we reason logically.[24]

To see what the difference really is, consider the difference between a *material* and a *logical* conditional. Suppose a dog thinks: *if* I stand by the door, *then* I will be let out. That is a *material* conditional, represented as "→." The dog may indeed be let out, but there is no guarantee of this. The obtaining of the antecedent condi-tion does not guarantee that the consequent condition will also obtain. Suppose now that the dog thinks: "either the food is under A or B, and it is not under A, *so then* it has to be under B." In this sentence, "then" expresses a *logical* condi-tional, represented as " | =." The material conditional, ->, can be employed in causal reasoning: if I put this stick in the termite mound, then termites will climb on it. But the logical conditional | = is required for logical reasoning. However, the distinction between material and logical conditionals is not captured by the idea that in the former case I am thinking about the world and in the latter case I am thinking about thoughts. In both cases I am thinking about the world (i.e., the various ways it is or might be and the relations between these ways). What differs is the strength of the connection between antecedent and conditional ways the world might be. In the material conditional, the way the world is (the dog standing by the door) raises the probability of the world becoming another way (the dog is let outside). But the former by no means guarantees the latter. In the logical conditional, one way the world is (the food is either in A or it is in B and it is not in A) guarantees—*necessitates*—another way the world might be (the food will be in B). There is, very roughly, a certain *guarantee, assurance,* or kind of *necessitation* involved in | = that is not involved in ->. When | = is in play, the existence of the antecedent way the world is guarantees or assures the existence of the consequent state of the world, and this sort of guarantee is lacking in the case of the material conditional, ->.

In other cases of causal reasoning, there often is a type of necessity involved, which goes beyond mere regularity—the sort of regularity by which an owner will let a dog out to the garden when it stands by the door. If a New Caledonian crow drops stones in a narrow pipe containing water, then, all things being equal, the

---

[24] How odd would that be? Logic would never be about the world but only about the relations between thoughts.

level of the water *must* rise. This sort of necessity is known variously as *physical*, *nomic*, or *causal* necessity. This sort of necessity is distinct from logical necessity: it is weaker, holding only in a subset of all possible worlds—the worlds that instantiate the same natural laws as ours. Logical necessity, on the other hand, holds in all logically possible worlds, including the ones that have different natural laws than ours. The difference between logical and causal reasoning, therefore, is not a matter of what that reasoning is about: it is about ways the world is or might be in both cases. Rather, it is a matter of the nature of the connection—the strength of the necessity—that holds between these ways.

It is, of course, perfectly possible to engage in logical reasoning without knowing any of the above facts. One can engage in causal reasoning on some occasions and logical reasoning on others without having any idea that there is a difference between the two. *A fortiori*, one can engage in both logical and causal reasoning without understanding the notion of necessity, and that the sort of necessity that is involved in logical reasoning differs from that involved in causal reasoning, and so on. A child will be able to employ *modus tollendo ponens* long before he or she understands any of these things. To understand the basis of a guarantee or assurance is, clearly, not required to use the assurance in reasoning. One can engage in logical reasoning even if one does not understand that the logical conditional ( | =) carries with it a special kind of assurance that is lacking in other domains.

An animal—or child, for that matter—who successfully engages in logical reasoning can do so even if he has no idea that this is what he is doing, has no conception of what logical reasoning is or of what causal reasoning is, or that there is a difference between the two. He need not be able to think about his thoughts, and need not possess the concepts of truth and falsity. To suppose that an individual that engages in logical reasoning needs to have or do any of these things is to artificially inflate the requirements of logical reasoning.

## 4. LOGICAL REASONING AND THE LANGUAGE OF THOUGHT

As we saw in Section 2, one of the alternative algorithms that might be used to explain apparent animal successes in disjunctive syllogism was Rescorla's suggestion that they use cognitive maps to represent the possible locations of objects, assign subjective probabilities to the likelihood of an object being at a given location, and then update those probabilities as experience unfolds.[25] The general assumption is that if an animal were to employ this kind of Bayesian apparatus, then it would

---

[25] Rescorla (2009).

not be executing a deductive inference but merely simulating the results of such execution. This is what I want to question.[26] I am not sure the distinction between the execution of a deductive inference and the simulation of the results of such an execution is as clear as is commonly supposed—even, perhaps especially, in the case of humans.

Some have argued that the ability of humans to engage in deductive reasoning is underwritten by a *language of thought*.[27] The rationale for this language of thought hypothesis (LOTH) is that thought has certain properties that language also possesses. Language has these properties because it has a certain structure. The relevant properties of thought are, therefore, best explained by supposing it has this same sort of structure. LOTH is the hypothesis is that thought has essentially the same structure as language. The relevant features of thought that, according to LOTH, necessitate its possession of linguistic structure are:

(a) Systematicity: any creature that can think that John loves Janet can also think Janet loves John.
(b) Generativity: it is possible to generate an unlimited number of sentences from a finite base of lexical elements.

The explanation of systematicity and generativity appeals to the *recursive* structure of language. Language comprises a relatively small number of lexical elements (i.e., words) together with rules for combining these. As a result, lexical elements can be combined and recombined in various ways with the result that language is both systematic and generative. There is a third feature of language that is particularly germane to our concerns: language has a structure that makes it a peculiarly useful vehicle for deductive reasoning. Deductive inference is sensitive to the internal structure of sentences. Many inferences (for example, those involved in classical syllogism) only make sense if sentences have an internal structure. For example, the classical syllogism (1) All men are mortal, (2) Socrates is a man, therefore (3) Socrates is mortal will not work if we assume sentences are unstructured.[28] The logical connections between these sentences hold, in part, because of the internal structure of each sentence. We can make the same inferences in thought as we can in language—the logical structure of language and thought is isomorphic.

---

[26] Not reject, necessarily, but question. The ultimate answer, as we shall see, is complicated.

[27] *Locus classicus*, Fodor (1975). See Fodor (2008) for an updated version.

[28] That is how they are represented in classical propositional logic, where each proposition is treated as unstructured. In propositional logic, this argument would have the form p, q, therefore r, which is clearly invalid.

The best explanation of this, according to LOTH, is that language and thought have the same structure.

It is standard to distinguish between weak and strong versions of LOTH. According to its weaker version, LOTH is the hypothesis that thought has combinatorial structure. This does not entail that thought has the same structure as language, for the simple reason that not all combinatorial structures need be specifically linguistic in character. What is required for combinatorial structure is a number of primitive elements and rules that specify how these elements can be combined and recombined. This is true of language, of course, but can also be true of other, non-linguistic, forms of representation, such as models or maps.[29] The strong version of LOTH makes a distinct, additional claim: not only do representations have combinatorial structure but, in addition, this combinatorial structure is specifically linguistic structure. Henceforth, when I talk of LOTH, I should be understood as referring to the *strong* version of this hypothesis.

If LOTH is true, then at some level of analysis the neural activity that is responsible for thought has linguistic structure—the same general structure as sentences or propositions. If a person thinks that the cat is on the mat, then part of the activity occurring in her brain must correspond to the subject (the cat) and part to the predicate (is on the mat). More generally, strong LOTH is committed to the claim that, *at some appropriate level of analysis*, neural activity is structured in the way sentences are structured: that it can be parsed into subjects, predicates, prepositions, objects of prepositions, nouns, verbs, adjectives, adverbs, and so on. The "appropriate" level is generally thought to be a relatively abstract one: linguistic structure will not be evident when looking at a pattern of spreading activation across neurons in a MRI, for example. Nevertheless, strong LOTH commits its advocates to the claim that there is some level of analysis at which neural activity can be parsed into the sort of lexical structure characteristic of language. The problem is that there seems little reason for supposing that this specifically linguistic form of lexical structure will be replicated in the neural activity of creatures that do not have the kind of language possessed by humans. After all, why would an animal that does not use sentences think in sentences?[30]

---

[29] As Elizabeth Camp (2007, p. 159) puts it: "[M]any maps employ discrete, recurring constituents with a highly arbitrary semantics, and combine them according to systematic rules to produce systematically related whole representations. But at the same time, the principle according to which those constituents are combined relies on a spatial rather than a purely logical isomorphism between the structure of the constituents and the structure of the corresponding elements in the content. This demonstrates in concrete terms that there is more than one way in which the syntactic structure of mental states can mirror the semantic relations among their intentional objects."

[30] As Jacob Beck (2017) puts it, "Because we human animals speak a public language, there has always been a special reason to accept LOTH as true of us. Our linguistic utterances are naturally construed as direct translations of our internal thoughts, which suggests that our internal thoughts mirror the structure of

5. MODELING REASON

Suppose it is true, as Rescorla hypothesizes, that it is mental models or cognitive maps that underlie the cognitive performance of animals. Does this mean that deductive reasoning is forever beyond them? An ape, monkey, raven, or dog can solve an exclusion problem; but it does this, we are supposing, by way of some model-based, Bayesian, architecture. Is it appropriate to describe the animal's performance as deductively rational? The question is more complicated than it appears. And any satisfactory answers will, I think, be nuanced. The argument I am going to develop, an argument that will lead—eventually—to these nuanced answers, comes in two stages.

The first stage is indebted to some ingenious work by Elizabeth Camp, showing the logical power of model- or map-based representations. Camp argues, persuasively, that something akin to logical operations such as conjunction, disjunction, and conditionals can be instantiated in map-based systems. For example, on a map of a certain region, the presence (i.e., conjunction) of two items can be trivially registered. This is trivial because maps "automatically conjoin information about the spatial locations of all the objects and properties they represent."[31] The fact that there is a Starbucks *and* a church on the corner of 57th and 23rd is precisely the sort of thing that a map can represent. Nor is it difficult to extend maps to represent negative information. For example, one might color map icons and background to reflect positive and negative information. The default state might be a gray background, which expresses neutrality about the presence or absence of any given object or property. A black icon could then represent certainty that a given object is at the represented location, and a white icon could represent certainty that the represented object is *not* at that location. A white background could, similarly, represent certainty that there were no other objects or properties in that region (except for those explicitly represented by icons placed on the region).

One can also represent disjunction, or something akin to disjunction, on a map. For example, one might arrange it so that pairs of icons repeatedly flash on and off in bright yellow lights to indicate either one or the other object is at the represented place. Similarly, one might use a flashing blue light to indicate the antecedent of a conditional together with a solid blue light to indicate its consequent.

---

their public-language expressions. When it comes to nonhuman animals (hereafter: animals), this special reason is missing." However, proponents of LOTH, such as Fodor, insist that, if they think, animals do have a language of thought. The question is: how plausible is this insistence?

[31] Camp (2007), p. 161.

There is no need, certainly not for our purposes, to suppose that the operators described are real—genuine, whatever that means—logical operators. More modestly, and less contentiously, we can regard them as *simulacra* of logical operators: operators that behave in more or less the same sort of way, and so yield more or less the same results, in restricted contexts, as real operators. The important point, for our purposes, is that functions that are really quite like— really not too very far away from—genuine logical operations can be performed through maps. A creature whose cognition is grounded in map- or model-based mechanisms could, in principle, have the resources to make inferences—or, if you prefer, "inferences"—that yield the same sorts of results, at least within restricted contexts, as a creature whose logical abilities are underwritten by a language of thought. One can easily see, for example, how the ability of a creature—an ape, monkey, raven, or dog—to pass the kind of exclusion tests we looked at in Section 2 could be purchased by this sort of model. Initially, for example, the icons on the animal's map that represent cup A and cup B are both flashing orange. Then the cup A icon turns a solid red, while the cup B icon simultaneously turns a solid green. Camp also shows how to extend map-based models to incorporate representations of past and future, and, with limited success, intensional and quantificational contexts.

Whether or not it involves "real" logical operations, the kind of map-based representational architecture proposed by Rescorla has the means and wherewithal to allow a creature to engage in behaviors that are, at least, quite like what we do when we execute deductive inferences. They are "quite like what we do" in the sense that they will yield the same results as the execution of deductive inferences—not in all cases, certainly, but in many.

## 6. A TWIST IN THE TAIL, PART 2

The twist in the tail in Chapter 4 was that tracking begins at home. I shall explore a similar idea with regard to deductive reason. This is the second stage in the advertised argument for the aforementioned nuanced conclusion. To see why there might be a twist in the tail, one should understand, first, that (strong) LOTH is a controversial thesis. The guiding assumptions that structured discussion in the previous section were that (1) humans possess a language of thought, but (2) animals do not. Questions were, thereby, raised about animals' ability to execute deductive inferences give their (presumed) reliance on a model-based architecture. In the absence of a language of thought, we can understand how animals can do things that are *in the ballpark* of deductive inferences—perform operations that are *not so very different from* deductive inferences in that they yield similar outputs—but are, nevertheless, not quite deductive inferences. But assumption (1) is questionable. And if (1) is false, then we might find ourselves in the same kind of boat as (the one in which we have placed) animals. That is, it may turn out that the kinds of model-based cognitive architectures that I have, following Rescorla, assigned to animals may be precisely the kinds of architectures that underwrite the cognitive abilities of humans.

There are some fairly compelling reasons to think LOTH does not provide an adequate account of human cognition in general and of the ability to engage in logical reasoning in particular. With respect to logical reasoning, the problem facing LOTH is not so much that it is unable to explain our ability to engage in logical reasoning. It's our *lack* of ability in this regard that is more pertinent. If LOTH were true of us, it would indeed explain how we are so *good* at logical reasoning. The problem is that it cannot explain how we are so *bad* it. When engaged in logical reasoning we make mistakes—a lot of them! It is the mistakes we make, and the characteristic pattern of errors we exhibit, that is difficult to square with LOTH.

When neural network approaches to cognitive modeling—versions of a model-like cognitive architecture—first started challenging the idea of a language of thought, and the computational paradigm more generally, their allure was based not only on their supposed neural realism (which is, in fact, quite limited) but also on the fact that the abilities of such systems seemed to align more closely with human abilities. Neural networks are very good at certain tasks, and very bad at others. Crucially, the sorts of tasks humans can do well are precisely those tasks most readily implementable in a connectionist system. Conversely, the sorts of tasks humans do badly are ones most difficult to implement in a neural network. The tasks that humans and neural networks perform most easily number, broadly, tasks that can easily be reduced to pattern mapping—recognizing, completing, transforming, and associating operations. These include visual perception/recognition tasks, categorization, recalling information from memory, and finding adequate solutions to problems with multiple partial and inconsistent constraints. The tasks that humans and neural networks both do relatively poorly are, you've guessed it, logical and mathematical calculations and formal reasoning in general.

For traditional symbolic systems—and a language of thought would qualify as one of these—the situation is reversed. The tasks that humans do well are precisely those tasks that are most difficult to implement in traditional symbolic systems. And the tasks that humans do poorly—formal reasoning of various stripes—are the ones that symbolic systems do very well. In short, neural networks are good at the sort of things humans do well and bad at the sort of things humans do poorly, while for traditional symbolic systems, the reverse is true. This, for many, is a good *prima facie* reason for supposing that neural networks are more promising models of human cognition than are symbolic systems. The type of representations employed in neural networks are analog, model-based representations. That the cognitive strengths and weaknesses of human and neural networks align, while the opposite is true when we compare human and symbolic systems, suggests that we too might, biologically speaking, be model-based thinkers.

## 7. EXTENDING THE LANGUAGE OF THOUGHT

The general response of LOTH to the capacities of neural networks has been to argue that the same is true of them as, according to the hypothesis, is true of brains: there must be some level of analysis at which the activity occurring in a neural network has sentential structure.[32] At some level of analysis, that is, this model-based architecture *implements* a language of thought. However, the foregoing reflections on the case of animals point us in the direction of another possibility.

The possibility—that we might, in common with other animals, be model-based thinkers—leaves us with a puzzle. Whether or not animals can execute deductive inferences, it is clear that our deductive reasoning capacities outstrip those of all other animals. *Modus tollendo ponens* is one thing. But there is no evidence that any other animal can execute, say, De Morgan's theorem. Part of what needs to be explained is why human deductive reasoning abilities came to outstrip those of other animals if we both share a model-based cognitive architecture. A response available to LOTH is that at some level of description, our neural activity has sentential structure, and this is not true of other animals. But, even if correct, this would provide only half of an answer. A complete answer would explain precisely why there is such a level of description for human neural activity but not for animals. The general contours of this explanation are, of course, already clear: we *speak* a language with rich recursive, combinatorial structure, and this structure—*somehow*—became reflected in our neural activity. Filling in the details, however, is a little trickier.

The strong LOTH assumes that thinking is neural activity and, therefore, at some level of analysis, neural activity has the structure of language. This assumption has been challenged by recent accounts that see cognition in so-called 4E terms: embodied, embedded, enacted, or extended—or some combination of

---

[32] See, for example, Fodor and Pylyshyn (1988).

these.[33] The details of these views need not detain us. The general idea is that cognitive processes are often the result of a combination of neural and environmental factors. For example, in solving a jigsaw puzzle, we typically manipulate the individual pieces—physically rotating them, bringing them into proximity to see if they fit, etc. If we were not allowed to do this, jigsaw puzzles would become much more difficult. We would have to form detailed mental representations of the individual pieces, and then mentally rotate these representations to determine their mutual fit. By physically manipulating the pieces, we offload some of the task onto the environment, and thereby reduce the complexity of the task we have to accomplish with our neural hardware.[34]

There is another example that is particularly germane to our purposes. Consider, for example, how difficult it would be to perform mathematical operations in one's head if one were unable to use external formal structures. [35] Simple multiplication between one-digit numbers is easy enough—this can be done by pattern-mapping operations that are easily implementable in the brain's neural architecture. When we have a pen and paper available, we can create an external formal structure— 842 × 343. Then we can break down the task into individual steps—3 × 2, 3 × 4, etc.—each of which can be achieved by pattern mapping. After each step is complete, we make written modifications to the external structure, and these then direct us to the next step. In this way, a formal operation can be achieved through a combination of pattern mapping plus manipulation of an external structure. Once again, a cognitive task is partially offloaded onto the environment, thereby reducing the complexity of the task we have to accomplish internally, using our naked biological hardware.

That this sort of cognitive offloading is commonplace is no longer doubted. The significance of these sorts of cases, however, is still a matter of debate. On the one hand, there are those who argue that cognitive processes *extend* into the offloading—that cognitive processes straddle both neural processes and the wider environmental processes whereby we manipulate external structures.[36] On the other hand, there is the more conservative view that this shows that cognitive processes are *embedded* in a wider environmental scaffolding that facilitates cognition.[37] The embedding interpretation of the claim is less controversial, and that is all I need to assume for the purposes of the argument I am going to develop.

---

[33] See, for example, Clark (1997), Rowlands (1999, 2010), Noë (2004), Gallagher (2005), Menary (2007, 2010).

[34] Kirsh and Maglio (1994).

[35] Rumelhart, McClelland et al. (1986).

[36] Clark (1997), Rowlands (1999, 2010), Menary (2007, 2010).

[37] Classically, the idea of scaffolding dates back to Vygotsky (1986) and Vygotsky and Luria (1993).

The crucial feature of scaffolding, for our purposes, is that when appropriate scaffolding is available to us, we do not need to replicate external structure—in the form of detailed internal representations—but, rather, can avail ourselves of the structure in the world around us. I do not need to construct a detailed internal representation of the jigsaw pieces, but can instead use the pieces I find around me. I do not need to hold in my head a detailed internal representation of the entire long multiplication problem, but can instead return to the external representation as and when I need to. The information that would be contained in a detailed, internal, representation is, instead, stored in the world outside me, and I do not need to store information internally if it is available externally. The function of the brain, in many cases, is to avail itself of external structure—hence information—rather than replicate this structure internally.

Given this general idea, the relevance of cognitive scaffolding for the ability to engage in deductive inference can be understood in two different ways. The first is as a *synchronic* claim: often—not always, not necessarily, but often—we avail ourselves of external structures in the performance of deductive inferences. This may be true of individual cases or it may not—it depends on the complexity of the inference. More germane to my purposes, however, is a second, *diachronic* or *developmental*, claim. Our ability to engage in deductive inference develops through the contribution of both internal and external factors—of both neural activity and our ability to manipulate formal structures in our environment.

According to this hypothesis, then, what makes us so much more adept at deductive reasoning than other animals is not so much our biological hardware but our environmental scaffolding. In terms of biology, the brains of humans and many other animals are not fundamentally different—we are both, biologically, model-based thinkers. Models, not sentences, are the natural currency of the brain. Humans, however, have something at their disposal that no other animal has: external systems of representation. And some of these external systems of representation have logical structure.

Model-based systems, like neural networks, are good at modeling any type of cognitive process that can be reduced to some sort of pattern-mapping operation. The processes involved in formal reasoning do not seem reducible to these sorts of operations. However, once we give a model-based brain opportunity to use formal schemas outside—by embedding it in an environment that contains such schemas, and embodying it in such a way that it can use them—things change. Our model-based cognitive architecture affords us access to external formal structures, and the two, in tandem, allow us to complete a given cognitive task. Eventually we learn, to a greater or lesser degree, to *internalize* these structures. Those who learn to do long multiplication in their heads do this by internalizing larger patterns.

Instead of merely transforming the pattern "2 × 2" into the pattern "4," someone who does long multiplication in her head is able to internalize a larger pattern, 842 × 343, and hold this in her head while she transforms, in the correct order, the patterns implicated in it. Human powers of internalization of this sort vary between individuals and are, in some cases, very impressive.[38]

## 8. GOOD TO THINK, AGAIN

Many of the raw materials of deductive inference—or something very close to deductive inference—can be built into a model-based architecture. Model-based representations can, at the very least, provide good approximations of logical operators such as conjunction, disjunction, and negation. Some animals, in virtue of their map- or model-based neural architecture, would have a basic ability to engage in the sorts of operations, and something like this might explain their ability to pass tests for exclusion reasoning of the sort involved in *modus tollendo ponens*. In terms of our naked, biological cognitive hardware, we are likely in the same boat as other animals. But we have surrounded ourselves with cognitive scaffolding that enhances and expands our abilities to reason deductively, and the ability to (partially) internalize this scaffolding allows us to give a pretty good impression of being formal machines—devices, like classical symbolic systems, in which logical or linguistic structures have been directly built.

The important thing is that we are talking about a continuum not a dichotomy. Neither we nor other animals are, in all probability, formal machines in this sense. But both of us can do quite good impressions—simulate the performance— of such machines. The possibility of such simulation is built into our biological neural architecture—allowing us to simulate the function of logical operators and so perform operations that are very like what is going on in deductive inference. However, our human capabilities in this domain are enhanced by scaffolding and, often, the subsequent ability to internalize such scaffolding.

It is now possible to appreciate the misleading character of the question of whether animals can execute deductive inferences. Can we humans execute deductive inferences? The natural home, and primary locus, of deductive inference

---

[38] Consider, for example, the incredible mental calculations performed by children, usually from South and Southeast Asia, who have learned mathematical operations on an abacus. Their internal calculations are invariably accompanied by movements of fingers and arms—of the sort involved in manipulating an abacus. They have, in effect, internalized the abacus, and their bodily rehearsals of manipulating an abacus—when no abacus is present—help them mentally manipulate this internalized representation of the abacus. The result: output that is almost indistinguishable from a formal system achieved by the model-based, pattern-mapping, analog machinery of the brain. See, for example: https://www.youtube.com/watch?v=zECqhrsWSx8.

may well be on paper—in external formalisms more generally—rather than in the brain. The basic ability to approximate such inferences is found in the biological cognitive architecture of both humans and animals. But we humans can more closely approximate the behavior of formal systems in virtue of the scaffolding we have erected around us—external symbol systems that do possess logical structure—and in our subsequent capacity, partial and limited though it undoubtedly is, to internalize these external systems. Both humans and animals can simulate formal systems, but humans, for these reasons, can do it more completely and effectively than other animals. Nevertheless, even in humans, this imposition is always partial, and falls short of perfect—that is why we are so prone to mistakes in our formal reasoning of the sort of involved mathematics and deductive logic.

Can animals engage in deductive inference? I did say the answer was going to be nuanced. But no amount of nuance, of course, detracts from the general idea that animals can be rational. Many animals clearly can engage in causal reasoning. There is good evidence for supposing that animals can engage in logical reasoning of the sort involved in *modus tollendo ponens*. And the idea that when they do this they are doing something fundamentally different from what we do when we engage in such reasoning—that we execute deductive inferences but they do not—is based on an untenably dichotomous way of thinking about what we do versus what they do. Hume was right, animals clearly meet the rationality condition of personhood.

# 6

## BEYOND THE LOOKING GLASS

John Locke, as we have seen, defines a person as: "a thinking intelligent being, that has reason and reflection, and can consider itself the same thinking thing, in different times and places, which it does only by that consciousness which is inseparable from thinking and seems to me to be essential, to it; it being impossible to perceive without perceiving that he does perceive."[1] In this passage, Locke ties the possibility of personhood not only to mental complexity—intelligence, reason, and reflection—but also to self-awareness. To be a person a creature must be able to "consider itself the same thinking thing, in different times and places." If animals are not able to do this, then they are not, according to this Lockean conception, persons. This raises at least two questions:

(1) What is it for a creature to be able to "consider itself"?
(2) Why is this ability crucial to being a person?

Locke also stipulates that a person need not just be able to consider itself, but to consider itself in two specific ways: "the same thinking thing" and "in different

---

[1] Locke (1689/1979), p. 188.

times and places." The former condition seems to require *metacognition*: the ability to think thoughts about thoughts (and other mental states). Accordingly, the idea of metacognition will feature prominently in this chapter. The latter constraint points to the ability of a person to keep track of itself through space and time. I shall postpone discussion of this until Chapter 8.

So important do I regard the issue of self-awareness to personhood, and so complex will this issue prove to be, that I am going to devote four entire chapters to it. The argument I am going to develop in these chapters looks like this. First, there are two quite different conceptions of self-awareness, hence two quite different conceptions of what it means for a creature to be able to "consider itself." This distinction is not introduced to advance the cause of Locke scholarship—my interests lie in the distinction itself rather than working out precisely what Locke had in mind. (Although there are, I shall suggest, good reasons for thinking that Locke had one of these in mind rather than the other.) Second, while there are some reasons for being skeptical of the idea that animals can be self-aware in one of these senses—not necessarily overwhelming reasons, but reasons nonetheless—there are compelling reasons for thinking they must be self-aware in the other sense. Third, it is this other sense of self-awareness—the sense in which many animals qualify as self-aware creatures—that is relevant to personhood. Animals, that is, are self-aware creatures in the sense of self-awareness that is relevant to personhood. Therefore, they cannot be denied the status of persons simply by appealing to their (alleged) lack of self-awareness.

These three claims, outlined in the preceding paragraph, will be developed and defended over the course of the coming chapters. The present chapter focuses on the first sense of self-awareness—the sort that animals do not, arguably, have. Personally, I do not endorse the claim that animals lack this form of self-awareness, but I am, for tactical reasons, making life as difficult as I can for myself. Even if animals lack this form of self-awareness, they are still persons—that is where I am going with this. The general structure of this form of self-awareness that animals allegedly lack will be identified, reasons will be assayed for thinking that most animals lack it, and arguments will be developed for thinking that there must be another form of self-awareness that is not captured under this general model. The goal of Chapter 7 is to provide an account of this second form of self-awareness— the sort that many animals almost certainly have. In Chapter 8, I shall further develop the account of this second form of self-awareness, with particular reference to the "different times and places" facet of Locke's definition. In Chapter 9, I shall argue that this second—animal-friendly—sort of self-awareness is the one that is relevant to being a person.

## 2. INTENTIONAL SELF-AWARENESS

Many mental states are about things. Some claim that all mental states are about things. Others demur. We do not need to take a stand. It is sufficient for our purposes that many mental states are about things. When you think, you don't just think: you think something. When you believe, you don't just believe: you believe something. You desire something, hope something, fear something, expect something, and so on. These sorts of mental states are all *about* something. Philosophers call this aboutness *intentionality*. The objects of this intentionality are what are known as *contents*. The notion of content is best understood by contrasting it with that of a *state of affairs*. A state of affairs is, very roughly, a combination of objects and properties. Oedipus being married to his mother is a state of affairs. Although he was married to his mother, Oedipus did not believe that he was—the eventual dawning of this belief came as a bit of a shock. The reason Oedipus could be married to his mother without believing this is, of course, that he did not realize that the woman he had married—Jocasta—was his mother. He believed of a certain woman—Jocasta—that she was his wife, but he did not realize that this woman was his mother, even though she was. A state of affairs exists whenever objects and properties are combined in an appropriate way. But mental contents—the contents of thoughts, beliefs, desires, and so on—require more than this. They require that the object, or properties, or both be *presented* in a certain way. Oedipus did not believe that he was married to his mother because, in his beliefs about her, Jocasta was presented as his wife but not as his mother. One and the same object can be presented in different ways. Content arises, minimally, when an object is presented in a certain way. Intentionality, therefore, has a tripartite structure: it involves (1) a mental act (such as thinking, believing, etc.) to (2) an object (in this case, Jocasta) where the object is presented as falling under what is known as (3) a *mode of presentation* (his wife, but not his mother).

The idea of self-awareness *can* be understood in terms of this general model of intentionality. The result is what I shall call, for obvious reasons, an *intentional model of self-awareness*.[2] I am intentionally self-aware when I have a mental state that is intentionally directed either toward me or toward some aspect of me. This is one way of interpreting Locke: of explaining what goes on when a subject, in Locke's sense, "consider[s] itself the same thinking thing, in different times and places." There is first, the intentional act—*considering*, which we might understand

---

[2] The reasons may be obvious, but I did agonize over this label. Right up until the final run-through I was going with *positional*—an archaic variant on *intentional*. My old eyes are not what they were, and so if you do encounter any unexpurgated occurrences of *positional*, please read these as *intentional*.

as a type of thinking or recognition. There is, second, the object of the act—*itself*. And there is, third, the mode of presentation of this object: *the same thinking thing*. This characterization is not as clear as it might be, however, because of a lack of clarity surrounding the relevant notion of *itself*—the object of my intentional act of self-awareness. There are various things this term might mean.

*Bodily Self-Recognition*

I am looking in a mirror—one that I do not initially realize is a mirror. I see a reflected body and quickly come to recognize that I am this body. Or—in G. E. Moore fashion—I look at my hands and recognize these hands are mine (and then, optionally, go on to prove the existence of the external world). Or when I look in the mirror, see the lines on my face, and think: Jesus, I'm getting old! These are all cases of bodily self-awareness. I am bodily self-aware when I recognize my body as me, or some part or facet of my body as mine. This sort of self-awareness will count as intentional if my body, or some part of my body, is an object of an intentional act—such as thinking. If I think, when looking in the mirror, "That's me!" or "I look old!" then my body, or some facet of my body (e.g., its conspicuous aging), is an (intentional) object of my thought. In such circumstances, I am bodily self-aware in an intentional sense.

*Non-bodily Self-Recognition*

When I wake up in the morning I know who I am. I know this before I have opened my eyes, and certainly before I have looked in a mirror. *That* I know this is obvious; *how* I know it is perhaps deeply puzzling. In a famous passage in the *Treatise*, David Hume, Locke's empiricist successor, wrote:

> For my part, when I enter most intimately into what I call myself, I always stumble on some particular perception or other, of heat or cold, light or shade, love or hatred, pain or pleasure. I never can catch myself at any time without a perception, and never can observe anything but the perception.[3]

Hume is talking of what we now call *introspection*. When I introspect, I encounter things such as sensations, feelings, and emotions. To this list we might add thoughts, beliefs, desires, hopes, fears, and so on. Hume's point is that we never encounter a self that has these things. If I introspect, then I might encounter pain or pleasure, disappointment or hope, love or hate, and a desire for a slug of

---

[3] Hume (1739/1975), Book 1, Part 4, Section 7.

bourbon. These sorts of things can all be intentional objects of my introspective acts. But I do not encounter any self that has these things. The self is not revealed in introspection as an intentional object among other such objects.

A way of reconciling the idea that I know who I am when I wake up in the morning with the idea that the self is not an intentional object of awareness involves the idea that to be aware of one's mental states is to be aware that they are one's own. This is independently plausible. "Here is a thought, I wonder to whom it belongs?" This generally doesn't happen. Maybe it never happens. To think is to realize that the thought is one's own. Suppose, now, we add to this the idea that I am aware that a thought is my own to the extent that this thought is an object of another intentional act of mine. I do *not*, I must emphasize, endorse this idea—certainly not as a general account of the sense of ownership of one's mental states—and later I shall argue against it. But, at present, I am merely using it for purposes of exposition—to explain what non-bodily intentional self-awareness would be. Thus, for example, one might think that I am aware that a thought is my own to the extent that I am thinking that this thought is mine. This would be an intentional model of our awareness of our mental states. My mental states—thoughts, beliefs, desires, feelings, and the like—are objects of higher-order thoughts. I have thoughts *about* my own mental states—thoughts to the effect that they are *my* mental states—and, therefore, am intentionally aware of these states. This would be non-bodily intentional self-awareness.

Intentional self-awareness, therefore, comes in two forms: bodily and non-bodily. What is common to both is that some or other part or aspect of me is the object of an intentional act of mine. Accounts of the specific nature of this act vary. Some accounts think of it as quasi-perceptual—introspection, on this view, is a form of *inner perception*. Other accounts see it as a cognitive act of some sort—typically, an act of *thinking*. My purposes being what they are, I do not need to get involved in this sort of dispute. Rather, what is crucial is the following idea: whether the object of intentional self-awareness is bodily or mental, and whether an act of intentional self-awareness is cognitive or quasi-perceptual, intentional self-awareness always involves an act intentionally directed toward something else—toward the so-called intentional *object* of the act, and this intentional object will be the person or some facet of the person.

To be intentionally self-aware, animals would have to be able to do two things. First, they would have to be able make their bodies (or some part or aspect thereof) or their minds (i.e., their mental states) into objects of their intentional states and, second, they would represent these objects under the mode of presentation: *me* or *mine*. There are reasons—not necessarily insurmountable ones, but reasons nonetheless—for supposing they cannot do one or both of these things. The reasons differ depending on whether we are dealing with bodily or non-bodily self-awareness. It is often thought that (most) animals lack the requisite bodily form of self-awareness because they fail the *mirror self-recognition* (MSR) test. And it is also often thought that they lack non-bodily self-awareness because they do not possess *metacognitive* abilities. Let us consider each of these in turn.

## 3. MIRROR SELF-RECOGNITION

The MSR test was originally developed by Gordon Gallup[4] and is still widely regarded as a test for self-awareness. In the classic form of the test, a mark (typically dye) is placed on an animal subject—typically when the animal is anesthetized—in a position where this mark is visible only in a mirror. The animal's subsequent behavior in front of a mirror is observed. If it appropriately engages with the mark—using the mirror to inspect it, for example, or touching the relevant part of its body after viewing the mark in the mirror—then it is deemed to recognize that the body reflected in the mirror is its own body. This seems to qualify as a form of bodily self-awareness.

It is not entirely clear which animals pass this test. It is generally accepted that humans (over the age of 18–24 months), common chimpanzees, bonobos, and orangutans consistently pass the test. Animals that have been argued to pass the test include elephants, dolphins, and pigeons. I gather that manta rays have been patiently building a case.[5] Gorillas, to be quite frank, have struggled with the test, although this is probably because they regard eye contact as an aggressive gesture, and so avoid looking at each other's faces—including faces that stare back at them in a mirror.[6]

Also unclear is precisely what one has to do to pass. Dogs, for example, are deemed to fail the test, on the grounds they show no interest in any marks placed on them. This highlights the first shortcoming of the test: it only applies to creatures that are suitably *motivated*. Dogs get crap on themselves all the time—sometimes quite literally and deliberately, especially if you live next to cows—and just don't seem to care. So, why should we expect them to show any interest? Second, the mirror test is, of course, designed for creatures whose primary sense is visual. Dogs are driven by olfaction at least as much as by vision. Thus, one thing that they care far more about than how they look in the mirror is *urine*. Marc Bekoff ran a very nice experiment along these lines—colloquially known as the *yellow snow* experiment.[7]

---

[4] Gallup (1970).

[5] Ari and D'Agostino (2016).

[6] Andrews (2011).

[7] See Bekoff (2001).

Marc recorded how long his dog, Jethro, spent sniffing urine deposited by dogs in the snow. To make sure he could not identify his own urine by remembering where he left it, Marc shoveled up Jethro's yellow snow and moved it to new locations. Jethro spent significantly less time sniffing his own relocated urine than he did that of other dogs—suggesting he is able to differentiate between urine that is his from urine that is not.[8] Does this show that Jethro has a concept of "mine" and, therefore, the related concept "me"? Unfortunately, no matter how imaginative one's experiments are, there is always some deflationary killjoy out there who will try to negate them. Perhaps—if I may briefly assume the role of deflationary killjoy—Jethro merely discriminates yellow snow that is "more interesting" from snow that is "less interesting." He is driven to pay more attention to some patches of yellow snow over others without understanding why. I'll leave the reader to determine the plausibility of this counterhypothesis, but it does illustrate a general problem with attribution of the concept of *me or mine* to an animal. Any observed behavior of the animal that might be thought to prove possession of a self-concept might—not necessarily can, but might—equally be explained in terms of *stimulus generalization*. In this case, the class of "interesting" urine is (postulated as being) extensionally equivalent to the class of urine that belongs to other dogs: any instance of interesting urine is also an instance of another dog's urine and vice versa.

There are further problems of interpretation of evidence. In informal, non-experimental, contexts involving not the mirror test as such but a dog's more general reaction to its reflection, a dog will usually exhibit one of two reactions to its image in the mirror. The first: utter indifference. The second: it attacks the mirror—the opposite, in effect, of utter indifference. Both have been taken as indications of the dog's failure to recognize the reflection as itself. But it is difficult to see how you can't have it both ways. If indifference equates with likely failure, how can its opposite also be a symptom of failure? Hugo, the family German shepherd, saw his reflection in a full-length mirror every day, a circumstance to which he was casually indifferent. Knowing Hugo rather well, I can say that, without a shadow of a doubt, if he saw an unfamiliar dog in his house, casual indifference would not be the way he would choose to deal with it. So, if he did see a dog reflected in the mirror—and if he did not, the test would be inapplicable anyway— this would seem to be pretty good evidence that he knew that he was that dog. Indifference, in fact, might be evidence of passing the test and not, as it is commonly thought, evidence of failure.

---

[8] Roberto Gatti (2016) has supplied a more formal validation of this experiment, admittedly with a small sample class of four dogs. See Horowitz (2017) for a more recent version of the olfactory mirror test involving altered rather than relocated urine samples.

I shall put these issues aside as they are largely irrelevant. The important issue, for our purposes, is not which animals pass the test, and not what behavior qualifies an animal as passing the test. Rather, what is important is the conception of self-awareness implicated in the test. To pass the test, the animal must recognize the body in the mirror as its own body. That is, it must have a thought of the form: "This is me!"—where the demonstrative "this" denotes the body reflected in the mirror. Thus, the intentional act (of recognition) is directed toward an object (the body that appears in the mirror), and this object is subsumed under a certain mode of presentation (identical with me). This, therefore, is a case of intentional self-awareness, in the sense introduced in the previous section. MSR is, thus, a test for intentional self-awareness.

## 4. METACOGNITION

The other form that intentional self-awareness might take is the non-bodily form. The non-bodily form of self-awareness seems to presuppose *metacognitive* capacities: abilities to make one's mental states into objects of one's own intentional acts. These capacities can enter the picture in two distinct ways. In some forms of non-bodily self-awareness, mental states may be the objects of intentional acts. For example, I may be self-aware, in a non-bodily sense, in virtue of thinking about my mental states. This belief is a consequence of that belief, I might think. This desire, one I wasn't sure I had, is troubling. This memory is so indistinct, I'm not sure if it ever really happened, and so on. In such cases of non-bodily self-awareness, I am self-aware in virtue of certain of my mental states being objects of my intentional act of thinking (or some similar intentional act).

There is a second sense in which metacognitive abilities might be implicated in non-bodily self-awareness—a way suggested by Locke's idea that a person can "consider itself the same thinking thing." In this form of self-awareness, an object (i.e., "itself") is subsumed or presented under a given mode of presentation—"same thinking thing." Thus, in exhibiting this form of self-awareness, I am aware of myself as a thinking thing. And I cannot be aware of myself in this way unless I am able to think about thinking—and so must possess metacognitive abilities.

*Metacognition* is, roughly, the ability to think thoughts about other mental states. The other mental states in question might be one's own or those of someone else. In the latter case—when the mental states belong to someone else—metacognition takes the form of what is known as *theory of mind* or *mindreading*. A creature that can think thoughts about the mental states of another individual, using these thoughts to predict or explain that individual's behavior, is said to have a theory of mind or, equivalently, is capable of mindreading. That any animal, other than human, possesses a theory of mind is a controversial claim, which we shall explore in more detail in Chapter 10.

If you have a theory of mind, you are able to engage in what we might call *third-person metacognition*. It is "third person" in the sense that the thoughts you have are about the mental states of someone else—a third party. Correspondingly, *first-person metacognition* would be the ability to have thoughts about your own mental states. The question of which type of metacognition comes first—either logically or developmentally—has exercised philosophers for some time. There are three basic options.

(1) The forms of metacognition are independent.
(2) First-person metacognition comes first. That is, third-person metacognition presupposes, either logically or developmentally, first-person metacognition.
(3) Third-person metacognition comes first. That is, first-person metacognition presupposes, either logically or developmentally, first-person metacognition.

If first-person and third-person metacognition are independent of each other, then neither depends on the other. You might be able to think thoughts about your own mental states but not those of others, or you might be able to think thoughts about the mental states of others but not your own. First-person metacognition is not required for third-person metacognition, and third-person metacognition is not required for its first-person counterpart. This is a possible view, but has attracted few adherents. It is far more common to think that one of these abilities is a precondition—either a logical prerequisite or a developmental one—of the other. To many, it has seemed natural to suppose that one's metacognitive abilities develop initially in the first-person context: one learns to think about one's own mental states first and then—subsequently and/or consequently—learns to think about the mental states of others.

There is, however, a famous line of argument that challenges this perhaps natural supposition—an argument developed by Ludwig Wittgenstein.[9] As we saw

---

[9] Wittgenstein (1953).

in Chapter 2, Wittgenstein argued that an individual could not learn the meaning of mental words by associating them with processes occurring in his or her own mind. This would entail the possibility of a logically private language—a language that can, in principle, only be learned by one person. Wittgenstein argued that this is impossible, on the grounds that there could be no standards of correctness in such a language: no standards governing when a term has or has not been correctly applied. Therefore, Wittgenstein thought, we learn the meaning of mental words in a public context—the same way we learn the meaning of any word. That is, we apply mental words in varying public situations, and our application is either confirmed or corrected by competent speakers of the language. By such a process, we learn to adjust our use of words to bring them into line with community norms. To mean something by a word is to have the ability to adjust one's use of it in this way.

If Wittgenstein is right, our understanding of mental states begins with other people and not ourselves. We learn concepts like happiness, sadness, disappointment, grief, anger, and the like in a public context. "That man is angry," says the child, and her use of *angry* is either reinforced, "Yes, he is," or corrected, "No, he is happy." We learn what mental states are first by attributing them to others and then, on this basis, learning to attribute them to ourselves. If this is correct, it entails that third-person metacognition comes first, and the ability to engage in first-person metacognition is dependent on its third-person counterpart. Wittgenstein's arguments are found compelling by some, myself included, but rejected by others.

There are, therefore, various possibilities on the table. Fortunately, there is no need for us to adjudicate. Metacognition, whether first- or third-person, is a form of *intentional* self-awareness. Meta-cognition is thinking *about* thinking (and, of course, other mental states). The case for animal personhood I am going to develop does not, in any way, depend on animals being intentionally self-aware. Animals can still be persons, I shall argue, even if they lack intentional self-awareness. Of course, if they do pass the mirror test, or if they do turn out to have metacognitive abilities—whether first- or third-person—this is hardly going to *weaken* my case for animal personhood. But even if we assume—and for dialectical and strategic purposes, I find it useful to operate on the basis of worst-case scenarios—that intentional self-awareness, in both its forms, is beyond the abilities of all nonhuman animals, it does not matter one bit. There is another form of self-awareness. Many animals have it. And this other form of self-awareness is what is relevant to personhood. Establishing these claims is the task of the remainder of this chapter and the three that follow it.

## 5. "CONSIDER" RECONSIDERED

There are good reasons for thinking that the category of self-awareness is not exhausted by intentional self-awareness. The rest of this chapter will discuss and defend these reasons. The possibility of this other form of such awareness is, in fact, implicit in Locke's definition of a person. Locke's full definition, we should recall, is actually this: "a thinking intelligent being, that has reason and reflection, and can consider itself the same thinking thing, in different times and places, which it does only by that consciousness which is inseparable from thinking and seems to me to be essential, to it; it being impossible to perceive without perceiving that he does perceive."[10]

Taken literally, of course, the claim contained in the final clause is nonsensical. When I see, for example, I do not see (or hear or taste, etc.) my act of seeing. Nor do I see *that* I see (in the way that I might see, for example, *that* the book is on the table). Presumably, Locke is using the term *perceiving* as equivalent to *being aware of*: when I perceive, I am aware of perceiving. There are two problems with trying to understand this claim by way of the intentional model of self-awareness.

First, the claim seems implausible on grounds of phenomenology. If we adopt the intentional model, then Locke's claim would be that whenever I perceive, or think, I would have to possess a higher-order intentional state that takes my act of perceiving or thinking as its object and presents this act to me under a certain mode of presentation—for example, as something I am currently doing or engaged in. But things certainly do not seem this way. Most of the time I simply get on with perceiving things or thinking things. There is no suggestion, from the standpoint of experience, that when I do so I must simultaneously be thinking that I am thinking or thinking that I am perceiving, or that I am the subject of any other higher-order state that is about my perceiving or thinking.

Second, the intentional model of self-awareness will have a difficult time handling Locke's claim that awareness of thinking is *inseparable* from thinking. The claim that two things are inseparable is stronger than the claim that they are not, in fact, separated. If they are inseparable, they *cannot* be separated, even in principle. But the intentionality is a tripartite structure, comprising act, object, and mode of presentation. And not only are these three components separable, they often do, in fact, come apart. I can think this is a dagger I see before me, while there is no such dagger. A distinct, higher-order thought (or other higher-order state) that is about my first-order act of thinking or perceiving can always, in principle,

---

[10] Locke (1689/1979), p. 188.

be separated from the first-order act.[11] Thus, if we take seriously Locke's claim that awareness of thinking is *inseparable* from the thinking, then we cannot employ the intentional model of this awareness.

These factors do at least *suggest* that the term *consider*, as Locke uses it, should not be understood in higher-order—intentional—terms. And *suggest* is probably about as far as we can get by focusing on Locke alone. There is, however, an alternative available to the intentional model of self-awareness—an alternative that I shall develop in the course of this chapter and the next. In the rest of this chapter, I shall marshal some considerations for thinking that there is a kind of self-awareness—awareness of one's mental states and processes—that does not conform to the intentional model of self-awareness. At the core of my case will be the idea introduced in the discussion of Locke. The intentional model of self-awareness makes awareness of one's mental states and the mental states of which one is aware unacceptably independent of each other: it grants them a degree of independence that is ultimately unworkable.

## 6. WITTGENSTEIN AND KNOWLEDGE OF MENTAL STATES

In *Philosophical Investigations*, Wittgenstein remarks: "It can't be said of me at all—except perhaps as a joke—that I *know* I am in pain."[12] At first glance, this claim seems incredible. If I were in pain, then, surely, I would know it. Indeed, I would know this better than I know most, perhaps all, other things. If I am in pain, and my pain has reached a certain level of intensity, then, surely, I would be certain I am in pain. According to a venerable tradition associated with Descartes, I can know what is going on in my own mind better than I know anything else. Wittgenstein's point, however, is really a very good one. It concerns the uncritical application of the idea of knowledge to one's awareness of what is going on in one's own mind.

Suppose I say, "I know there is a book on the table." This is a standard (or fairly standard—knowing is an atypically factive attitude) intentional act: an act of knowing, an object known (a book), and a mode of presentation of this object (on the table). To this claim, someone might legitimately respond: "How do you know this?" And then I could provide that person with a list of factors that support my

---

[11] Thus, as we saw in Chapter 3, one of the counterintuitive implications of the higher-order thought vision of consciousness is that I might be in pain my whole life without ever being aware of it. Consciousness is added to my pain from the outside, by a state that is separable from it.

[12] Wittgenstein (1953), Section 246.

claim: I can see both book and table, the lighting conditions are good, I have not been experimenting with hallucinogens in the recent past, and so on. Suppose, however, that someone questions my claim to know I am in pain. How could I respond? Any attempted response (e.g., "I can *feel* it!" "It hurts!" and so on) would just be a reiteration of my original claim to be in pain. Supporting reasons, here, are not independent of the fact that they purport to support: to feel pain is to be in pain, and vice versa. The moral Wittgenstein drew is that knowledge of mental states is very different from knowledge of non-mental items. We use the same word—*know*—in both cases, but this common usage masks an underlying difference. Knowledge of mental states is not independent of those states: knowing that I am in pain is part of what it is to be in pain rather than a separate act that has my pain as its intentional object. We might put the point this way: whenever we have the familiar apparatus of intentional act, intentional object, and mode of presentation of that object, the act and object can typically come apart: at the very least, the object can exist without the act. This sort of independence of act and object is a standard feature of intentional contexts. But there is no such independence of being in pain and knowing one is in pain.

Wittgenstein's point applies *a fortiori* if we replace talk of knowing with talk of awareness. I can claim to be aware of the book being on the table and, if I do, my claim can be legitimately met with the question: "What makes you think that?" (or variations on this general theme). Then I can give reasons supporting my contention that there is a book on the table. The book's being on the table is independent of my awareness of the book being on the table. But my pain is not independent of my awareness of being in pain. If someone were to question what makes me think I am aware of being in pain, any answer I might offer in response would simply be a reiteration of my being in pain ("I can feel it!" "It hurts!" etc.). We use the term *awareness* in both cases—I am aware of the book being on the table and I am aware of being in pain—but the meaning of this term must be different in each case.

## 7. IMMUNITY TO ERROR THROUGH MISIDENTIFICATION

The idea of a kind of awareness that cannot be captured in terms of the intentional model of self-awareness is also what underlies the idea of *immunity to error through misidentification*.[13] This expression, introduced into the philosophical literature by Sydney Shoemaker, is actually elliptical. It's complete, and more accurate, version is, immunity to error through misidentification *relative to the first-person*

---

[13] Shoemaker (1968).

*pronoun.* One can, it is generally accepted, be mistaken about one's mental goings on: you think you dislike someone, but you are, in reality, attracted to him or her. You think you are afraid, but what you really feel is excitement. These sorts of errors are not at issue. Rather, the sorts of errors ruled out by immunity to error through misidentification are errors "relative to the first-person pronoun"—and this denotes a specific type of error. To claim that certain uses of the first-person pronoun are immune to this specific sort of error does not entail that one is infallible about what is going on in one's mind, nor does it entail that one's access to these goings on is incorrigible, etc.[14]

In explaining the idea of immunity to error through misidentification, Shoemaker distinguishes between two uses of *I*. The first-person pronoun can be used as an *object* or as a *subject*. Examples of its use as object include, "My arm is broken" and "I have grown six inches." This use of the first-person involves (a) the identification of a particular person and consequently (b) the possibility of an error of identification. To see why, consider an example, borrowed and adapted from David Kaplan.[15] I look in a shop window, see a reflection, and think, "My pants are on fire!" Happily, at least for me, it turns out that I am mistaken. Standing next to me is a man who rather looks like me, and has the same kind of sartorial proclivities, and it is his pants that are on fire. My judgment that my pants are on fire is based on misidentification. I judged the man whose pants are on fire to be me, and I was mistaken in this. This sort of mistake may be unlikely but, and this is Shoemaker's point, it is always *possible.*

On the other hand, the first-person pronoun can always be used as a *subject.* Examples of such use include, "I see so and so," "I am trying to lift my arm," "I think it will rain," and "I am in pain." In this usage, Shoemaker argues, there is (a) no possibility of an error of identification (relative to the first-person pronoun), and so (b) the usage cannot be regarded as involving identification. There is no possibility of an error of misidentification in this sense: if I say "I see so and so," it makes no sense to ask, "Are you sure that it is you that sees?" You might be mistaken about your seeing—you are, in fact, hallucinating not seeing. But what you can't be mistaken about is that it is *you* who is doing the seeing (or hallucinating). Similarly, if I sincerely profess to feel pain, this kind of error is

---

[14] In line with standard industry practice, Shoemaker provides a definition of the idea of error through misidentification that (a) is numbingly precise and (b) may take several hours of hard graft to understand. I include it here for any philosophers who might be reading, but I propose to explain the idea a little more informally. Shoemaker writes: *"Error through misidentification* = df. 'a is phi' is subject to error through misidentification relative to the term 'a' means that the following is possible: the speaker knows some particular thing to be phi, but makes the mistake of asserting 'a is phi,' because, and only because, he mistakenly thinks that the thing he knows to be phi is what 'a' refers to."

[15] Kaplan (1989).

not possible: I am mistaken in saying "I feel pain" because, although I do know of someone who feels pain, I am mistaken in thinking that person to be myself. In these sorts of claim, it is not possible to mistake yourself for someone else. This is immunity to error through misidentification relative to the first-person pronoun. If there is no possibility of misidentification concerning who is doing the seeing, or feeling the pain, or thinking that it will rain, then it does not make sense to think these uses of the first-person pronoun involve identification. Identification entails the possibility of misidentification. Thus, Shoemaker concludes: "My use of the word 'I' as the subject of my statement is not due to my having identified as myself something of which I know, or believe, or wish to say, that the predicate of my statement applies to it."[16]

The claim that identification entails the possibility of misidentification— that you cannot identify something unless there is at least the possibility of misidentification—is a consequence of the way identification, in this sense, works. Identification works via the recognition of certain properties and the attribution of them to an object. For example, when I identify myself in the mirror, in a reflection that contains numerous people, I may do so by way of various properties or qualities—properties of looking a certain way, broadly construed—and judge that I am the person with those properties.[17] This always comes with the possibility of misidentification. It may be that someone else has those same properties, or that I do not, in fact, have the properties I took myself to have.

A fruitful way of thinking about the idea that identification presupposes the possibility of misidentification is by seeing it as a version of a more general and, to some eyes at least, more familiar claim: *representation entails the possibility of misrepresentation*. The reasons this is so are well known. Essentially it is because the concept of representation is a *normative* one. Suppose I have the belief that grass is green. Then, given that I have this belief, grass *should* be green. If grass were not green, something would have gone wrong—not with grass but with my belief. A belief—which I employ here as a standard example of a representational state—stakes out a claim on the world: if I have a belief with, or otherwise represent, the content that *p*, then the world *should* be *p*. If the world is not *p*, then something has gone wrong. Any representational state, in this sense, has normative status.

---

[16] Shoemaker (1968), p. 558.

[17] One way of working out that it is your reflection in the mirror, for example, is seeing if the reflection moves when you do, and in the way you do. I include this in the notion of "looking" a certain way. Even that is not conclusive—if, for example, your twin, who also happens to be a skilled mimic, is behind the pane of glass.

The possibility of misrepresentation derives from the normativity of representations. Something can misrepresent only if it is *supposed* to represent some things and not others. But normativity, in turn, requires that representation and what it represents be at least *logically independent* of each other. In that case, a representation, R, can be activated when the world does not contain what R is supposed to be about. And it might not be activated when the world does contain what R is supposed to be about. In this way, we can have errors of representation— misrepresentation. Thus, representation presupposes the possibility of misrepresentation. The possibility of misrepresentation presupposes normativity. And normativity presupposes the logical independence of a representation and what it is about.[18]

The idea of error through misidentification, then, can be understood as a version of the idea of error through misrepresentation. Identification proceeds through recognition of properties, and the assigning of an object to those properties. Identification, in this sense, makes a normative claim. Given that a given identification has been made, a certain object *should* possess those properties that form the basis of the identification, and no other (contextually-present) object should possess those properties. But it is always possible that the object does not possess those properties or that some other object does. The object, and which properties it has, are logically independent of the act of identifying it—that is, of assigning properties to the object. Underpinning both the normativity of identification and the possibility of misidentification is the logical independence of the object identified and the identification of it by way of certain properties.

The upshot is this. In any genuine case of identification, there is always the logical possibility of misidentification. The latter logical possibility is purchased by the logical independence of the identified and the act of identifying it. Conversely, any immunity to error through misidentification would indicate that we are not dealing with a case of identification. And the reason we are not dealing with a case of identification is the same as the reason adduced by Wittgenstein in his discussion of our "knowledge" of our mental states: in self-awareness, that which we are trying to identify and the processes of identifying it are not logically independent of each other.

Immunity to error through misidentification provides a reason for rejecting the intentional model of self-awareness. The logical independence of the act of awareness and the object of awareness lies at the heart of the intentional model. On the one hand, there is the higher-order mental act, such as a thought, and, on the

---

[18] See Rowlands (2006) and (2012b) for elaboration of this general theme.

other, there is the first-order mental act that the higher-order act takes as its intentional object. As such, the intentional model will be unable to accommodate immunity to error through misidentification relative to the first-person pronoun. Where there is independence of a higher-order act of awareness and the first-order mental state that is the object of awareness, there will always be the possibility of such error. Immunity to error thorough misidentification indicates that in self-awareness there is no such independence of act and object.

## 8. THE ESSENTIAL INDEXICAL

John Perry has argued that, in statements of certain kinds of self-awareness, it is not possible to do without first-person indexicals (*I, me, my, mine*, etc.) of some sort. That is, such indexicals cannot be analyzed out in favor of anything else, in particular anything description-like. Suppose I am aware that the only Welsh person working in the Philosophy Department of the University of Miami is writing a book. Does this guarantee that I am aware that I am writing a book? It does not, Perry points out, unless I am aware that I am the only Welsh person working in the Philosophy Department of the University of Miami. To guarantee self-awareness, then, we would have to add the rider: *I* am the only Welsh person working in the Philosophy Department of the University of Miami, and our description has, therefore, invoked an indexical. Any attempt to characterize the content of self-awareness will, necessarily, have to invoke some or other first-person indexical. This, when properly contextualized, also counts against the intentional model of self-awareness.

The description "the only Welsh person working in the Philosophy Department of the University of Miami" is only contingently related to me. We can, that is, come apart. The department fires me, and hires another Welsh philosopher, for example. Or, it turns out I am mistaken about the place of my birth and I am not Welsh at all. The description still has the same meaning, irrespective of who it actually picks out—and even if it picks out no one at all. A description and the object (contingently) picked out by the description are, in this sense, logically independent of each other.

Indexicals, on the other hand, are not like this. A first-person indexical such as *I* gets its meaning, in a demonstrative context, by direct reference to the person it picks out. A failure of reference for an indexical would result in a statement that had no meaning. It is, as we shall see, impossible to imagine a failure of reference in the use of a first-person pronoun as subject.[19] But, for now, consider other

---

[19] Shoemaker (1968) makes this point. I'll discuss it further in the next section.

indexical uses. If I say, "Look at *that* dog" and there is no dog there, then what I have said has no meaning. In general, failure of reference in the case of a demonstrative utterance makes that utterance meaningless. The meaning of an indexical statement and the object picked out by the embedded indexical are not, therefore, logically independent of each other. The meaning of an indexical utterance is, as it is sometimes put, *object involving*, in two senses. First, if the utterance is meaningful, then the object demonstrated must exist. Second, one cannot substitute in another object—for example, replacing one dog with an exact duplicate—without changing the meaning of the utterance.

The significance of Perry's argument should now be apparent. The content of self-awareness cannot be captured in non-indexical terms. Some or other indexical will be a non-eliminable component of the content of any act of self-awareness. However, the content of an indexical utterance or statement is object-involving, and therefore not logically independent of what it is about. Combining these two claims yields the following corollary: at least in some cases, an act of self-awareness is not logically independent of the self or mental state it takes as its object. Once we accept this, we must—for reasons outlined in the preceding section—abandon the intentional model of self-awareness—at least as a general model of all self-awareness. The intentional model of self-awareness is committed to the logical independence of the (higher-order) act of awareness and the (first-order) object of awareness. If Perry is correct, this sort of independence cannot, in general, be sustained.

## 9. WHY SELF-AWARENESS IS NON-DEMONSTRATIVE

Reflections on the arguments of Perry might suggest that we can understand self-awareness in demonstrative terms. Ultimately, I do not think this idea is going to work, for reasons adduced by Shoemaker.[20] Demonstratives behave differently than acts of self-awareness in at least two crucial respects. First, in a demonstrative, there is always the possibility of a failure of reference (e.g., in hallucination). "That dog is big," I say, but there is no dog and my utterance is, accordingly, meaningless. There is no parallel possibility of failure in the case of self-awareness. Second, suppose I say, "This is red." The denotation of *this* is fixed by the speaker's intentions. Or, suppose I say, "I name this the *SS Cutty Sark*." What does *this* refer to? The ship? The champagne bottle I'm breaking on it? The act of breaking a bottle of champagne over the hull of a ship? The ambient air temperature when

---

[20] Shoemaker (1968), p. 559.

the bottle is broken? In the early, heady, days of the causal theory, there was an idea doing the rounds to the effect that we explain reference by way of an initial act of baptism and subsequent causal history. These examples show that, at the very least, we need a sortal: "I name this *ship* the *Cutty Sark*." And which sortal is involved is fixed by the intentions of the speaker, shaped in many cases by social and linguistic conventions. There is no parallel for this in the case of self-awareness. For example, when I use *I* as a subject, in Shoemaker's sense, it is not as if there are various candidates for what *I* might pick out, with the correct one being determined by my intentions or by socio-linguistic conventions. It is unlikely, therefore, that we can understand self-awareness as a form of demonstrative self-reference.

## 10. UP NEXT

If the arguments of this chapter are correct, we do not have, yet, a workable model of self-awareness. The intentional model had the advantage of being both relatively clear and familiar. But there are good reasons for supposing that this model will not provide a general account of self-awareness. There is, I have argued, a form of self-awareness in which the act of awareness is not logically independent of the object of awareness. It is not possible to capture this latter form of self-awareness by way of the intentional model—for this model is committed precisely to such independence of act and object of awareness.

This is not—and I wish to emphasize this—to deny that we can make ourselves, our bodily states, and our mental states into objects of our awareness. I can think that I need to lose a bit of weight. I can bemoan my thinking being not as sharp today as it was yesterday. There is no reason for denying that this is self-awareness, and so no reason for denying that self-awareness can take intentional form. But if the arguments of this chapter are correct, the intentional form is not the *only* form that self-awareness can take. Indeed, this sort of intentional self-awareness is a relatively unusual phenomenon. Certainly: it happens. But it does not happen most of the time. Most of the time we just get on with things—experiencing, thinking, and acting. The sort of higher-order, intentional, reflective attitude that one can take with respect to oneself and one's bodily and mental states is relatively uncommon. There is, I shall argue in the next chapter, another, far more pervasive form of self-awareness—a *non-intentional*, or as I shall prefer, *pre-intentional*, form of self-awareness. This pre-intentional self-awareness is present whenever we "get on with things"—that is, whenever we experience, think, and act. Intentional self-awareness involves considerable cognitive sophistication—including, in one of its forms at least, metacognitive abilities—and is relatively sparse and derivative. Pre-intentional self-awareness involves far less cognitive sophistication, is far more pervasive, and arguably makes intentional self-awareness possible. *What*, precisely, pre-intentional awareness is, *why* it is so pervasive, and *how* it makes intentional self-awareness possible are the subjects of the next chapter.

# 7

## PRE-INTENTIONAL AWARENESS OF SELF

### 1. KANT: EMPIRICAL AND TRANSCENDENTAL SELF-CONSCIOUSNESS

There are some ideas that seem to spend much of their existence curiously—perhaps unfairly, perhaps even outrageously—neglected. But they will not go away entirely because they are just too good. Such ideas will resurface every now and then, quickly become forgotten again, and will be subsequently reinvented by a new, historically myopic, generation. The idea that there is a form of awareness that is not, and does not reduce to, intentional self-awareness is one of these ideas. It is an idea that pops up in the most unexpected of places. Prior to its popping up in this book, recognizable versions of the idea can be found in the work of Edmund Husserl, Jean-Paul Sartre (and the rest of the phenomenological tradition for that matter), Ludwig Wittgenstein, Sydney Shoemaker, Hector-Neri Castaneda, John Perry, and Gareth Evans, among others.[1]

---

[1] The view that self-awareness comes in different forms and in different degrees is not an uncommon idea. Recent defenders of this general idea include Bekoff (2003), Bekoff and Sherman (2004), DeGrazia (2009), and Evans (2016). I have in mind, however, a quite specific version of this idea that identifies a basic and broad distinction between two forms of self-awareness, each of which has distinctive properties. I have discussed the views of Wittgenstein, Shoemaker, and Perry in the previous chapter. See also Castañeda (1966) and Evans (1982). Zahavi (2005) can be added to this list. The daddy of this distinction, however, is almost certainly Kant (1781/1787).

Historically, however, the idea is perhaps most closely associated with Immanuel Kant.[2]

Kant distinguishes two forms of self-awareness: "the I that I think is distinct from the I that it, itself, intuits. I am given to myself beyond that which is given in intuition."[3] This is, perhaps, not particularly helpful, but we're dealing with Kant and so you had better get used to it. The general distinction Kant wished to draw is relatively clear, at least in outline. Someone may be conscious of himself and his psychological states through what Kant called *inner sense*. This Kant referred to as *empirical self-consciousness*. Empirical self-consciousness corresponds to what, in the previous chapter, I labeled intentional self-awareness. In empirical self-consciousness, there is an act of awareness that takes me, or some facet of me, as its intentional object.

According to Kant, empirical self-consciousness is not the only form that self-awareness can take. Someone may be conscious of herself and her psychological states in a quite different way: through engaging in conscious acts such as perceiving and thinking—not perceiving or thinking specifically about oneself but perceiving and thinking more generally. A form of self-consciousness, Kant thought, is implicated in acts such as these. This latter form of self-consciousness Kant often called *transcendental apperception* or, sometimes, *transcendental designation*. Neither of these expressions is ideal. Kant's use of *transcendental apperception* was far from univocal. Sometimes he used it to refer to a kind of self-awareness. But sometimes he used it to refer to the *basis* of this self-awareness: the *acts of synthesis* that make this form of self-awareness possible (we'll get to that later). The expression *transcendental designation*, on the other hand, appears only in the A edition of the *Critique of Pure Reason*—being completely excised from the B edition.[4] Rather than employ either of these expressions, but modeling my usage on Kant's use of the expression *empirical self-consciousness*, I shall talk of *transcendental self-consciousness*. Kant's core idea, then, is that transcendental self-consciousness is bound up, or implicated, in the possession of conscious acts in general.

Suppose I see a dog running across a field. I am, then, engaged in a mental act—an act of seeing—that makes me aware of the dog. But, according to Kant, I am not simply aware of the dog. In engaging in this conscious act of seeing, I am also

---

[2] Kant (1781/1787).

[3] Kant (1781/1787), B155.

[4] For the non-philosophers, a little explanation might be useful. Kant's *Critique of Pure Reason*, a rather large and difficult book, but enormously influential, was published twice. The first edition—known as the A edition—was published in 1781. The second—B—edition was published in 1787. There are some differences between the two editions, not all of them insignificant.

aware both of myself and of the act of seeing. Awareness of object, awareness of self, and awareness of mental act are bound up together. But my awareness of myself, and the mental act of seeing, is of a different kind than my awareness of the dog.

My awareness of the dog is intentional awareness: the dog is an intentional object of my perception. It is not, of course, intentional *self-awareness*. Intentional awareness occurs whenever I engage in an intentional act (seeing, thinking, etc.) that has an object. Intentional *self*-awareness, on the other hand, occurs when I, or some aspect or facet of me, is that object. In this case, I am intentionally aware of the dog. I *might*, of course, be thinking about myself or my act of seeing at the same time, in which case I would be intentionally aware of myself also. But I *need* not be thinking about myself or my act of seeing. And if I am not, I would still be aware of myself and my act of seeing in another way, for, according to Kant, having such awareness is part of what it is to see the dog. In this other way of being aware of myself, I am not an object of any intentional act of mine, and neither is my act of seeing. My awareness of myself and of my act of seeing is transcendental, or, as I shall put it, *pre-intentional*.[5]

While Kant is clear that transcendental self-consciousness—pre-intentional self-awareness, as I am calling it—is bound up, or implicated, in the possession of any conscious act, he is, unfortunately, less perspicuous on why and how this is so. Kant is clear that this transcendental self-consciousness is characterized by certain *peculiarities*:

Through this I or he or it (the thing) which thinks, nothing further is represented than a transcendental subject of the thoughts = X.[6]

And:

In attaching "I" to our thoughts, we designate the subject . . . only transcendentally, without noting in it any quality whatsoever—in fact, without knowing anything of it either directly or by inference.[7]

---

[5] This is a modified borrowing from Sartre (1943/1957), who would talk alternately—sometimes in the same sentence—of *pre-reflective* awareness, *non-positional* self-awareness, *non-thetic* self-awareness, and *unreflective* awareness. These all mean more or less the same thing, although he did also use *unreflective* awareness in another way. Also, the notion of "reflective" contains the notion of self: all reflective and pre-reflective awareness is self-awareness. This is not true of *positional*. I can be positionally aware of many things, myself included, but only non-positionally self-aware.

[6] Kant (1781/1787), A346/B404.

[7] Kant (1781/1787), A355.

Kant also claims that in transcendental self-awareness "nothing manifold is given."[8] Moreover, in such self-awareness, one does not "represent" oneself but merely "denote" oneself. [9]

To see what Kant is getting at with this idea of designating the subject "without noting in it any quality whatsoever" we can, I think, usefully return to Shoemaker's notion of *identification* discussed in the previous chapter.[10] I see a book, let us suppose, in virtue of seeing various properties or features of it: its size, color, the words on its dust jacket, and so on. Some of these properties may not uniquely identify the book. Many books can have a yellow cover, for example. But some properties, or combination or properties, may uniquely identify the book—such as the title and author printed on the cover: Mark Rowlands, *Running with the Pack*. Of course, there may be—and it goes without saying that I hope there are— many copies of this book. But further properties might be used to identify specific tokens of this book (one has been chewed by a puppy, on another my sons have drawn a moustache and spectacles on my author photo, etc.). On the basis of such properties, I can judge or determine the identity of specific tokens of the book. In this sort of case, my identification of an object proceeds by way of my recognizing that it has a certain set of properties. This is *identification through property—or quality—recognition*.[11]

The same sort of procedure can also apply to self-identification. If I see myself reflected in a shop window, I may initially not recognize who this person is (my eyesight is not what it was, or the window is dirty, or I don't realize there is glass in front of me, and so on). But then I see that this person is wearing the shirt I put on this morning, and I realize that I am that person. I have identified myself by way of a property—the wearing of a particular shirt—that I have. Once again, we have a case of identification through property recognition.

This, however, is a rather unusual case. While awareness of myself might be like this, it is not typically like this. When I wake up in the morning, before I have opened my eyes and looked at myself, I am aware of who I am. I don't have to be thinking thoughts of the sort "I am Mark Rowlands." That would be a strange way to wake up. More likely, I am thinking thoughts about the coming day—running through a list of all the shit I am going to have to deal with in the next sixteen hours or so. This does seem to be a form of self-awareness: I am aware of myself— of who I am. But, the crucial point is that this self-awareness does not involve, or

---

[8] Kant (1781/1787), B135.

[9] Kant (1781/1787), A382.

[10] Here, I am grateful to Brook (2001), who also explores this comparison.

[11] From Shoemaker's perspective, the expression *through property recognition* would be redundant since property recognition is built into his conception of identification. I include it here for the sake of clarity.

proceed through, recognition of a property or collection of properties I happen to have. Rather, the explanation has far more to do with the fact that the shit that must be dealt with is, precisely, *my* shit. And, a brief recollection of Perry's argument should convince us of the folly of thinking that this *mine-ness* of the shit in question can be explained in non-indexical, property-recognition, terms (e.g., the shit that must be dealt with by the only Welsh philosopher working in the Department of Philosophy of the University of Miami, etc.).

This peculiarity of self-consciousness explains why it should be *immune to error through misidentification*—in Shoemaker's sense that we explored in the preceding chapter. Identification that proceeds via properties, or qualities, always carries with it the possibility of errors of identification: the properties one thought it possesses it, in fact, does not possess, and properties one thought it does not possess it, in fact, does, etc. Such identification is always, therefore, fallible. Self-consciousness, in Kant's transcendental sense, should be immune to error through misidentification precisely because, and to the extent that, it does not proceed via property or quality recognition.

It is one thing to establish that self-consciousness comes in two distinct forms. It is quite another to explain what these forms are. Thus far, Kant, on this interpretation, has supplied a distinction: empirical self-consciousness is grounded in identification through property or quality recognition; transcendental (or pre-intentional) self-consciousness is not. But to say what transcendental self-consciousness does not involve is not to say what it does involve. Moreover, the crucial question that Kant's account needs to answer is obvious: *why* is it that engaging in a conscious act (seeing, thinking, remembering, and so on) guarantees that you are aware not only of what the act is about but also of oneself and the conscious act?

Kant's answer to this question begins with what we might think of as the *unity of experience*. Experience is—at least typically, and perhaps necessarily—unified. If I see a bright red tomato and hear a loud claxon simultaneously, then I experience these two occurrences as part of one larger experience. Moreover, the successive appearances of the tomato are presented precisely as appearances of an enduring object, rather than merely as a succession of unrelated, evanescent, appearances. All these occurrences are parts or moments of this larger—or, as Kant puts it, "general"—experience:

When we speak of different experiences, we can refer only to the various perceptions, all of which, as such, belong to one and the same general experience. This thoroughgoing synthetic unity of perceptions is indeed the form of experience; it is nothing else than the synthetic unity of appearances in accordance with concepts.[12]

For a general experience, in this sense, to exist, acts of *synthesis* must be performed: the various elements of experience (sights, sounds, and so on) must be united into a whole, and assigned to enduring objects. This *seems* to be the key to transcendental self-consciousness. But how, *precisely*, do acts of synthesis whereby elements of experience are united in a general experience yield, or result in, transcendental self-consciousness? Kant's answer lies in a notoriously obscure passage:

> The mind could never think its identity in the manifoldness of its representations . . . if it did not have before its eyes the identity of its act, whereby it subordinates all [the manifold] . . . to a transcendental unity.[13]

Putting aside the questionable metaphors,[14] the idea seems to be that an individual can only be transcendentally self-conscious ("think its identity") if it is aware of ("have before its eyes") the identity of an act(s) by which it combines the individual elements of experience into a synthetic whole or, as Kant puts it, "general experience." But, as an explanation of the connection between acts of synthesis and transcendental self-consciousness, this seems poorly targeted for at least two reasons. First, as stated, it only provides a *necessary* condition of transcendental self-consciousness: to be self-conscious in this way I must "have before my eyes" the acts of synthesis responsible for the combination of experiential elements into a unified general experience. Part of what we want to know is what transcendental self-consciousness is. Thus far we have only been told what it is not and the way it does not work. Necessary and sufficient conditions might help us out in this respect. But a merely necessary condition really does not. All we are told is that unless we are aware of our acts of synthesis we can't be transcendentally self-conscious. But this does not tell us what it is to be transcendentally self-conscious.

Second, this account seems merely to explain transcendental consciousness of oneself with consciousness of the identity of one's mental acts of synthesis. This yields a dilemma. The consciousness of one's mental acts of synthesis must, it seems, be either transcendental or empirical. If the former, then this account does not explain transcendental self-consciousness but presupposes it. If the latter,

---

[12] (1781/1787), A110. See also Brook (2001).
[13] (1781/1787), A108.
[14] The mind has eyes, ffs!

then the worry is that the distinctiveness of transcendental self-consciousness would be lost: transcendental consciousness of self turns out to be nothing more than empirical consciousness of one's mental acts (of synthesis). Transcendental self-consciousness is, in fact, empirical self-consciousness. This, it is reasonably clear, is *not* Kant's view.

I'm missing something, I'm sure. But if there is one thing I have learned from decades of wrestling with the Old Jacobin, it is this useful, albeit bitterly acquired, lesson: if you have a problem to solve, it is usually far easier, quicker, and less cognitively demanding to solve it yourself than to try and work out how Kant solved it. Who knows? Perhaps the view upon which I shall ultimately alight is, in fact, Kant's. I can't tell.

## 2. SARTRE: REFLECTIVE AND PRE-REFLECTIVE CONSCIOUSNESS

Like Kant, Sartre thought that a form of self-awareness was built in to any conscious act. Rather than using the term *transcendental* to label this form of consciousness, Sartre preferred the term *pre-reflective*. He also used the equivalent expression *non-positional*. Whenever one engages in a conscious act, Sartre thought, one is pre-reflectively/non-positionally aware of both oneself and the act in which one is engaged. Pre-reflective or non-positional self-awareness is opposed to reflective awareness. I am reflectively aware of myself when I, or some facet of me, is an object of an intentional act of mine (an object of a thought, of an act of introspection, and so on). I can be reflectively aware of myself, but much of the time am not. But whenever I have conscious experience at all, I am aware of myself pre-reflectively. Reflective consciousness corresponds to what I have labeled intentional self-awareness and, at least roughly, to Kant's notion of empirical self-consciousness. Its pre-reflective counterpart corresponds to what I have called pre-intentional self-awareness.

When I am pre-reflectively self-aware, according to Sartre, I am aware of myself without making myself, or any facet of me, into an intentional object of my awareness. Like Kant, Sartre thought that this sort of pre-reflective awareness is bound up with, or implicated in, the possession of any conscious mental act. Sartre's position can be factored into two components. The first is the claim that whenever I am conscious (i.e., engaged in a conscious act), I am also self-conscious. The second is the claim that this self-consciousness that necessarily accompanies the act should not be understood as *reflective* (i.e., intentional).[15] With regard to the

---

[15] To reiterate: this is not to deny that self-consciousness can take reflective, or positional, form. It is to

second claim, Sartre levels a regress argument. In stating this argument, he takes *knowledge* to be a standard exemplar of positional consciousness: when I know, I know *something*. He writes:

> The reduction of consciousness to knowledge in fact involves our introducing into consciousness the subject–object dualism which is typical of know-ledge . . . but then a third term will be necessary in order for the knower to become known in turn, and we will be faced with this dilemma: Either we stop at any one term of the series—the known, the knower known, the knower known by the knower, etc. . . . Or else we affirm the necessity of an infinite regress. . . . If we wish to avoid an infinite regress, there must be an immediate, non-cognitive, relation of self to self.[16]

We encountered this type of argument earlier, when identifying problems with the higher-order thought (HOT) model of consciousness. This is unsurprising because the HOT account just is an expression of the idea that in order to be conscious I must be reflectively—intentionally—aware of my mental states. Suppose we ac-cept that (1) whenever there is a conscious mental state there is consciousness of that state and (2) this consciousness is reflective. If the consciousness is reflective, then we have to accept that the mental state and the higher-order state (thought, knowledge) are distinct states—as was the case in the HOT model. But, then, if the higher-order state is to be conscious, there will have to be a distinct higher-higher-order state to make it so, and so on. As I argued in Chapter 3, the argument can be strengthened considerably by regarding the regress issue as one horn of a dilemma. But there is little need to revisit this issue now since it is tangential to our current concerns.

It is Sartre's claim that whenever there is consciousness there must also be self-consciousness that is germane to current concerns. When he introduces this idea Sartre, curiously, provides no argument for it. He seems to think it is so obvious that no argument needs to be given. The closest he comes to an argument is here:

> However, the necessary and sufficient condition for a knowing consciousness to be knowledge *of* its object is that it be consciousness of itself as being that knowledge. This is a necessary condition, for if my consciousness were not consciousness of being consciousness of that table, it would be consciousness

---

deny, however, that the form of self-consciousness that is necessarily built into conscious experience is reflective or positional self-consciousness.

[16] (1943/1957), p. 12.

of that table without being consciousness of being so. In other words, it would be a consciousness ignorant of itself, an unconscious—which is absurd.[17]

Is it really absurd, and if so, why? It might be that Sartre is simply being a little too blasé, and that what seems obviously absurd to him may, in fact, be neither obvious nor absurd. Or, it might be that Sartre's insouciance is due to his belief that he has *already* supplied such an argument. To see what this argument is—or, at least, might be—we must return to the opening pages of *Being and Nothingness* where Sartre discusses the nature of objects:

> Modern thought has realized considerable progress by reducing the existent to the series of appearances that manifest it . . . the dualism of being and appearance is no longer entitled to any legal status within philosophy. The appearance refers to the total series of appearances and not to a hidden reality that would drain to itself all the *being* of the existent.[18]

The "modern thought" in question is the phenomenological program instigated by Husserl. An "existent" is an existing thing—an object, event, process, etc. "Appearances," as Sartre uses them, should not be confused with experiences. The guiding idea behind Husserl's phenomenological reduction or *epoché*—the initial step in the application of his phenomenological method—is that we are to focus on the way things appear, and bracket the question of what sorts of things— mental, physical, etc.—these appearances are. Sartre continues:

> The phenomenal being manifests itself; it manifests its essence as well as its existence, and it is nothing but the well-connected series of its manifestations. . . . Yet the existent in fact cannot be reduced to a *finite* series of manifestations since each one of them is a relation to a subject constantly changing.[19]

Objects (existents) are series of appearances. This is an ontological claim: a claim about what objects are (although it is a fairly minimal ontological claim since it takes no stand on what appearances are).[20] What is important for our purposes is

---

[17] (1943/1957), p. 11.

[18] (1943/1957), pp. 1–2.

[19] (1943/1957), p. 5.

[20] Also, it is an ontological claim that is fashioned by the application of the Husserlian epoché—and the basic function of this is to make us rescind from ontological claims. So, the idea is best stated: from the perspective of the epoché we shouldn't think of objects as anything more than series of appearances. By the way: none of this matters at all. Forget I ever said it.

not this claim as such, but its implications for what it is to see an object. The idea of seeing an object *as* something—as an object of a particular sort—is crucial. The idea I am going to develop in the next section is that pre-reflective—or, as I am calling it, pre-intentional—self-awareness is implicated in seeing an object *as* something. Whenever one sees an object as something—and there is no way to see an object other than *as* something or other—one is also aware, pre-intentionally, of oneself. This argument may be Sartre's or it may not. I don't think there is sufficient textual evidence to definitively adjudicate. But it is an argument, and I hope it's a good one because I am going to try to do a lot with it.

## 3. SEEING AS

In recent years, the opening class of any course of phenomenology I teach has always seemed to start in the same way—my once plentiful pedagogical innovations having melted away like *les neiges d'antan*. I hold up a bottle of Coke—my most faithful and enduring educational manipulative—and ask the students what they see. They're philosophy majors, some of them anyway, and suspect a trap. So, sometimes they tell me they see a collection of colors and shapes. Sometimes they tell me they see the front of a Coke bottle. They're far too suspicious, too infected by philosophy. All I want them to do is tell me what is obvious: it's a bottle of Coke, stupid!

There are two facets of the obvious that are important for our purposes. First, to see that which I hold in my hand as a bottle of Coke is to see it as an *enduring object*, rather than a series of evanescent sense impressions of colors or shapes. Second, it is to see this enduring object as belonging to a certain kind: bottle of Coke. But it is also true that, at any given time, they see—or, at least, are in direct visual contact with—only the part of the bottle that is facing them, and this part that is facing them might be broken down into a series of shapes and colors. So, why is it, then, that they see it as a bottle of Coke, rather than a bottle of Coke façade, or a series of sense impressions?

The phenomenological tradition provides a clear and consistent answer to this question: they see the item in my hand *as* a bottle of Coke because they have certain *expectations* or *anticipations* regarding how what appears to them will change in the event of certain *contingencies*—that is, in the event of certain things happening. That is, they anticipate that if, for example, I were to rotate the bottle, the appearances that are presented to them would change in a certain way: the Coca-Cola logo on the front of the label will progressively disappear from view, being replaced by the smaller writing that appears on the back of the label, and so on. If, on the other hand, the item in my hand were a bottle façade, the succession of appearances would be very different: the thin edge of the cardboard would quickly become visible, and so on. The same sorts of points apply whether the Coke bottle is moved (rotated, relocated) relative to me or I move relative to the Coke bottle (I move to the left or to the right, I walk around it, and so on). In both cases, I have expectations about how the appearances will change in these circumstances. When we see an item as a Coke bottle rather than a Coke bottle façade it is because what we see has generated in us a certain set of expectations that are specific to a Coke bottle. To have these expectations is precisely what it is to see this little piece of the world as a bottle of Coke.

The same sorts of points apply to other forms of perception. If I hold the bottle in my hand, it would seem to me that I am holding a bottle in my hand. But, at any given time, my fingers are in contact with only portions of the bottle. Why does it seem to me that I am holding a bottle in my hand? (Suppose I am in the dark, and can't see the bottle.) The feel of the bottle in my hand has generated various expectations about how my experience will change in given circumstances: if I slide my fingers up, my tactile sensations will change in a certain way—consistent with the narrowing of the neck of the bottle, for example—and will change in a certain distinct way if I slide my fingers down the bottle, etc.[21]

This general picture of perception as constituted by expectations was a common refrain in early phenomenology. More recently it has been usefully appropriated by the *enactivist* tradition in philosophy of mind: to see an object, as an object, is to have mastered various *sensorimotor contingencies*. Here, for example, is Alva Noë, whose preferred inspirational object in this case is a tomato rather than a bottle of Coke:

> Our perceptual sense of the tomato's wholeness—of its volume and back-side, and so forth—consists in our implicit understanding (our expectation) that the movements of our body to the left or right, say, will bring further bits of the tomato into view. Our relation to the unseen bits of the tomato is mediated by patterns of sensorimotor contingency. Similar points can be made across the board for occlusion phenomena.[22]

---

[21] For a lucid discussion of these issues, by a psychologist influenced by the phenomenological tradition, see Mackay (1967).

[22] Noë (2004), p. 63.

Even more recently, this general idea forms the backbone of what is known as the *predictive processing* paradigm. According to this paradigm, brains are constantly active in that they attempt to predict the streams of sensory stimulation before they arrive. What is most important in this process are sensed discrepancies or deviations from the streams they have predicted, which form the basis of further refinement of the prediction. In seeing the Coke bottle, my visual experience reflects a multi-level neural guess that best reduces visual prediction errors. When there is a deviation from what my brain predicts—when I begin to circumnavigate the bottle and see the thin edge of a cardboard façade instead of the rounded back side of the bottle—this provides critical information that allows my brain to refine its guesses. When I visually perceive the bottle, my brain has, in effect, already predicted the scene, and any subsequent mismatch between prediction and experience results in refinement of further predictions until equilibrium is reached.[23]

The idea that perception is to be understood in terms of anticipations, expectations, or predictions is, thus, a well-entrenched view, straddling different times, traditions, and disciplines. I am going to rely on it in developing the case for non-positional self-awareness. The crucial point, for my purposes, is this: *I am implicated in many—indeed, arguably all—of these expectations or predictions.* For example, some of the relevant anticipations involve either *my* doing something or something being done to the bottle relative to *me*. I anticipate that if *I* were to move five meters to the left, the appearance of the bottle would change in a certain manner. And it would change in a somewhat different way if *I* were to move to the right. I am able to anticipate that if the bottle were to move relative to *me*, then the appearances it presents would also change in a certain way. Even when the bottle is rotated, the changes of appearance I anticipate depend on my remaining stationary: if I orbit the bottle as it rotates, the appearances of the bottle would not change.[24] Thus, to see these appearances *as* the appearances of a certain, enduring, object involves a kind of awareness of myself. It is I, one and the same I, that is implicated in these expectations: if *I* were to move five meters to the right, if the bottle were to move relative to *me*, if the bottle were rotated while *I* remained stationary, and so on. This awareness I have of myself is required for me to see these appearances as appearances of a bottle (rather than as appearances of something else). This is one example of what I have labeled pre-intentional self-awareness.

---

[23] See, for example, Hohwy (2015), Clark (2016).

[24] The appearances of the background would, of course, change. In any appearance there is, as Sartre pointed out, always a *figure* and a *ground* (1943/1957, p. 41). The rotating bottle is the figure, and the appearances of this may stay the same as I orbit it in time with its rotation. But the ground—the background—would be changing.

In seeing the bottle, I am pre-intentionally aware of myself to the extent I am implicated in the anticipations in virtue of which I see it *as* a bottle.

## 4. I KNOW WHAT YOU ARE THINKING . . .

. . . You are thinking that there is a glaring problem with this account: it is question-begging. Not so, I shall argue. At least, ultimately not so. But I can see why you might think that. The problem is that the account, as it has been developed so far, makes the capacity of pre-intentional self-awareness dependent on the capacity for intentional self-awareness. The anticipations involved in seeing the bottle *as* a bottle are intentional states that have me as their object—if I were to move relative to the bottle, if the bottle were to move relative to me, and so on. Therefore, I can't have anticipations of this sort unless I am capable of thinking thoughts about myself.

This apparent dependence of pre-intentional self-awareness on intentional self-awareness does not square with the views of Kant and Sartre. Sartre, in particular, is very clear that pre-reflective self-awareness is prior to reflective self-awareness in the sense that it makes the latter possible:

> If I count the cigarettes which are in that case . . . it is very possible that I have no positional consciousness of counting them. . . . Yet at the moment when these cigarettes are revealed to me as a dozen, I have a non-thetic consciousness of my adding activity. If anyone questioned me, indeed, if anyone should ask, "What are you doing there?" I should reply at once, "I am counting". . . . Thus reflection has no primacy over the consciousness reflected on. It is not reflection that reveals the consciousness reflected on to itself. Quite the contrary, it is the non-reflective consciousness which renders the reflection possible; there is a pre-reflective cogito which is the condition of the Cartesian cogito.[25]

Reflective self-awareness, according to Sartre, depends for its existence on pre-reflective self-awareness. I can be reflectively aware of myself only because I am, first, pre-reflectively aware of myself.

Moreover, not only is this Sartre's view, it is also the view I require given the overall dialectical purposes of this book. In the face of skepticism, in some quarters at least, of the possibility of intentional self-awareness (mirror self

---

[25] Sartre (1943/1957), p. 13.

recognition, metacognition, etc.) in animals, I have argued that there is another, pre-intentional, form of self-awareness. That argument will prove spurious if pre-intentional self-awareness turns out to require intentional self-awareness.

Happily, this is not so. The account of pre-intentional self-awareness, as I have so far developed it, is an overly—and unnecessarily—intellectualized one. It describes pre-intentional self-awareness as it would exist in a creature that is also capable of intentional self-awareness. However, I shall now argue, it is possible to purge the offending intellectualist strains of this account of pre-intentional self-awareness, and thus arrive at an account of pre-intentional self-awareness that does not presuppose intentional self-awareness. To do so, we must first properly identify these intellectualist strains, for the seeds of their replacement can be found in their proper identification.

The worry is *not* that seeing an object, O, as such-and-such requires *consciously thinking* numerous thoughts of the sort, "If I were to move relative to O, then the appearances would change in a such-and-such manner"; "If O were to move relative to me, then appearances would change, thus-and-so," and so on. There is no reason to suppose that the relevant anticipations that allow me to see O as such-and-such must be take the form of conscious, occurrent thoughts.

Nor, second, is there any reason to suppose that these anticipations must take the form of unconscious thoughts. The pre-intentional is not a sub-category of the unconscious. Rather, it is to be understood as a distinctive—*sui generis*—form of self-awareness. When I see an object as such-and-such, this seeing-as must be grounded in an indefinitely large array of anticipations—but these anticipations are *implicit* rather than unconscious. The categories of the implicit and the unconscious are quite different. If an anticipation is unconscious, it is actually present, but in unconscious rather than conscious form. However, if an anticipation is implicit, it exists in dispositional rather than actual form. An anticipation of mine is implicit if I have a tendency, or disposition, to (actually) have this anticipation under certain conditions but do not, as things stand, (actually) have it.[26]

Nevertheless—and this is the real worry—even if only implicit, the existence of these anticipations seems problematic. If the anticipations exist in dispositional form, then while I might not actually be thinking them, consciously or unconsciously, I must, nevertheless, be *able* to think them. And these anticipations are, in effect, thoughts about me. Therefore, it seems, I must have the *capacity* for intentional self-awareness in order to be pre-intentionally self-aware. Thus, if animals cannot be intentionally self-aware—and this is a common view—then it

---

[26] I am working with what is sometimes called a *formation-dispositional* account of the implicit.

seems they cannot be pre-intentionally self-aware either. The key to avoiding this problem can be found by taking a closer look at the notion of the dispositional.

An anticipation of mine is implicit if I have a disposition, to (actually) have this anticipation under certain conditions but do not, as things stand, (actually) have it. However, the conditions under which I will actually have this anticipation can vary. Sometimes these conditions will be relatively common. But sometimes they are far rarer, obtaining infrequently or even never. And sometimes—and this is the possibility that interests me—they not only do not obtain but, as things stand, *cannot* obtain. The sense in which a circumstance cannot obtain is a matter of *physical* necessity. I doubt we can make sense of the idea that one can have a disposition to φ in circumstances C, where C does not occur in any logically possible world. But if the impossibility is merely physical, then I think we can certainly make sense of this idea. In a circumstance where pigs had wings, pigs might indeed have a disposition to fly—even though such a circumstance is, given certain plausible constraints on evolutionary development, physically impossible.

This is the idea I am going to exploit: the claim that the required anticipations are implicit does not, in fact, entail that the individual who has these anticipations is capable of thinking or entertaining them. If things were different—in some logically possible but perhaps not physically possible way—then the individual would be able to entertain these anticipations. But, as things stand physically, it cannot do so. The key to whether an individual is pre-intentionally self-aware lies in what anticipations it would have in certain logically possible circumstances and not what anticipations it actually does have. More precisely, I shall argue that pre-intentional self-awareness is best understood in a way akin to that in which, in Chapter 4, we understood narrow content: as a *function*. In this case, however, the function in question is from a *context* to an *act of intentional self-awareness*.

## 5. PRE-INTENTIONAL SELF-AWARENESS DE-INTELLECTUALIZED: THE SUBJUNCTIVE-DISPOSITIONAL MODEL

Let us suppose I am a wide receiver trying to catch a football.[27] The ball is thrown in a parabola, reaching a zenith and beginning its descent back to earth. How do I make sure I intercept it? I could, at least at one point in my life, do the math. But, even on a good day, this would have taken around twenty minutes and so could not help me with my current predicament. So, instead, I do something

---

[27] Here, I am drawing on the work of McBeath, Shaffer, and Kaiser (1995), which actually concerned catching a baseball not a football.

much simpler: I start moving. If I can get my path just right—a path that mirrors that of the ball—our respective motions will cancel each other out, and the ball will look as if it is traveling in a straight line. Moreover, if I can match my speed with that of the ball, then the ball will appear as if it is moving at a constant velocity. The result of these actions I can take is that the ball comes to appear *catchable*. And making the ball appear catchable is, in general, a pre-requisite of catching it—at least with any degree of reliability. On the other hand, if my path is incorrect, or if my speed is not quite right, then I will experience the ball as, for example, going to fall just out of reach, or behind me. It will, then, not appear catchable—or appear, as things stand, as uncatchable. To catch the ball, I have to get myself in position to catch the ball, and this means, fundamentally, acting in such a way that the ball will appear catchable. I do this by performing certain actions vis-à-vis the ball.

Catching the ball requires mastering the relevant sensorimotor contingencies. A sensorimotor contingency can be thought of as made up of two components: (1) a contingency and (2) a consequence. The contingency will involve some change in either the object perceived or the perceiver: the object moves relative to the perceiver, the perceiver moves relative to the object, and so on. The consequence will be a change in the appearance of the object perceived. In the event that I move in such-and-such a trajectory (the contingency) the ball will appear in such-and-such a way (as catchable or not, the consequence). In this case, and this is what differentiates it from the case of simply seeing a bottle, I am trying to catch the ball. Thus, in this case, I *desire* to enact, or bring about, certain contingencies in order that certain consequences (e.g., the ball appearing catchable) may ensue. The difference between trying to do something and merely seeing something is the *desire* to enact, or bring about, the contingencies. In seeing the bottle as a bottle, I simply anticipate—believe, broadly construed—that certain contingencies will result in certain consequences for the appearance that present themselves to me. But in trying to catch the ball, I *desire* to bring about certain contingencies precisely *because* these will result in certain consequences for the way the ball appears: as a result of my bringing about these contingencies, the ball appears progressively more and more catchable, and this, all things being equal, will impact on the likelihood of success in my goal of catching the ball. Nevertheless, in trying to catch the ball, I am aware of myself and my trying for the same reason that in seeing the bottle I am aware of myself and my act of seeing: I am implicated in these anticipations concerning the relations between contingencies and consequences.

So far, of course, this has done nothing to expunge the unwanted intellectualist strain of this account of pre-intentional self-awareness. That part comes now.

Suppose a dog is very good at catching a Frisbee. This would constitute evidence that the dog has mastered the relevant sensorimotor contingencies pertaining to the interception of the Frisbee. She knows the steps she needs to take in order to make the Frisbee catchable. [28] And part of the process of making the Frisbee catchable is taking steps that make the Frisbee appear catchable. This is, ultimately, why the dog is good at catching the Frisbee: the dog is good at putting herself in position to catch the Frisbee, which is equivalent to being good at making the Frisbee appear catchable to her. Let us call the state of mastering these sensorimotor contingencies state φ. State φ is, in effect, the de-intellectualized version of pre-intentional self-awareness. Being in state φ, by itself, does not entail that the dog is capable of the intentional self-awareness—that it is capable of thinking thoughts of the form, "If I were to φ, then such-and-such would happen," etc. Whether an individual can think these thoughts is crucially dependent on features of what we can call the *context*, C.

The most important feature of this context will, of course, be a metacognitive machinery that allows an individual to think thoughts about itself and its actions: if I were to move here, then . . . ; if the object were to move there, then . . . ; and so on. Without this apparatus, state φ will not yield the requisite thoughts. Nevertheless, the absence of the apparatus and resulting thoughts, does not entail that the individual is not pre-intentionally self-aware—in this de-intellectualized way. We can understand the de-intellectualized act of pre-intentional self-awareness in a way analogous to that in which we understood the idea of narrow content in Chapter 4: in this case, as a function from a context to an act (or acts) of intentional self-awareness. Take a state of (de-intellectualized) pre-intentional self-awareness, φ, plug it into the right context (i.e., one involving the requisite metacognitive machinery), and you end up with an act, or acts, of intentional self-awareness. If the context is different, however—lacking in the metacognitive machinery—you end up with no such thing. Nevertheless, in these latter circumstances, the individual is pre-intentionally aware of itself in virtue of being in a state such that *if* this state were plugged into an appropriate metacognitive apparatus, it would yield an act of intentional self-awareness. That is, an individual X is pre-intentionally aware if:

> X is in state φ, such that *if* X were to instantiate (metacognitive) context C, *then*, as a result of being in φ, X would also be the subject, in dispositional form, of at least one mental act of intentional self-awareness.

---

[28] Dogs, the evidence suggests, put themselves in position to catch Frisbees in precisely the same way a wide receiver puts himself in position to catch a football, or an outfielder to catch a baseball. See Shaffer et al. (2004).

We might call this a *subjunctive-dispositional* model of pre-intentional self-awareness. The possession of state φ, to be clear, is *neither* a subjunctive *nor* a dispositional matter. The subject, X, is actually in state φ. That is, X actually is pre-intentionally self-aware. However, what makes φ a state of pre-intentional self-awareness is a subjunctive matter. It is a matter of what φ would do when inserted into an appropriate context—that is, a context involving the requisite metacognitive apparatus or abilities. The acts of intentional self-awareness that φ, when inserted into an appropriate context, will yield are not acts in which the subject must actually engage. It is enough that X is disposed to engage in these acts. This is so even though X has the metacognitive apparatus that allows it to think such thoughts.

I have talked of pre-intentional and de-intellectualized pre-intentional self-awareness. But I do not mean to suggest that there are two things here—two different forms of pre-intentional self-awareness. There is only one thing: state φ. We can explain this in an intellectualist way: in terms of anticipations that have the subject and her mental acts as part of the content of anticipations. Or we can explain state φ in de-intellectualized terms: as the mastery of sensorimotor contingencies that allow it to interact with objects in successful ways. There is one state, a state that can be inserted into different contexts, and therefore described and explained in different ways.

## 6. THE SITUATED ANIMAL

I have argued that an animal, X, is in a state of pre-intentional self-awareness when it is in a certain state φ such that, if φ were inserted into an appropriate metacognitive context, this would yield dispositions for X to engage in acts of intentional self-awareness. For φ to qualify as a state of pre-intentional self-awareness, it is not required that φ actually be inserted into the appropriate metacognitive context. The status of φ as an act of pre-intentional self-awareness is a matter of what would happen in certain circumstances, whether or not those circumstances ever actually obtain. In other words, pre-intentional self-awareness is a function from a context to an act of intentional self-awareness.

In Chapter 4, I used essentially the same apparatus to explain the notion of narrow content that was crucial to the idea that our beliefs can *track* the beliefs of animals—and therefore can be used to explain the behavior of animals even though they cannot, actually, have those beliefs. Thus, the conclusion we should draw, it seems, is that pre-intentional self-awareness stands to intentional self-awareness as narrow content stands to content. Both pre-intentional self-awareness and narrow content are subjunctive-dispositional states.

It is no accident that this apparatus of functions should be useful here. It is an apparatus originally devised in and for situated semantics—the key element of which is, of course, situatedness. It applies so naturally to the case of animals precisely because the situatedness of animals is very different to our own situatedness. In attempts to understand animals and their capacities, some form of de-anchoring is always going to be required. And that is precisely the idea I have brought here to the understanding of pre-intentional self-awareness.

The account of pre-intentional self-awareness developed thus far is rather skeletal. I have been concerned with the rudiments of the idea, with the general framework for thinking about pre-intentional self-awareness. The task of the next chapter is to fill in the details—to put some meat on the bones of this subjunctive-dispositional skeleton.

# 8

## IN DIFFERENT TIMES AND PLACES

The preceding chapter provided an account of pre-intentional awareness based on sensorimotor anticipations. A way of de-intellectualizing these anticipations by way of the subjunctive-dispositional model was also defended. In this chapter, I shall assume that this account of how to de-intellectualize pre-intentional self-awareness is correct. With that in the bag—at least, that's how I see it—much of the discussion of this chapter will be conducted, largely for ease of exposition, in intellectualist terms. The guiding assumption is that these terms can always be de-intellectualized by way of the subjunctive-dispositional model as and when required.

To begin the process of putting some meat on the skeleton of this account of pre-intentional self-awareness, consider how the account might be extended from awareness of self—of the I that is implicated in sensorimotor anticipations—to awareness of mental *acts*. Extending this account of pre-intentional self-awareness to the act of *seeing* is relatively easy. The account of pre-intentional self-awareness outlined in the previous chapter appealed to what are sometimes known as *sensorimotor contingencies*. These contingencies pertain to various things that might happen to the bottle of Coke, or to me: if the bottle moves relative to me, or I move relative to the bottle, etc. However, as we have seen, sensorimotor contingencies effectively come in two distinct forms: *environmental* and *bodily*. The Coke bottle's moving relative to me is an environmental sensorimotor contingency—a contingency that pertains to an environmental object. But my moving relative to the bottle is a bodily contingency, a contingency that pertains, in the first instance, to me.

There are certain kinds of bodily sensorimotor contingency that underwrite pre-intentional awareness of the act of seeing. Most obviously, I anticipate that if I were to close my eyes, the bottle, and indeed my visual field, would disappear and be replaced with nothing. Conversely, I anticipate that if I were to block my ears, or hold my nose, my current visual field would, all things being equal, remain unchanged. The act of seeing is implicated in these sorts of bodily sensorimotor contingencies. In virtue of these sorts of contingencies, I am pre-intentionally aware of my act of seeing.[1]

## 2. PERCEPTION FOR ACTION: AFFORDANCES AND THE LIVED BODY

An important category of seeing-as is perception for action. *Perception for action* is perception of the world in terms of the various possibilities it *affords* for action— whether these possibilities are positive or negative, beneficial or harmful.[2] That is, one sees things in the world *as* offering or affording certain opportunities or dangers. Perception for action involves a specific set of anticipations concerning what the perceived object can do for or to you. Since all of these anticipations will involve you, pre-intentional self-awareness is built into perception for action.

In perception for action, one important form that pre-intentional self-awareness can take is awareness of one's body. Let us suppose I walk into a room, spot an empty chair, walk over to it, and sit down. In doing so I may have noticed very little about the chair: its color, shape, fabric, and construction may all have escaped my notice. What I did notice, however, was one salient fact: it is empty. And because it is empty it is what we might call *sit-able*. To put the matter in Gibsonian terms: unlike all the chairs that are occupied, this chair *affords* sitting. It is the affordance I see, and not the other properties of the chair. But seeing the world in this way involves pre-intentional awareness of my body. I see the chair as sit-able because of various anticipations I have concerning the opportunities this chair

---

[1] That is, in de-intellectualized mode, I am in a state, φ, such that should this state be inserted in the appropriate metacognitive context (which, in my case, it is) will yield intentional acts of self-awareness with content such as IF I CLOSE MY EYES, THE VISUAL SCENE WILL DISAPPEAR, etc.

[2] Obviously, I am borrowing this notion of affordances from James Gibson (1979). Sartre (1943/1957, p. 425) also talked in similar terms, describing the world I inhabit as a "vast skeletal outline of my possibilities." Sartre's inspiration is clearly Heidegger's (1927/1962) notion of being ready-to-hand.

offers vis-à-vis my goal of sitting. But that the chair offers these opportunities is dependent upon my having a body of a certain sort. If I were twelve feet tall, or twelve inches tall, or had four legs, then the chair would not afford sitting. Awareness of the body is, thus implicated in awareness of the sit-ability of the chair. To be aware of the affordances of an object is, at the same time, to be aware of my body, its dimensions, shape, limitations, and other characteristics.

I am aware of this body in a very different way than I am aware of the body I see when standing in front of a mirror—the body I recognize as mine when I pass the mirror test.[3] The body in the mirror is the *body as object*: something I am aware *of* when I look at it. It is an intentional object of my act of seeing. When I see the chair as sit-able, I am aware of my body in a quite different way. The body is not the object of my awareness—that object is a certain affordance of the chair. My body, here, is not something I am aware *of*, but something I am aware *with* or *in virtue of*: I am, in part, aware of the affordance—the sit-ability—of the chair in virtue of my body being a certain way, having certain properties rather than others. The chair has the affordance it does only because my body has certain characteristics, and my having a body of a certain sort is, therefore, implicated in the anticipations through which I see the chair as sit-able. Thus, in being aware of the affordance, I am also aware of my body. I am intentionally aware of the affordance and thereby, at the same time, pre-intentionally aware of my body. This awareness of my body is immune to error through misidentification. There is no question of whose body this is because there is no question, in this specific case, of for whom the chair affords sitting. The body as object is not immune to error through misidentification. But this *lived body* very much is.

The distinction between the *lived body* and the *body as object*—between *leib* and *körper*, as Husserl put it—is a common theme in the phenomenological tradition.[4] When I see my body in the mirror, the body I am aware of is the body as object. If I look at my hands, then the hands I am aware of are the hands as objects. If I am caught doing something embarrassing, and I imagine how I must look to other people, then the body I imagine is the body as object. My body can appear to me, in this way, as an object. But that is not the way I ordinarily experience it. As Sartre puts it:

---

[3] Sartre actually regarded the two bodies as having different kinds of being. The body I see in the mirror, the body as object, has being in-itself (*être en-soi*). The body that walks across the room and sits in an empty chair has being for-itself (*être pour-soi*). The latter body is the same thing as consciousness—a type of revealing activity. I think Sartre is right about this. But I do not need this stronger, ontic, claim about the type of being possessed by these two bodies and, therefore, shall not assume it here. Even rescinding from this claim, it is clear that the two kinds of awareness are very different. See Sartre (1943/1957), pp. 401–70, for discussion.

[4] Husserl (1912/1980).

My body as it is *for me* does not appear to me in the midst of the world. . . . It is true that I see and touch my legs and my hands. Moreover, nothing prevents me from imagining an arrangement of the sense organs such that a living being could see one of its eyes while the eye that was seen was directing its glance upon the world. But it is to be noted that in this case again I am the *Other* in relation to my eye . . . I cannot "see the seeing."[5]

Most of the time, I just get on with doing things. I walk into a room prior to a long meeting, and sit down in the empty chair. I neither think about nor see what I am doing. I just do it. Experiencing my body as an object is something that happens only in comparatively rare circumstances. Most of the time I live *through* my body, rather than experiencing it as an object.

Mirror self-recognition is a symptom only of the ability to recognize the body as object. The most common form of bodily self-awareness is not of this sort. One is aware of the lived body when one sees the world in ways that are correlated with, or dependent on, one's body. To see the chair as sit-able is, at the same time, to be pre-intentionally aware of the aspects of one's body that make it so. One is not aware of these aspects as objects of one's thoughts or perceptions—that would be the case only when the body is the body as object. Rather, one's awareness of one's bodily characteristics consists in one's being aware of other objects *as* being a certain way—a way that is tied to the nature of one's body. This is what it is to be pre-intentionally aware of the body as lived.

## 3. PRE-INTENTIONAL AWARENESS OF GOALS, INTENTIONS, AND DESIRES

When I see the chair as sit-able, I am pre-intentionally aware of more than my lived body: I am also pre-intentionally aware of my *goals, intentions,* or *desires*. Suppose my goal in going into the room is to attend a lengthy, and almost certainly less than scintillating, meeting. On the basis of this, I intend, or desire, to find somewhere comfortable, and ideally unobtrusive, where I can pass the time without being asked any awkward questions. Once again, I will overlook most of the features of any given chair, and instead see the features of the chair—being sit-able (because empty) and unobtrusive (because tucked away in the corner)— that are pertinent to my intention or desire. That these particular features should stand out for me is a result of my having this specific intention or desire.

---

[5] Sartre (1943/1957), p. 402.

We can put this idea in terms of the language of expectation. Possibilities are cheap: there is an indefinite number of possible things I might do with or to the chair. However, my intention or desire results in my generating a limited set of expectations—being able to sit comfortably and unobtrusively for a somewhat lengthy period—and these expectations are responsible for my seeing certain features of the chair rather than others. However, both I, and my intention or desire, are implicated in many of these expectations. This is a chair on which *I* will be able to *sit comfortably* and *remain unnoticed*. The goal, intention, or desire generates a specific set of expectations and, because of this, is implicated in these expectations. I am intentionally aware of the chair and its salient properties: they are objects of my perception and thought. But in being intentionally aware of these features of the chair rather than others, I am pre-intentionally aware of my goal, intention, or desire. My pre-intentional awareness of my goal, intention, or desire or goal *consists in* my seeing the world in terms of certain of its features rather than others.

## 4. FROM PERCEPTION TO MEMORY

The story so far: I have argued that pre-intentional self-awareness is built into the possession of conscious experiences. The reason is that such experiences present objects to subjects *as* being a certain way. When an object is presented as being a certain way this is because of a specific set of anticipations generated in the experiencer. And, crucially, in many of these anticipations the subject, her body, or her mental states, or some combination thereof, is implicated. The upshot is this: if an animal can have conscious experience at all—and the burden of Chapter 3 was to show that many of them do—then it is pre-intentionally aware of itself. If this is correct, pre-intentional self-awareness is neither rare nor a particularly sophisticated cognitive achievement. Intentional self-awareness *may* be like this, requiring metacognitive abilities and concepts of mental states, but its non-intentional counterpart is a pervasive feature of the animal kingdom.

In some ways, it is tempting to continue with this investigation on the foregoing sort of case-by-case basis. I have focused on perception. But the same general principles would apply to any type of mental act that presents objects *as* being a certain way. On one way of thinking about emotions, for example, they are intentional states akin, in many ways but not all, to perception. Thus conceived, emotions present objects in numerous ways: an accident scene is presented as horrific, the knife-wielding intruder is presented as terrifying, and so on. [6] This sort of

---

[6] See Solomon (1984, 2004) for a defense of this intentionalist conception of emotions. Other accounts

presentation is a function of anticipation, and so we should expect pre-intentional awareness of oneself and one's horror or terror to be involved in the having of emotions of this sort. The knife-wielding intruder is presented as terrifying because of my anticipations of what he might do next, of the damage the knife could do to my body, and so on. Implicated in these anticipations will be awareness of oneself and one's terror. In experiencing the intruder through these anticipations, I am pre-intentionally aware both of myself and of my terror.

In the rest of this chapter, however, I am not going to extend these ideas on a case-by-case basis but, rather, focus on a type of mental act that is particularly important in the overall project of establishing that animals are persons. The emphasis on self-awareness as a condition of personhood is inspired by Locke's idea that a person is the sort of thing that can "consider itself." But there is another aspect of Locke's claim with which we have not yet dealt. A person, according to Locke, is the sort of thing that can "consider itself the same thinking thing *in different times and places*." One might harbor a suspicion that the kind of pre-intentional awareness we have looked at so far is too temporally circumscribed to underwrite the "in different times and places" condition. If I see a bottle of Coke *as* a bottle of Coke, I may thereby be pre-intentionally aware of myself. But this pre-intentional self-awareness need, it seems, extend through time only as long as it would take the relevant anticipations to be satisfied or stymied. Thus, while there is some temporal duration built into these anticipations, one may doubt that this will be enough to underwrite any robust notion of self-awareness through time. The question is whether pre-intentional self-awareness can be temporally extended in this way. I'm sure it will come as no surprise to find out that I am going to argue that it can: adding a suitable temporal dimension to pre-intentional self-awareness is the primary task of the remainder of this chapter.

In developing this temporal dimension of pre-intentional self-awareness, my focus switches from perception to *memory*. In particular, I am going to argue for the existence of a certain kind of pre-intentional self-awareness that is embodied in memory experience.[7] This kind of pre-intentional self-awareness is, I shall

---

of emotion are non-intentionalist, most notably the James-Lange theory which understands emotions as awareness of bodily disturbances. See Prinz (2004) for a defense of this sort of view. In my view, the James-Lange conception of emotions is untenable. But if I'm wrong I would have to revise my idea that emotions, like perception, present objects *as* being a certain way and so involve pre-intentional self-awareness. Happily, I'm never wrong. But even if I were in this case, that would not matter for the overall project of this book: pre-intentional self-awareness can be established simply on the basis of conscious perceptual experience.

[7] Stan Klein (2013), a man who has seemingly made a career of working things out before I do, seems to hold something like this view also. Fortuitously, for me, it is not clear that we share the same conception of pre-intentional self-awareness, and his arguments are certainly somewhat different than mine.

argue, extended through time and so is the sort self-awareness that can underwrite Locke's "in different times and places" condition.

## 5. EPISODIC MEMORY AND EXPERIENCING *AS*

In humans, it is *episodic* memory that is largely responsible for grounding diachronic awareness of the self through time.[8] Endel Tulving introduced the idea
of episodic memory by way of a distinction between this and what he called *semantic* memory.[9] Semantic memory is memory of facts. I remember that Paris is
the capital of France. Some of these facts might be about me: I remember that
I have climbed the Eiffel Tower. This sort of memory is a semantic *autobiographical*
memory. On the other hand, I also remember looking out over Paris from high up
on the tower. I also remember the excitement on the faces of my children as we
reached each new floor on our climb, and prepared to take another look out over
the city. These are two examples of episodic memories.

While both qualify as episodic memories, however, we should not overlook quite
significant differences between the two. In the first memory—of looking out over
Paris—I am the intentional object of that memory: it is I that I remember, looking
out over the city of Paris. But in the second memory, the intentional objects of
my memory are my children—specifically the excitement on their faces—rather
than myself.[10] We might be tempted, following the corresponding distinction in
semantic memory, to say that the former memory is, whereas the latter is not,
an episodic autobiographical memory. However, this would overlook something
rather important. There is a clear sense in which I am "in" my episodic memories
even when they are not about me. That is, there is a clear sense in which *all* episodic
memories are autobiographical. Even when the episodic memory is not about me
specifically, an episode is presented precisely *as* one that *I* formerly encountered
(witnessed, orchestrated, etc.). When I episodically remember the excitement on
my children's faces, this excitement is presented, precisely, *as* something *I* formerly witnessed.

---

[8] I say "largely" because semantic autobiographical memory can also play some role in grounding this
awareness. This complication does not affect my argument. In fact, given that the existence of semantic
memory in animals is easier to establish, this would, if anything, help my argument. As usual, however,
I want to make things as difficult for myself as I possibly can.

[9] Tulving (1983).

[10] I could, of course, remember *my* looking at the excitement on my children's faces—it is *I* that I remember looking at the excitement on my children's faces. That, however, would be a different memory
than the one I am considering here, which should be taken to be a memory of the excitement on my
children's faces rather than a memory of me remembering the excitement on my children's faces.

Episodic memory is not simply the memory of an episode: semantic memories can be memories of episodes. When I remember that Vesuvius erupted in 79 A.D., I am, it seems, remembering an episode—the instantiation of a property (of erupting), by an object (Vesuvius), at a time (79 A.D.). Rather, episodic memory requires that an episode be remembered in a quite specific way—*as* an episode I formerly encountered. More generally, in any episodic memory there is (1) an act of remembering, (2) an episode remembered, and (3) the way in which this episode is presented—the *mode of presentation* of the episode. Episodic memory is defined by a quite specific mode of presentation—the episode must be presented, precisely, *as* one that the subject formerly encountered (witnessed, orchestrated, etc.). Thus, in the memory of the faces of my children, even if I am not part of the episode remembered—this episode consists in the excitement on my children's faces—I am still implicated in the memory because I am part of the mode of presentation of this episode: the excitement is presented as something that *I* formerly witnessed.[11]

Therefore, we should expect pre-intentional self-awareness to be built in to episodic memory experiences. This is because such memory involves a defining experiential mode of presentation: an episode is experienced *as* one I have encountered before. Thus, if animals can episodically remember, this will guarantee them a form of pre-intentional self-awareness that is extended through time. Unfortunately, and more than a little ironically, it is this idea that memory involves a defining experiential mode of presentation of an episode that provides the biggest hurdle—or what is generally taken to be the biggest hurdle—to supposing that animals can remember episodically. While animals may be capable of *episodic-like* memory, it has been argued, it is impossible to establish that they are capable of episodic memory.[12]

## 6. EPISODIC-LIKE MEMORY IN ANIMALS

The history of human thought has been littered with attempts to identify a feature that decisively—qualitatively rather than quantitatively—distinguishes humans

---

[11] Moreover, this mode of presentation must have an *experiential* character. I might remember that I once saw Led Zeppelin at Knebworth in '77 without having any experiential recollection of doing so. This would qualify as a semantic autobiographical memory but not an episodic one. Episodic memory requires that I experience an episode as one I have encountered before, and not merely think that the episode is one I have encountered before. See Rowlands (2016), Chapter 2, for a proper defense of this way of understanding episodic memory.

[12] Klein (2015) is skeptical of the idea that animals can remember episodically for precisely this reason. In an extremely rare disagreement with him, I am going to argue against this skepticism.

from other animals. Rationality, language, intelligence, tool use, toolmaking, culture, play, and a variety of other characteristics have, at one or more times, and by one or more persons, been advanced as the feature that differentiates us from, and elevates us above, the rest of the animal kingdom. History has not been kind to these proposed features.[13]

In the eyes of some, episodic memory is the latest off the production line of—demarcating, elevating—characteristics that set humans apart from other animals. This has everything to do with the idea that episodic memory involves a defining experiential mode of presentation of an episode—a way of presenting an episode of which some think, for varying reasons, animals are incapable. The only evidence we have for episodic memory in animals cannot establish that they present remembered episodes in this defining experiential way—or so one may think. Instead, this evidence can establish only that animals possess what we might think of as the *objective correlate* of such memory: the *what, where,* and *when* (and, occasionally, *who*) of an episode. *What* was the episode? *Where* did it occur? *When* did it occur? This objective correlate of episodic memory can be studied in animals, but given that such studies do not capture the subjective, presentational, component of episodic memory, the memory tested for by the what, where, and when paradigm is usually called *episodic-like* rather than episodic memory.

There is a large and growing body of evidence for episodic-like memory in a variety of animals. In a seminal study, Clayton and Dickinson investigated whether scrub jays are capable of episodic-like memory using a food caching and recovery paradigm.[14] Specifically they tested the ability of the birds to remember what, where, and when they have cached a particular food. The food in question was either a wax worm or a peanut. Jays prefer wax worms and, in normal circumstances, would preferentially recover them over peanuts. However, these worms perish relatively quickly. In the study, jays were allowed to cache both wax worms and peanuts, and recover these items after specific intervals of 4 and 124 hours. For one group of jays, the wax worms became inedible after 124 hours but not 4 hours, whereas for a second group of jays wax worms were edible after both the short and long retention intervals. For both groups, peanuts remained edible

---

[13] If we were less anxious and determined about this, our endeavor might, ironically, have provided us with a significant clue. If there is one feature that decisively demarcates humans from other animals, it is, surely, this: humans are those animals who are always looking for one feature that decisively distinguishes them from the rest of the animal kingdom. You will not find *that* characteristic in any other animal! To cut a long story short, humans are like some ghastly middle-class species: never comfortable in their skins like all the other proletarian species out there, always anxious about their status, and, therefore, always on the lookout for ways to elevate themselves above the bestial *hoi polloi.* Below the angels but above the animals: the Great Chain of Being indeed.

[14] Clayton and Dickinson (1998).

after both intervals. The group of jays given the perishable worms rapidly adopted the strategy of visiting worm locations before peanut locations after 4 hours but visiting peanut locations before worm locations after 124 hours. The other group, with the non-perishable worms, recovered worms independently of the duration of the retention interval.

In follow-up studies, Clayton and colleagues demonstrated that scrub jays have detailed representations of what, where, and when the food was cached.[15] Similar studies have been replicated with other species, including rodents,[16] birds,[17] and non-human primates.[18] Collectively, these sorts of studies provide good evidence for the existence of episodic-like memory in several species of nonhumans. However, as we have seen, evidence of episodic-like memory is not, by itself, evidence of episodic memory. These studies all test for the objective correlate of episodic memory: what, where, and when. More is required to show that these animals are capable of episodic memory. We also need the subjective component: the episode recalled needs to be subsumed under a specific mode of presentation—it needs to be presented, experientially, *as* an episode that the animal formerly witnessed, encountered, or orchestrated Nothing in these tests establishes that the animals do this. Indeed, it is difficult to imagine how to test for this.

These deficits are serious enough to even call into question the label *episodic-like*. As Suddendorf and Busby have pointed out, the memory tested for in these sorts of study might more aptly be called *www-memory*—what–where–when memory—than episodic-like memory.[19] It is not clear why we should think of the sort of memory tested for in these studies as even episodic-like let alone episodic: it is possible, for example, that a scrub jay might remember what food it cached and when and where it cached it simply by using semantic memory (as when I remember, semantically, the order of my children's birthdays).

One type of response to these shortcomings is to try and bolster the objective correlate in such a way that it becomes more and more likely that episodic-like memory is, in fact, occurring. The general strategy is to show that the observable what–where–when behavior has certain additional features that make it very likely that episodic-like memory is occurring. For example, Clayton et al. emphasize the

[15] Clayton and Dickinson (1999a, 1999b, 1999c), Clayton, Yu, and Dickinson A (2001), deKort, Dickinson, and Clayton (2005).

[16] Ergorul and Eichenbaum (2004), Babb and Crystal (2005, 2006), Ferkin et al. (2008), Roberts et al. (2008), Zhou and Crystal (2009).

[17] Zinkivarsky, Nazir, and Smulders (2009); Henderson et al. (2006) indicated that hummingbirds could identify when and where but not what.

[18] Martín-Ordás et al. (2010).

[19] Suddendorf and Busby (2003).

flexibility and structure of the behavior.[20] *Flexibility*, here, denotes the ability to use the encoded information in a variable, context-sensitive, manner. The behavior has *structure*, on the other hand, to the extent that the remembered "what," "when," and "where" are bound together in such a way that retrieving of one of these components will significantly increase the likelihood of the retrieval of the remaining components. Both flexibility and structure are empirically tractable. Fortin et al. have identified flexibility in the www-memory behavior of rats.[21] Clayton et al. have identified structure in the www-behavior of scrub jays.[22]

Another version of this same type of approach begins with the idea that evidence for episodic-like memory using what–where–when behavior is based on food-reward behavior. This typically requires extensive training up of the animal subjects, and this is more likely to lead to the animals encoding the episode information semantically rather than episodically. Given that this is so, a useful antidote would be to employ a spontaneous unique trial paradigm. Kart-Teke et al.[23] and Dere et al.[24] have employed this strategy in studies of rodents.

Assessment of these kinds of approach is well beyond the scope of this book. However, even if such approaches increase the likelihood that an animal is displaying episodic-like recall—and they are, indeed, promising in this regard—they will not, presumably, be able to take that extra step and show that the animal is engaging in episodic memory, in the sense of having experiences with the defining experiential mode of presentation identified in Section 5. It may be that the sorts of approach that seek to augment the objective correlate of episodic memory ultimately have to remain silent on this issue. Whether or not this is true, the strategy I shall pursue is quite different. Instead of focusing on the objective correlate of episodic memory, I am going to take a closer look at the subjective correlate: the idea of an episode being presented *as* one the subject has formerly encountered.

## 7. BATH TIME FOR HUGO

Hugo was a dog who actually liked his baths. He had quite a lot of them: being somewhat allergic to the ubiquitous south Florida pollens, he had a tendency to get skin infections, especially during the high pollen seasons of April–May and

---

[20] Clayton, Yu, and Dickinson (2001).
[21] Fortin, Wright, and Eichenbaum (2004).
[22] Clayton, Yu, and Dickinson (2001).
[23] Kart-Teke et al (2006).
[24] Dere, Huston, and De Souza Silva (2005).

September–October. To prevent these, it was necessary to give him a bath with a medicated shampoo. In April–May, in particular, these were an almost daily occurrence. Happily, he loved these. The "baths" in question involved me hosing him down with a garden hose, rubbing in the shampoo, waiting for twenty minutes, and then hosing him down again. Whenever I would say to him, "Do you want a bath?" he would bounce up and down excitedly, and when I opened the back door would run over to the hose. He clearly knew what was going to happen next. And if he knew this, it seems he must have remembered previous bath time episodes. These are, of course, unscientific observations—and are not offered in any spirit of scientific rigor, I assure you. Hugo was a real dog, but here he features *only* as a thought experiment: a useful way of organizing our thinking about the subjective, presentational, aspect of episodic memory.

Suppose we accept that Hugo does, in some sense, remember his previous baths. This assumption is harmless: it does not commit us to the claim that he can remember episodically—for it may be that his memory of these previous bath times is semantic. To episodically remember, Hugo would have to have a memory experience of a specific sort: an experience with a specific mode of presentation of the form, roughly: I HAVE SEEN THIS BEFORE—or some variation on this theme.[25] Given this is so, it seems there are three sources of possible skepticism vis-à-vis the idea that Hugo can present an episode in this way.

(1) *General skepticism about experience/phenomenology.* Hugo's presentation of the episode in this way must have an experiential phenomenology. And there is no reason for thinking that Hugo can have experiences of this sort.

(2) *Skepticism concerning possession of temporal concepts.* There is no reason to suppose that Hugo possesses the *temporal* concepts, specifically a concept of the past, necessary to present an episode as one that I HAVE SEEN **BEFORE**.

(3) *Skepticism about metacognition.* There is no reason to suppose that Hugo has the metacognitive abilities required to think thoughts either about himself or his mental states necessary for presenting an episode as one that **I** HAVE **SEEN** BEFORE.

---

[25] I HAVE ENCOUNTERED THIS BEFORE, I HAVE DONE THIS BEFORE, etc. Variations that exclude, or apparently exclude, the "I" do not seem to be adequate. THIS HAS HAPPENED BEFORE, for example, does not explain Hugo's behavior. His excitement would not be the same if he remembered another dog getting a bath—an event from which he was always excluded. His excitement seems to be based on the fact that this episode that happened before happened to *him*.

Let us consider each of these sources of skepticism in turn.

### General Skepticism About Experience/Phenomenology

Skepticism about whether Hugo could have subjective experience in general is part of a more general skepticism about other minds. We have already dealt with this in Chapters 2 and 3, and I shall, therefore, be brief. Hugo's seemingly excited reaction to his upcoming bath is not atypical. Animals often exhibit strong behavioral reactions to remembered episodes. For example, a common way of testing memory—and deficits of memory—in rodents involves conditioning them to associate two random stimuli: for example, they are conditioned to associate a loud noise with an electric shock. This provides the basis for further memory testing: for example, once the rats have formed this association, you can, for example, inject them with a protein-synthesis inhibitor, and gauge whether the association remains intact.[26] The salient point is that the evidence for the retention or loss of the association is entirely behavioral. The rats exhibit fear behavior on hearing the loud noise—freezing in place, shaking, etc. If we take this behavior at face value, it is indicative of an underlying phenomenology: the feeling of fear. One might reject this via appeal to the problem of other animal minds—relying on the idea that no behavior is sufficient to justify the attribution of experience to animals. But we examined the problem of other animal minds in Chapter 2—and found it lacking. If we accept that animals are phenomenally conscious—and the burden of Chapter 3 was to show that we should accept this—then there is little doubt that experiential phenomenology regularly accompanies their memories. This is true whether those memories are episodic or semantic. If there is a problem with the idea that animals lack episodic memory, it is unlikely that this problem lies in their lack of experiential phenomenology in general.

### Skepticism About Temporal Concepts

In the second worry, the focus changes from an alleged deficit of consciousness to an assumed conceptual deficit—a deficit of cognition. In this sort of objection, it is not his lacking in phenomenology that denies Hugo episodic memory, but his lacking in phenomenology with a quite specific content—a sort that can only be had if he possesses concepts that he does not, in fact, possess. In this second objection, the phenomenology-shaping concepts are temporal ones: Hugo lacks the concept of BEFORE.

---

[26] See, for example, Nader (2003).

This skeptical objection is, however, difficult to sustain. The concept of BEFORE seems to be required for the possession of what–when–where (www) memory—even if such memory is purely semantic. Recall the dialectical situation: it is difficult to dispute the idea that many animals can possess www-memory of a purely semantic sort. As we saw in Section 6, the evidence for the possession of this sort of memory by a number of animals is substantial. The question is not whether animals possess this sort of memory but whether they possess episodic memory, for this requires not just www-memory but the kind of experience required for an episode to be presented *as* one that the subject formerly witnessed or encountered. However, as soon as we accept that animals have www-memory—in particular, the *when* component of www-memory—we are compelled to accept they have the ability to distinguish past from present. This is true even if the www-memory is merely semantic. The point of the Clayton and Dickinson scrub jay studies, for example, is that how long a wax worm has been cached is crucial to its edibility. The scrub jay must be able to gauge how long—before the present time—the worm has been cached. But to estimate the time that has elapsed between caching and the present the jay must have an idea of *before* now—and hence a concept of BEFORE. Note that the behavior of the jays cannot be explained simply in terms of the degradation of a representation over time: that a representation of caching a particular food at a particular place becomes less effective over time. Recall, there were two groups of jays, one for whom the worms became inedible after 124 hours, one for whom they did not. Simple degradation of a representation of what and where should yield identical behaviors. But the behavior of the two groups was different. The concept of BEFORE is required for even www-memory. Thus, if animals lack episodic memory, it is unlikely to be because they lack the concept of BEFORE.

*Skepticism About Metacognition*

The final worry about Hugo's ability to entertain the content I HAVE SEEN THIS BEFORE focuses on his presumed metacognitive deficits. Hugo can only entertain this content if he is able to represent himself (I) and his mental states (SEEN). But if that is the worry, then the preceding arguments of this chapter and the last give us the raw materials to handle it. The precise details of this handling are the focus of the rest of this chapter, but the basic outlines of my proposed solution will, I'm sure, easily be anticipated: even if Hugo lacks metacognitive abilities—and so is able to make neither himself nor his mental states into objects of intentional awareness—he can still be pre-intentionally aware of himself and his mental states. In particular, I shall argue, there is a type of pre-intentional self-awareness that is peculiar to episodic memory, and this provides animals such as Hugo with a form of self-awareness through time.

## 8.  AUTONOESIS AND THE FEELING OF PAST-NESS

When Tulving initially introduced the idea of episodic memory, he characterized it in terms of what he called "feeling tones"—the feeling that the episode one recalls is an episode one has experienced in the past. This idea later evolved into what he called "autonoesis."[27] And the concept of autonoesis has gone on evolving, to the extent that its use in the literature is now far from univocal. Sometimes it seems there are almost as many definitions of autonoesis as there are people who discuss it in the literature. I have captured the idea of autonoesis in terms of the idea of a mode of presentation of an episode: an episode is presented *as* one formerly encountered by the individual who remembers.[28]

In Tulving's hands, the idea of autonoesis is presented as a more mature and articulated version of his original idea of a feeling of past-ness. I, on the other hand, suspect there is a useful distinction lurking in this general vicinity. This distinction is important for my purposes, and so I need to capture it in some way or other, and Tulving's alternate locutions seem useful in this regard even if it is not what he had in mind. Thus, by *autonoesis* I propose to understand the fully fledged representation of an episode *as* one the subject has encountered (seen, witnessed, orchestrated, etc.) before. Autonoesis, therefore, involves intentional awareness of oneself and one's mental states: in autonoesis, I understand that this is an episode that *I* have *seen*, or otherwise *experienced*, before. Thus, to be capable of autonoesis, I shall assume, one must have the sorts of metacognitive abilities that allow one to subsume an episode under the appropriate mode of presentation. A feeling of past-ness, on the other hand, is quite different—at least in the way I shall put this idea to work. Colloquially, a feeling of past-ness can come in a variety of forms, some more sophisticated than others. But what I have in mind is a very basic version of this feeling that amounts to what we might call a *sense of familiarity*.

Familiarity is typically thought of as the poor cousin of memory—a simpler ability that neither entails nor requires episodic memory. Familiarity is a function

---

[27] Tulving (2002).

[28] See Rowlands (2016) for a defense of this way of thinking about autonoesis (although, there, to avoid the multiple ambiguities in the concept I did not talk of autonoesis but, instead, of what I called the "presence of self in memory").

of the strength of a perceptual match to a prior exposure: that is, to the extent one's current experience maps on to, or resembles, a stored representation. Something—a person, place, or event—can seem familiar without one having any idea when or where one encountered it, and certainly without mentally traveling back in time to this original encounter. Familiarity is, thus, distinct from both episodic and www-memory. Nevertheless, I am going to argue that, while clearly distinct, there is a deeper connection between familiarity and episodic memory than is generally recognized. A sense of familiarity, I shall argue, is the pre-intentional form that episodic memory can take.

## 9. A FEELING OF HOME

There is a passage in *The Wind in the Willows* that nicely captures a strange experience undergone by Mole. This experience is, perhaps, a memory of home. But if it is, it is a memory of a distinctly non-standard sort:

> We others who have long lost the more subtle of the physical senses have not even the proper terms to express an animal's intercommunication with his surroundings, living or otherwise, and have only the word "smell" for instance, to include the whole range of delicate thrills which murmur in the nose of the animal night and day, summoning, warning, inciting, repelling. It was one of those mysterious fairy calls from out of the void that suddenly reached Mole in the darkness, making him tingle through and through with its very familiar appeal, while as yet he could not clearly remember what it was. He stopped dead in his tracks, his nose searching hither and thither in its efforts to recover the fine filament, the telegraphic current that had so strongly moved him. A moment and he had caught it again; and with it this time came recollection in its fullest flood. Home! That is what they meant, those caressing appeals, those soft touches wafted through the air, those invisible little hands pulling and tugging, all one way.[29]

The relevance of this passage lies not in who or what has the experience but, rather, in the experience itself. The experience may be a form of memory, or it may not. But, at the very least it is something on the cusp of memory—it straddles the borderlands of memory—which at the end of the passage transforms into a

---

[29] Grahame (1908), p. 67. And, yes, I am aware that Mole is a fictional animal.

memory of a reasonably standard sort.[30] This is the most inchoate form that a sense of familiarity may take. One feels that there is something about this place— and these feelings may take many different forms—but one does not quite know what. These feelings Mole has do not generate in him anticipations about how appearances would change if certain circumstances were to transpire. Prior to his realization, therefore, his environment is not presented to him *as* his former home.

Consider, now, a situation that I think can plausibly be regarded as one step closer to standard episodic memory. It is another experience of home—specifically of returning to one's childhood home—this time supplied by Gaston Bachelard:

> But over and beyond our memories, the house we were born in is physically inscribed in us. It is a group of organic habits. After twenty years, in spite of all of the other anonymous stairways, we would recapture the reflexes of the "first stairway"; we would not stumble on that rather high step. The house's entire being would open up, faithful to our own being. We would push the door that creaks with the same gesture, we would find our way in the dark to the distant attic. The feel of the tiniest latch has remained in our hands.[31]

One may choose to regard this as an example of embodied memory, or one may not. It is clearly not a case of episodic memory in the usual sense. However, there are differences between this case and the experience had by Mole that make Bachelard's description closer to episodic memory. In this case, certain anticipations about how appearances will change in given circumstances are, in-deed, generated. However, these anticipations *only emerge in the bringing about of those circumstances*. I anticipate that the stair will creak, or that the door will squeak, only as I am about to step on the stair or open the door. Thus, I find my-self opening the squeaky door in the very particular way I did whilst sneaking out of the house as a youth—a way that mitigates its squeaking. And, I do this even though I retain no memory, in the standard sense, of the door's squeaking: my memory emerges only in and through my current manipulation of the door. The sense of familiarity, here, consists in knowing what to do in a situation—how to open the squeaky door, which step to avoid on the stairs, and so on—where this knowing what to do only emerges in the doing.

Contrast this with much more standard memories of one's childhood home. I can, sitting here at my desk in Miami, remember the layout of my childhood

---

[30] See Rowlands (2016), Chapter 3, for an extended discussion of this, what I call, *affective Rilkean memory*.
[31] Bachelard (1958/2014), p. 27. I discuss this case of what I call *embodied Rilkean memory* in Rowlands (2016), Chapter 3.

home in Wales. My memory of this layout consists, in part, in knowing where any turn would take me: after entering through the front door, if I take the first door on the left, I would enter the sitting room, with its piano and furniture I wasn't allowed to sit on. Taking the second, I would enter the living room, with its TV in the corner. If I continue through the door in front of me, I would enter the kitchen, and so on. The layout of the house in which I grew up is the content of my memory, and I know this content to the extent I know which actions would yield which consequences. These anticipations about which actions yield which consequences do not, as in Bachelard's case, occur only in the course of acting. Given that my childhood home is four thousand miles away and, indeed, may not even exist today, I think we have to conclude that my current anticipations are 100 percent offline. But my memory of the layout of the house consists in these kinds of anticipations of the results of my possible actions.

This is not intended as a reductive account of remembering. I am not claiming that to remember is *nothing more* than to have expectations or anticipations about how appearances will change in given circumstances. Rather, my point is simply to draw attention to just how much anticipation is bound up with the content of certain memories. The house of my childhood is presented in memory as having a certain layout precisely because, and to the extent that, I can anticipate the sensorimotor consequences of possible actions on a house that may no longer even exist. This more modest claim—that the presentation of some contents in memory is bound up with sensorimotor anticipations—is all I require for my purposes.

## 10. THE PRE-INTENTIONAL AWARENESS OF SELF THROUGH TIME

If the general apparatus of sensorimotor anticipations is applicable to the content of memory—if to remember at least some content is to have anticipations about how remembered appearances will change in given circumstances—then we can tell the same kind of story about pre-intentional self-awareness in memory as we did for the case of perception. Thus, Hugo's memory of bath time, it can be argued, is close to a standard episodic memory—even if we assume he lacks the cognitive apparatus required to think thoughts about himself and his mental states. Hugo remembers his previous bath times in the sense that these previous episodes, and his experiences of them, have generated in him, now, various anticipations. On hearing the utterance, "Do you want a bath?" Hugo runs to the back door because he anticipates what is going to happen next. He snaps at the water shooting out of the hose because he anticipates it will be pleasurable. He darts this way and that because he anticipates I will follow him with the water spout, something that will also be fun. While his medicated shampoo is soaking in, he stares wistfully at the pool but avoids going in the pool because he anticipates I will shout at him to stop if he tries. This is what it is to remember an episode, or a series of episodes, pre-intentionally. Hugo remembers the bath time episodes pre-intentionally because these previous episodes have generated in him certain anticipations over the likely unfolding of events given various circumstances. And he, as the other cases make clear, is implicated in many of those anticipations. Familiarity with a situation, scene, or episode is a matter of having certain appropriate anticipations concerning what will, or what would, happen in various circumstances. Since the person who anticipates will be implicated in many of those anticipations, we can regard familiarity as the pre-intentional awareness of the self through time.[32]

---

[32] I've developed this idea using the intellectualized version of pre-intentional self-awareness. The assumption—as I mentioned at the beginning of the chapter—is that the anticipations can be expunged in the same way as with perception: in terms of the idea that pre-intentional self-awareness, in its most basic form, is a function from a context to these sorts of intentional anticipations.

# 9

## SELF-AWARENESS AND PERSONS

1. THE STORY SO FAR

In the three preceding chapters, I argued for the existence of a form of self-awareness that, while a staple of the post-Kantian tradition in philosophy, will be unfamiliar to some. This form of self-awareness has been overlooked in contemporary discussions of self-awareness in animals. In such discussions, the guiding assumption—often implicit, but usually there—has been that self-awareness must take what I have called an *intentional* form. On such a view, I am self-aware to the extent that I, or some bodily or psychological aspect of me, is an intentional object of a mental act of mine. In the most common version of this idea, I am self-aware when I think thoughts about myself, or about my bodily or psychological features. Debates about mirror self-recognition and metacognition in animals are debates framed in, and guided by, the light of the assumption that self-awareness must take this sort of intentional form.

There is, I have argued, another form of self-awareness: pre-intentional self-awareness. When I am pre-intentionally self-aware, I am aware of myself but without making myself into an object of any intentional act of mine. Intentional self-awareness is hardly uncommon, but is nowhere near as widespread and pervasive as its pre-intentional counterpart. Pre-intentional awareness of self is implicated in the possession of any conscious experience. Whenever I experience something *as* something—whenever I subsume an object under an experiential mode of presentation—I am pre-intentionally aware of myself because I am implicated in the anticipations that allow me to thus subsume the object. Reflections on episodic memory allowed us to extend the temporal parameters of this pre-intentional self-awareness.

If we accept that there are these two, importantly different, forms of self-awareness, then, given the overarching concern of this book, an obvious question arises: which of these forms of self-awareness is relevant, or most relevant, to the question of personhood? Following Locke, I have identified self-awareness as a condition of personhood: an individual can be a person only if it is self-aware. But, which form of self-awareness are we dealing with here? Which form of self-awareness is most plausibly thought of as a condition of personhood? That is the subject of this chapter. The stakes are obvious. The sort of skepticism that attends the claim that animals are intentionally self-aware is far more difficult to maintain with respect to pre-intentional self-awareness. If pre-intentional self-awareness is a condition of personhood, and the intentional alternative is not, then many animals would satisfy this condition of personhood.

## 2. THE UNITY OF A MENTAL LIFE

With a certain inevitability, it is time for us to revisit Locke's definition of a person: "a thinking intelligent being, that has reason and reflection, and can consider itself the same thinking thing, in different times and places, which it does only by that consciousness which is inseparable from thinking and seems to me to be essential, to it; it being impossible to perceive without perceiving that he does perceive." In this passage, Locke emphasizes the ability of a person to, "consider itself the same thinking thing, in different times and places." This ability he then connects with a kind of self-awareness—the "consciousness which is inseparable from thinking." Thus, there are two distinct strands to this idea. One is the idea of unity: "the same thinking thing, in different times and places." The other is the ability of a person to "consider" itself as such. There has been a strong historical tendency to regard these two strands as intimately connected. But let us first consider each in turn.

Consider, first, the idea that a person is a unity—a unified mental life. Suppose there were a sequence of disjointed, disassociated mental states and processes, none of which has any connection to the others. One state or process occurs, quickly followed by another, but there is no connection—neither causal nor logical—between them. In this disjointed mental life—although it is doubtful we can really characterize it as a life—there really is just one damned thing after another. This disjointed sequence would, it seems, not be a person. For a person to exist these mental states and processes must, at the very least, form a reasonably coherent whole. There must be at least some salient connections between the states and processes, connections that make intelligible why one state or process follows another, and is, in turn, followed by another—where this sequence, overall, makes at least some sort of sense. Let us refer to a sequence of mental acts, states, processes, and the like as a *mental life*. The intuition, then, is that a person is a *unified mental life*—the *same* thinking thing in different times and places.

Various lines of argument may be used to support this intuition. One promising line of argument, for example, appeals to the idea that there is no principled criterion of identity for a mere sequence of disjointed mental acts, states, and processes. That is, in such a sequence, there is no principled answer to the question of whether two distinct time slices of the sequence belong together: of whether they are parts of one mental life or two different mental lives. Look at the sequence at time *t*, and again at a later time, *t\**, and then ask yourself whether these are parts of the same mental life or belong to two different lives. There does not seem to be any principled way of answering this question. But when we are dealing with a person, things cannot be this way. For a person to exist there must not only exist a mental life at time *t*, and a mental life at time *t\**, but the mental life that exists at *t* must be (part of) the same mental life that exists at *t\**—as two different segments of a river are parts of the same river. This is true even though there can be substantial qualitative changes in the stream that have occurred between *t* and *t\**. The thoughts or experiences occurring at *t* might be quite different from those occurring at *t\**, for example. This idea of *unity in diversity*—of something that persists through changes in the mental acts, states, and processes, something that binds all these act, states, and processes together—is a core component of the idea of a person. This does not mean that there must be something that lies behind the acts, states, and processes—a substratum to which these things attach. One can think of unity in this way, but one need not do so. It may be, as we shall soon see, that the unity in question can be explained in other ways. But whatever way we decide to think of the basis of this unity, a core component of the idea of a person is that a person is something that *persists* through time. A disjointed series of acts and processes does not persist through time, or does not in the same way. We might put the point this way: in a person, there is unity underlying the diversity of mental acts, states, and processes. In a disjointed sequence of mental acts, states, and processes there is only diversity.

The same is true if we switch our focus to the situation *at* a time rather than *through* time. You and I, let us suppose, are in the same room, conversing with

one another. Given our conversation, it is likely that there is some overlap between the mental acts, states, and processes I possess and the ones that belong
to you. Nevertheless, the mental life that I am must be distinct from the mental
life that makes you up. But it is not possible to make sense of the distinctness of
mental lives unless we can also make sense of the unified status of these lives.
The distinctness of two mental lives presupposes the unity of each of those lives.
If disjointed sequences of mental acts, states, and processes were—somehow—
inserted into the room, there would be no principled answer to the question of
how many sequences there were.

At the conceptual heart of the person, therefore, is the idea of unity through
diversity—the idea of a unified mental life. Locke's definition also hints at the
basis of this unity: *self-awareness*, the awareness of this mental life. This is a theme
that one finds strongly echoed in Kant. In a famous passage from the *Anthropology*,
Kant writes:

> The fact that man can have the idea "I" raises him infinitely above all the
> other beings living on earth. By this he is a person; and by virtue of the unity
> of his consciousness, through all the changes he may undergo, he is one and
> the same person—that is, a being altogether different in rank and dignity
> from things, such as irrational animals, which we can dispose of as we please.[1]

This passage is curious because, in it, Kant seems to claim that being a person—
and so having a unity of consciousness or mental life—requires the ability to have
an idea or representation of oneself. That is, Kant seems to associate both the
possibility of personhood and of a unified mental life with the ability to be intentionally self-aware. This is curious for two reasons. First, as we have seen, the idea
of pre-intentional awareness—transcendental self-consciousness—has its roots
in the work of Kant. Second, there is a line of argument that can (arguably) be
found in Kant—in particular in a chapter of the *Critique of Pure Reason* entitled
"The Paralogisms of Pure Reason"—that strongly suggests that intentional self-
awareness *cannot* be the basis of the unity of a mental life. If this is correct, and
if the relevance of self-awareness to personhood is that it provides the basis of
the unity of a mental life—as Kant certainly seems to believe—then intentional
self-awareness cannot be what is crucial to personhood. Whatever Kant's position
ultimately turns out to be, this is the idea I am going to explore—and defend—in
the remainder of this chapter. In particular, I shall defend two claims. First, intentional self-awareness is not the sort of thing that can provide the basis of the unity

---

[1] Kant (1974), 8: 127.

in a mental life. Second, pre-intentional self-awareness is a much more promising candidate for this basis.

## 3. UNITY, SELF-AWARENESS, AND "JUST MORE CONTENT"

As I am using it, the expression *mental life* denotes a stream or sequence of mental acts, states, processes, and the like. If a person is to exist, this succession of acts, states, and processes must form a unified whole. The suggestion under consideration is that self-awareness, in one or other form, can supply the requisite unity to the mental life. I shall argue, first, that intentional self-awareness cannot do this.

The intentional model of awareness of one's mental life involves two distinct components. On the one hand, there is the mental life. On the other, there is one's awareness of it. One's mental life, or some aspect thereof, is made into an intentional object of a thought or some other intentional state. The question: can we explain the unity of one's mental life by appealing to one's awareness of this life, where this awareness is understood as distinct from the mental life itself? The answer, I shall argue, is that we can't.

The idea that intentional self-awareness can ground the unity of a mental life essentially involves introducing further (higher-order) mental states—for example, thoughts to the effect that the original (first-order) states that make up the life all belong together, or belong to the same individual. The problem is that this strategy leads to a *regress*. The strategy would work only if it were guaranteed that these higher-order states belong together with the first-order states and processes that make up the mental life. To see this, consider the following situation.

(1) There are two series of mental states and processes, A and B.
$$A_1-A_2-A_3 \ldots A_n \qquad B_1-B_2-B_3 \ldots B_n$$
Let us call these the A series and B series.

(2) There are also higher-order thoughts—$T_1$, $T_2$, etc.—to the effect that (all and only) members of the A series and (all and only) members of the B series belong together (for example, $T_1$ is the thought that $A_1$ belongs with at least some of $A_2$, $A_3$, and $A_n$; $T_2$ is a thought to the effect that $A_2$ belongs with at least some of $A_1$, $A_3$, $A_n$, and so on). I say, "at least some of" because it would be rather overzealous to require that the subject be able to grasp all of its mental states at any given time. The question, then, is this:

(3) Do these higher-order states unify (and thus also underwrite the distinctness of) the two series?

There are good reasons for supposing that the answer to this question must be "no." The crucial problem is that:

(4) The higher-order thoughts are distinct from the series of mental states they are supposed to unify.

Thus, if a higher-order thought, $T_1$, is to unify, or even help unify, the A series, then it would have to belong with the A series as opposed to the B series. If it, instead, belonged to the B series, it could do nothing to unify the A series. However, the claim that $T_1$ belongs to the A series is equivalent to the claim that $T_1$ and $A_1$, $A_2$, $A_3$ . . . $A_n$ form a *unified* whole. Thus, the appeal to $T_1$ to explain the unity of the A series, in fact, *presupposes* unity rather than *explains* it. $T_1$ was invoked in order to explain the unity of the A series. But any such explanation will be forthcoming only if $T_1$ and the A series form a unified whole. The unity of a mental life has, therefore, not been explained but presupposed.

The problem, here, ultimately derives from the fact that $T_1$ is a *distinct* state from $A_1$, $A_2$, or any other member of the A series. Since it is distinct from any member of the series, the question can always arise as to whether it belongs together with the members of this series. Appealing to $T_1$, therefore, does nothing to solve the problem of unity unless we have reason for supposing that $T_1$ is unified with the A series. That is, $T_1$ can explain the unity of the A series only if the series $\{A_1 - A_2 - A_3 . . . A_n - T_1\}$ forms a unified whole. Appeal to $T_1$, on its own, presupposes an answer to the problem of unity and so cannot provide such an answer. The problem of explaining the unity of the A series has been replaced with the problem of explaining the unity of the A series plus the higher-order state.

This is all horribly abstract. So, let us consider a simple example. At time $t$, let us suppose, I see a red square (R) and hear a loud trumpet (L). The parenthesized (R) and (L) denote the experiences of the red square and loud trumpet, and not the square and trumpet themselves. You also see and hear these things at time $t$. Let us denote your experiences of these things as (R*) and (L*). Now suppose that I think a thought (T): the thought that (R) and (L) belong together. Clearly, my thought that (R) and (L) belong together is incapable of unifying *your* experiences of the red square and loud trumpet. My (T) does not belong with your (R*) and (L*), it belongs with (R) and (L). Thus, the moral seems to be this: my thought (T) that (R) and (L) go together can only unify my (R) and (L) if (T) belongs with my (R) and (L) and not your (R*) and (L*).

It might be thought that there is an easy way to solve this problem: my thought (T) is unified with my (R) and (L), rather than your (R*) and (L*), because it is *about* (R) and (L) and not about (R*) and (L*). That is, (T) is the thought that (R) and (L) belong together, and not the thought that (R*) and (L*) belong together. This suggestion, however, has two serious problems. First, and most obviously, I can think thoughts not only about my mental states but also about yours. For example, I might think that you are now seeing a red square and hearing a loud trumpet. But my having a thought about your mental states would not entail that my thought and your mental states together form part of a unified mental life. The intentional directedness of a mental state, such as a thought, toward another mental state is clearly not sufficient for those two mental states to belong together in the same mental life.

Second, this suggestion *presupposes*, rather than explains, the unity of a mental life. To see this, suppose it were to turn out—contrary to fact, I know, but for now just suppose—that (R) and (L) and (R*) and (L*) form a unified series. That is, (R) and (L) and (R*) and (L*) were just smaller parts of a larger whole. In such circumstances, my thought (T) that (R) and (L) belong together would, in fact, be a thought about the larger series ((R), (L), (R*), (L*)). Remember: it would be implausible to claim that, to play its unifying role, a higher-order thought such as (T) would have to be about all the individual states that make up a mental life. No one is capable of thinking such a thought. Rather, (T) would have to be able to play its unifying role in virtue of being about some of the individual states that make up a mental life. Thus, if ((R), (L), (R*), (L*)) were a mental life, (T) could play a role in unifying this mental life in virtue of being about some components of this life—such as (R) and (L)—rather than all of the components. According to the present higher-order account of unity, therefore, (T) could play a role in unifying the mental life ((R), (L), (R*), (L*)). There is a clear moral to be drawn from this. Our guiding assumption, of course, was that (R) and (L) and (R*) and (L*) are really parts of *distinct* mental lives. That is why (T) is about the ((R) and (L)) mental life but not the ((R), (L), (R*), (L*)) mental life. However, if we do want to say this, then we are committed to regarding (R) and (L), on the one hand, and (R*) and (L*), on the other, as parts of distinct mental lives. That is, to suppose that (T) is about the ((R), (L)) series and not the ((R), (L), (R*), (L)) series—and so helps unifies the former series but not the latter—is to assume that ((R), (L)) and ((R*), (L*)) belong to distinct series rather than being simply components of a larger series. But the distinctness of two series presupposes the unity of each individual series. No substance can be given to the idea that ((R), (L)) and ((R*), (L*)) form parts of distinct series—as opposed to parts of the larger ((R), (L), (R*), (L)) series—unless the ((R), (L)) series and the ((R*), (L*)) series are individually unified.

Therefore, as is so common with the appeal to higher-order states to explain a recondite phenomenon, this appeal to higher-order thought presupposes rather than explains its intended target—in this case, the unity of the series.

Higher-order states cannot act as the ground or basis of the unity of a mental life, for they inevitably—in one way or another—presuppose such unity.

Kant seemed to develop something very much like this line of argument in "The Paralogisms of Pure Reason." Much more recently, the late Susan Hurley wielded something like this argument to great effect, dubbing it the "just more content" problem.[2] The general form taken by the "just more content" problem is this: there is a question about whether two mental states ("contents" in Hurley's sense)—such as (R) and (L)—belong together. We cannot solve this problem by adding a third mental state because that merely raises the question of whether this third mental state belongs with the other two. If there is a question about whether two "contents" belong together, we cannot answer this question by appealing to a third "content" because that just raises the question of whether this third "content" belongs with the first two. Hurley used this "just more content" problem, as, she argues, did Kant, to argue against what she calls *subjective* accounts of the unity of consciousness. It is not possible, Hurley argued, to explain the unity of consciousness in terms of mental states and relations between them. Rather, we need an objective account—one that appeals, for example, to physical structures such as the brain and its various features.[3]

There are two points that should be noted at this juncture. First, as I mentioned in Chapter 1, physical accounts of the unity of a mental life are, all things being equal, far more hospitable to the idea that animals can have unified mental lives. Suppose one thinks, for example, that the brain is the relevant structure that grounds the unity of a mental life: mental acts, states, and processes form a unified whole to the extent they all occur in the same brain. Such a view is not very plausible, but let us simply assume it for the sake of argument. Animals have brains, and so if sameness of brain were necessary and sufficient for the unity of a mental life instantiated in that brain, animals would have unified mental lives. One might always try to find some physical structure that only humans possess and argue that *this* is the basis of a unified mental life. But if that is the strategy, one will have to accept that it has not yet been successfully pursued—and the more we find out about the deep commonalities between our brains and those of many other animals, the more unlikely it progressively becomes. But, this aside, the most notable challenge to the idea that animals can have a unified mental life locates the source of unity in psychological features—most notably, self-awareness.

<hr>

[2] Hurley (1998).

[3] Hurley was well aware of the difficulties involved in providing a physical account of the unity of consciousness, most notably a persistent danger of vehicle–content confusion. This leads her to abandon what she called the "classical sandwich" conception of cognition in favor of an embodied and extended account.

Second, while Hurley thought that the "just more content" problem is fatal to attempts to explain the unity of a mental life in psychological terms, she did not have at her disposal the idea of pre-intentional self-awareness. In the next section, I shall argue that such awareness does not generate a "just more content" problem, and to that extent should be preferred to understanding unity in terms of intentional self-awareness. Indeed, the idea of pre-intentional self-awareness allows us to see why the "just more content" problem is not really a problem at all.

## 4. PRE-INTENTIONAL SELF-AWARENESS AND THE UNIFIED MENTAL LIFE

The answer to the "just more content" problem is, I shall argue, this: there is no such thing as "just" content. Content is never "just" content. Therefore, there is no such thing as "just more content" either. The idea of pre-intentional self-awareness is crucial to establishing these claims.

There is a certain conception of mental states that gives rise to the "just more content" problem. Mental states are, in essence, *free agents*.[4] For any mental act, state, or process there is, in principle, always an open question to whom this act, state, or process belongs. In principle, the mental state could be mine or it could be yours. In principle, it could belong to anyone. The ownership of this "content" has to be supplied by adding something else to it—for example, a higher-order thought to the effect that I am (or you are, or someone else is) having it. Let us call this the *free agency assumption*. Once we accept this assumption, the "just more content" problem is unavoidable. The higher-order thought will also be a free agent, and so the question that arose with regard to the original first-order states will inevitably arise for the higher-order thought also. The key is not to face the problem head on—not to try to solve the "just more content" problem—but, rather, undermine the assumptions that led us to think there is a problem.

It is not difficult to understand how we came to find ourselves in a position where free agency seems to be a natural way of thinking about mental states. The primary culprit is the distinctness of mental state and awareness of it that is built into the idea of intentional self-awareness. On the one hand, there are the acts, states, and processes $A_1, A_2 \ldots A_n$, etc., that make up a mental life. On the other hand, there is our awareness of these things—awareness that takes the form of a higher-order state (typically, a thought) that has these acts, states, and processes as intentional objects. In intentional self-awareness, the act of awareness is

---

[4] I would like to thank Elizabeth Cantalamessa for this apt expression.

distinct from the acts, states, or processes of which it is aware. Let us call this the *distinctness assumption*.

The free agency assumption and the distinctness assumption are mutually reinforcing. If mental acts, states, or processes are free agents, in the way imagined, then something must be *added* to these to explain why they all belong together, in a single mental life. This something added will be different—distinct—from the acts, states, and processes it attempts to unify. Thus, the free agency assumption entails the distinctness assumption: it is because content is, in itself, a free agent that something must be added to it to account for the unity of a mental life.

To see why the distinctness assumption entails the free agency assumption, consider how different matters will look once we replace intentional self-awareness with the pre-intentional alternative. Pre-intentional self-awareness is not distinct from mental acts, states, and processes. Rather, it is built into these, implicated in the possession of such things. This means, to begin with, that the distinctness assumption does not apply to pre-intentional self-awareness. But, with regard to the free agency assumption, it is the *reason* for this lack of distinctness of awareness and object of awareness that is crucial. To see this, recall how the bare-bones idea of pre-intentional self-awareness was first motivated.

I see a book as a book, only because my initial perception of the part of the book that is facing me has generated a series of sensorimotor anticipations: expectations about how appearances will change in the event of certain contingencies, such as the book moving, my moving relative to the book, and so on. Crucially, however, *I* am implicated in many of these contingencies if the book moves relative to *me*, if *I* move relative to the book, if the book rotates while *I* remain stationary, and so on. In this sense, to see the book *as* a book involves awareness of myself. This awareness is pre-intentional. I am not, or need not be, an object of any intentional state on my part. The intentional object of my seeing is the book. My pre-intentional awareness of myself is a function of the way or manner in which this book is presented—in this case, *as* a book.

Understood in this way, the act of seeing is not a free agent. There is no question as to whom the seeing belongs because partly constitutive of the content of the act of seeing are the anticipations in virtue of which the object seen is seen *as* something. And implicated in many of these anticipations, perhaps all of these anticipations: the person who sees. The identity of the person who sees is, therefore, bound up in the act of seeing. There is no free agency involved in seeing. The content of the act of seeing—what I see when I look at the book—is a content that is, in this sense, *for me*. My fingerprints are, so to speak, all over this content.[5]

---

[5] See Rowlands (2016) for a far more detailed account of this.

Therefore, once we replace intentional self-awareness with its pre-intentional counterpart, the "just more content" problem simply disappears. If we accept that pre-intentional self-awareness is involved in any conscious mental act, then we also have to accept that mental acts are never free agents. It is never an open question as to whom a given mental act belongs. The identity of the person who engages in the mental act is infused into the content of that act. This infusion of person into content is what grounds the unity of a mental life.

## 5. THE UNITY OF ANIMAL CONSCIOUSNESS

In this chapter, I have worked with what I think is an intuitively natural idea: being a person involves more than simply having a mental life. For a person to exist, this mental life needs to be unified. There is a historically prominent line of thought that sees unity as a function of self-awareness. This chapter has argued that, if this is so, the only version of self-awareness that could confer unity on a mental life is pre-intentional self-awareness. But many animals—all those who are subjects of conscious experience—are pre-intentionally self-aware. Thus, if pre-intentional self-awareness is what provides the basis of the unity of a mental life, the mental lives of many animals will be unified mental lives. And if having a unified mental life lies at the core of personhood, this suggests that many animals can be persons.

In the next chapter, the focus switches from self- to other-awareness—the fourth and final condition of personhood. The strategy I shall adopt is to apply some of the lessons learned in this lengthy discussion of self-awareness to the question of other-awareness—the awareness of others as persons. I shall argue that just as there is a distinction between intentional and pre-intentional self-awareness, so too is there a corresponding distinction between intentional and pre-intentional other-awareness.

# 10

## OTHER-AWARENESS

### Mindreading and Shame

1. PRE-INTENTIONAL AWARENESS OF OTHERS?

In the preceding chapters, I argued that awareness of self is predominantly *pre-intentional*. Pre-intentional self-awareness does not involve taking the self, or any of its bodily and psychological states, as an object of awareness. Rather, awareness of the self is implicated in awareness of other things—items that are *not* the self, or any of its bodily or psychological states. The *way* in which we are aware of these other things is crucial. The key to pre-intentional self-awareness is that one is aware of something (that is not the self) *as* something. To be aware of something—an object, episode, process, and so on—*as* being a certain thing or *as* being a certain way requires having certain expectations or anticipations concerning how appearances will change in the event of certain contingencies, bodily or environmental. If I see something *as* a book, this will be because I understand that the appearances that are presented to me will change in certain ways in certain circumstances. If the book is rotated (and I am stationary), then I anticipate that the appearance of the front of the book will gradually transform into an appearance of the book's spine, and this in turn will gradually transform into an appearance of the back of the book. In such a case, I am not the object of my seeing or any other intentional state of mine—that object is the book (and the various appearances it presents). However, I am implicated in the expectations required to see the book *as* a book. In general, I am pre-intentionally self-aware to the extent that I am implicated in the expectations that allow me to perceive objects (episodes, processes, etc.) *as* being a certain way or *as* being of a certain sort. This does not require that I be able to think thoughts of the form, "If I move to the left, then . . ." Rather, on the subjunctive-dispositional account defended in Chapter 7, it means that I am in state φ such that if φ is situated into the right sort of metacognitive context—which, in my case, it is, of course—will result in my being disposed to have thoughts of this form. If I did not possess the requisite metacognitive abilities, the evidence that I am in state φ would consist in evidence of my mastery of a certain subset of sensorimotor contingencies vis-à-vis the object of my awareness. To the extent that conscious experience involves the presentation of an object *as* being a certain way, it will entail pre-intentional self-awareness.

Intentional self-awareness exists whenever I make myself, or my bodily or psychological states or characteristics, into an intentional object of my awareness. Thinking about myself—including higher-order thinking about my own mental states—is one way of doing this. So too is recognizing myself in a mirror. Many creatures can see themselves. Fewer, presumably, can think thoughts about themselves. And far fewer can think thoughts about their own mental states. But, whatever form it takes, intentional self-awareness is quite different from pre-intentional self-awareness. In the former, I am an object of one of my intentional acts (seeing, thinking, etc.). In the latter, I am not. Pre-intentional self-awareness is far more pervasive than its intentional counterpart.

If we accept the distinction between positional and pre-positional forms of self-awareness—and the burden of the preceding three chapters has been to argue that we should accept it—then an interesting possibility arises with respect to awareness of *others*. If it is possible to be pre-intentionally aware of oneself, then is it also possible to be pre-intentionally aware of others? This possibility is an intriguing one, for the possibility of pre-intentional other-awareness is one that has been roundly ignored in debates—such as the mindreading debate—that most clearly impact on the issue of awareness of others.

## 2. THE MINDREADING DEBATE IN APES

The standard test for self-awareness in animals is the mirror test. As we have seen, this only targets intentional self-awareness, and thus ignores the most prevalent form of self-awareness in humans and the most likely form of self-awareness in animals. When we switch to awareness of others, a corresponding form of myopia is not difficult to discern.

*Mindreading*—often also referred to as *theory of mind*—is the ability to predict and/or understand the behavior of another through the attribution to that other of mental states. If I explain the ability of an apocryphal chicken to cross a road by imputing to it the desire to get to the other side, I am engaged in mindreading. My imputation need not be correct—the chicken might have another reason entirely, or no reason at all for crossing the road. It may not even be the sort of thing that can have reasons. But the fact that I can at least attempt to explain its behavior in this way shows that I have (1) the ability to explain and/or predict the behavior of another by attributing to it mental states and therefore (2) a concept of the mental states of others.

Premack and Woodruff's classic paper, "Does the Chimpanzee Have a Theory of Mind?" first ignited the question of mindreading in animals.[1] Their original study was actually a question about whether chimpanzees understood human goals. The paper was widely questioned on grounds of methodology. There were further problems with the idea that chimpanzees, or any of the great apes, could engage in mindreading. First, research in the 1990s seemed to indicate that chimpanzees could not understand the idea that others could perceive.[2] Second, the apparent failure of any chimpanzee to pass the false-belief test further called into question their possession of a theory of mind. The false-belief test looks like this.[3] There is a puppet show. One of the puppets—Sally, in the classic version of the experiment—places a marble in a basket, and then leaves the stage. The other puppet—Anne—removes the marble from the basket and puts it in a box. The child spectator is then asked where Sally will go to retrieve the marble. Will she go to the basket or to the box? If the child responds with "basket," or points to the basket, she has passed the test. For this answer shows the child can distinguish the way the world is (marble in box) from the way Sally believes it to be (marble in basket). And to draw this distinction one needs to understand that others can have beliefs (and that these beliefs are not always true). Therefore, if any individual passes the false-belief test, she must have a concept of belief and be able to apply this concept to others.

Children only pass the false-belief task, in this form, when they get to around three and a half to four years of age, suggesting that theory of mind—at least in its more or less mature form—arises around this time. No ape has, as yet, provided any clear demonstration of being able to pass the false-belief test. However, prior to passing the test, younger children exhibit at least some behavior that suggests

---

[1] Premack and Woodruff (1978).
[2] Povinelli and Eddy (1996).
[3] *Locus classicus*, Baron-Cohen, Leslie, and Frith (1985).

partial or fragmentary understanding. Specifically, they exhibit *violation of expectation* and *anticipatory looking* behavior. First, children reliably look longer at a scene when an agent acts in a way that is inconsistent, rather than consistent, with their false beliefs. Thus, children will stare at Sally longer if she goes to the box (where the marble is) rather than the basket (where she should believe it is). This additional length of gaze is symptomatic of a violation of expectation. Second, prior to passing the false-belief test, children will visually anticipate where a subject with a false belief will search for the object—their eyes point to the basket rather than the box. Both violation of expectation and anticipatory looking evidence support the claim that children have at least some understanding of false belief—and hence of belief—from around two and a half years of age.

Various hypotheses have been enlisted to explain this discrepancy. For example, it might be that different sub-systems of the brain are involved in attributing beliefs to others and verbalizing those attributions. These do not concern us. What is germane for our purposes, however, is that apes exhibit the same kind of violation of expectation and anticipatory looking behavior as two and a half–year-old children, suggesting that they have at least some understanding of the idea of belief. This, however, is not enough to satisfy those who insist on a clear pass of the test for possession of a theory of mind.

Violation of expectation and anticipatory looking evidence aside, the failure to clearly pass the false-belief test is not the death knell for the idea that apes have a theory of mind. For it may be that whereas the currency of our mindreading efforts is (allegedly) beliefs and desires, the mindreading employed by apes employs different concepts. In particular, it has been suggested that the mindreading abilities of apes are underwritten by the concepts of *seeing* and *knowing*.[4] This way of thinking about the mindreading abilities of apes derives from a now classic experiment devised by Hare, Call, and Tomasello.[5]

The general contours of the Hare, Call, and Tomasello experiment look like this. Two chimpanzees are recruited, one dominant and the other subordinate. They are placed behind doors at opposite ends of a square enclosure. Food will be placed by an experimenter in the enclosure, under various conditions of visibility. Sometimes the dominant chimp can see the food being placed, and sometimes the placing of the food will be hidden from the dominant chimp behind a barrier. The subordinate chimp can see the food being placed, and is also, sometimes, in a position to know whether the dominant chimp can see the food being placed.[6] The

---

[4] Call and Tomasello (2008).
[5] Hare, Call, and Tomasello (2001).
[6] I say "in a position to know." Whether it actually knows this is precisely what the experiment is trying to establish.

chimps are then allowed to enter the enclosure, with the subordinate chimp given a few seconds head start—enough time to reach the food if it so desires.

The results are, perhaps, unsurprising: subordinate subjects retrieved a significantly larger percentage of food when they were in a position to know that their dominant counterpart lacked accurate information about the location of food. When the subordinate is in a position to see that the dominant can see the food, it does not, typically, approach the food. When the subordinate is in a position to see that the dominant cannot see the food, it does, typically, approach the food. When it is not in a position to see either way, it typically refrains from approaching the food. The question is: what do these result show?

One interpretation of the results is that they show that the subordinate chimpanzee has at least a limited capacity for mindreading. The subordinate chimp understands that the dominant *sees* the food placement and so *knows* where the food is. The subordinate chimp, therefore, has the ability to attribute mental states such as seeing and knowing to the dominant chimp. This was, in essence, the conclusion drawn by Hare, Call, and Tomasello.

There is, however, another interpretation, far more skeptical, championed by Daniel Povinelli and colleagues.[7] According to this skeptical alternative, the subordinate chimpanzee sees that the dominant chimp was *oriented* toward (i.e., facing) the food when it was placed. The subordinate is also in possession of other background knowledge concerning the behavior of dominant chimps. For example, it knows that when a dominant chimp is oriented toward food it will often go for it. This interpretation does not presuppose that the subordinate chimp has an understanding of the mental states of others. All it requires is that the chimp can identify regularities in the behavior of other chimps.

Povinelli and colleagues argue that their skeptical interpretation is to be preferred on grounds of explanatory parsimony. Their skeptical interpretation explains the subordinate's behavior thus: he sees that the dominant chimp was present and oriented toward the food when it was placed where it is now (and has identified relevant behavioral patterns such as "dominant chimps in such circumstances typically go for the food"). The mindreading interpretation, on the other hand, adds something extra: because the subordinate chimp could see that the dominant chimp was oriented toward the food when it was placed, the subordinate chimp believes that the dominant chimp *saw* where the food was placed and so *knows* where it is. The evidence, Povinelli and colleagues argue, can never establish anything more than the chimp's ability to identify behavioral regularities. The mindreading interpretation is therefore superfluous. More generally, any attempt

---

[7] Povinelli and Vonk (2003), Penn and Povinelli (2007).

to attribute mindreading abilities to chimpanzees or other animals faces what they call a *logical problem*: any behavior that seems to suggest the animal has a theory of mind can be reinterpreted in terms of *behavioral abstraction*—the identification of pertinent behavioral regularities.

The mindreading debate, in this form, is a debate about whether animals can be *intentionally* aware of the mental states of others. If the subordinate chip can think thoughts such as "the dominant chimp *saw* the food being placed and so *knows* where it is," then it is capable of making the mental states (seeing, knowing) of others into objects of its intentional acts (in this case, an act of thinking). Hare, Call, and Tomasello think that apes can be intentionally aware of the mental states of others, and the skeptical interpretation of Povinelli and colleagues denies this. The primary purpose of this chapter is to argue that this debate leaves untouched another way in which animals can be aware of the minds of others—a non-intentional form of mindreading. I shall postpone discussion of this idea until Section 4. First, I shall argue that even when restricted to the issue of mindreading in its usual, intentional, sense, the Povinelli-inspired, skeptical, interpretation has serious problems. It is to the latter, and for my purposes somewhat more tangential, issue that I now turn.

## 3. MINDREADING AND BEHAVIOR READING

The claim of Povinelli and colleagues is, in effect, this: we do not need to suppose that apes are mindreaders; we need suppose only that they are behavior readers. Instead of understanding that the dominant chimp *sees* the food being placed and so *knows* where it is, the subordinate need only be able to identify behavioral regularities such as when a dominant chimp is *oriented* toward food it will, when able, tend to go for it. The notion of *orientation* is doing a lot of work here, and that is where I am going to attack the argument. The Povinelli argument, I shall try to show, falls victim to a dilemma.

This is an experiment you can try at home—if you are suitably equipped with a dog. Put a tasty morsel on the ground around six feet in front of your dog. Stand behind the morsel and tell the dog to stay—just once. Then time how long he in fact stays. Then do the same thing, except turn your back to the dog, and time how long it is before he or she descends on the morsel. Third, face the dog again, repeat the stay command, but cover your eyes with your hands and, again, time how long the dog waits before eating the morsel. The first time I did this with my— at that time completely untrained—four-month-old German shepherd, Shadow, the following results were gleaned. When I was facing him, with uncovered eyes, he waited fifteen seconds before descending on the morsel. When my back was turned, and when my hands covered my eyes, he waited less than a second. In fact, "Stay" was still issuing from my lips as he sprang into action.[8]

I relate this story, not because the experiment is a model of rigorous scientific method. It isn't, obviously. Think of it, instead, as a *thought experiment*: a useful tool for assessing the idea that Shadow was able to identify relevant behavioral regularities by helping us work out precisely what it *means* to identify a behavioral regularity. Here, there are two distinct ways in which I might *not* be oriented toward the morsel: (1) I am facing away from it or (2) my eyes are covered. Therefore, there are two possibilities. One is that Shadow identifies two *different* behavioral regularities: (1) when I am facing away from a morsel he can go and get it and (2) when my hands are over my eyes he can go and get the morsel. Shadow, on this interpretation, identifies nothing in common, no common factor uniting these two regularities. The problem with this is that it will quickly become unwieldy. With a little ingenuity, we can expand the ways in which I fail to be oriented toward the morsel (blindfolds, bag over my head, opaque barriers between me and the food, etc.). On the present interpretation, Shadow would have to identify a distinct behavioral regularity for each of my failures to be oriented toward the morsel.

Povinelli and colleagues present their view as being more parsimonious than the alternative mindreading explanation. But, on this first interpretation, where an animal identifies a distinct behavioral regularity in each case, the parsimony spin seems to look more than a little ironic. The need for mindreading is obviated, perhaps, but only at the expense of a potential explosion of behavioral regularities that an animal is supposed to identify, and subsequent behavioral rules it is supposed to master. This is the first horn of a dilemma facing Povinelli and colleagues.

The second horn of this dilemma is based on the idea that it would, in fact, be far more parsimonious if Shadow were able to understand the *salience* of relevant objects or circumstances in the environment. The problem is that it is difficult to see how he can do this without an understanding of what another can *see*—and thus possessing some sort of mindreading ability. The notion of salience amounts to what an object or circumstance *affords* for a creature—but the notion of affordance, here, is relative to the ability to see. It is what an object or circumstance affords *for my ability to see the morsel* that is crucial.

To see this, consider Juliane Kaminski and colleagues' investigation into the visual perspective-taking capacities of dogs.[9] Each of two toys was placed on the

---

[8] Now he is trained, Shadow will wait indefinitely to get the food—whether I am facing him or facing away. The conclusion we should draw is obvious isn't it: training robs a dog of its theory of mind. ☺

[9] Kaminski et al. (2009).

dog's side of two small barriers. One of these barriers was opaque, and the other transparent. A human sat on the opposite side of the barriers, such that she could see only the toy behind the transparent barrier. The human then told the dog to "Bring it here!" without indicating either toy in any way. There were two controls. In the *Back Turned* control, the human also sat on the opposite side of the barriers but with her back turned so that she could see neither toy. In the *Same Side* control, she sat on the same side of the barriers as the dog, and so could see both toys. The result: the dogs preferentially retrieved the toy behind the transparent barrier in the experimental situation but did so in neither of the control conditions. Moreover, the dogs did not differentiate between the two control conditions. This strongly suggests that, even in the absence of behavioral cues, dogs are sensitive to the visual perspectives of others—even when this perspective differs from their own.

It is not immediately clear how one could supply a Povinelli-style behavior reading of these results. The problem is that the dog needs to understand the salience of the transparent and opaque barriers, and it is not clear how it could understand this without understanding the ramifications of each type of barrier for the ability of the experimenter to see. One could, of course, try to devise a behavior-reading explanation: when told to fetch an object, (1) fetch the one behind the transparent barrier and (2) don't fetch the one behind the opaque barrier. But one can easily multiply the variables—finding new ways to obscure the object behind different types of obstacle. And then we would face the kind of explosion of rules we encountered earlier in this section. In short, the most parsimonious way of explaining the dog's behavior is to suppose that it understands the salience of various objects. The dog must understand why an opaque barrier and the experimenter turning her back to the object have the *same* ramifications, and why a transparent barrier and the experimenter being on the same side of the barrier have the *same* ramifications. The dog cannot understand these things—the salience of these facts or circumstances—unless we suppose that it has some understanding of what is going on in the mind of the other. It must, at the very least, understand what the other can and cannot *see*—that it is capable of *perspective taking*. However, once we accept this, we are committed to the claim that the ape or dog is capable of at least some form of mindreading. This may not, of course, be the form human mindreading takes. It may be that, as Call and Tomasello suggest, apes and dogs work with seeing and knowing—rather than the believing and desiring that many assume is at the heart of human mindreading.[10] But this is a

---

[10] Call and Tomasello (2008).

matter of the details of mindreading strategies, rather than a question of whether mindreading abilities are being employed.

## 4. "SHAME": PRE-INTENTIONAL MINDREADING

The mindreading versus behavior-reading debate is a debate about *intentional* awareness of the minds of others. In mindreading, one must be able to think about, or understand, what the other sees and knows, or believes and desires. The guiding question is: do we need to suppose that animals have intentional awareness of the minds of others? Or does it suffice (for explanatory purposes) to suppose they have intentional awareness of only bodies and behavior? If the former, then animals must be capable of making the mental states of others—their *seeings* and *knowings*, for example—into objects of their intentional awareness. This debate is, actually, tangential to the primary concern of this chapter. This concern is to argue for another way of being aware of the minds of others—in effect, a nonintentional form of mindreading.

The idea that there can be a non-intentional form of awareness of the minds of others is a theme powerfully developed by Sartre. In Part 3 of *Being and Nothingness*, Sartre identifies a certain type of experience that he dubs *shame*. In Sartre's hands, this term has a technical meaning, somewhat divorced from our ordinary usage: shame is the non-intentional awareness of oneself as an *object* for the other. He explains the idea as follows:

> Let us imagine that moved by jealousy, curiosity, or vice I have just glued my ear to the door and looked through a keyhole. I am alone and on the level of non-thetic self-consciousness . . . there is no self in consciousness . . . my acts are in no way known; I *am my acts*.[11]

While Sartre does have a rather annoying habit of using different expressions to mean the same thing, often without explanation—here, "non-thetic" means the same thing as "what Sartre would call 'pre-reflective' or 'non-positional', and which I have chosen to call 'pre-intentional'—and while one should, perhaps, not underestimate the significant physical difficulties involved in simultaneously gluing one's ear to the door and looking through a keyhole, the kind of situation Sartre has in mind is reasonably clear. I am staring through a keyhole at a scene I really shouldn't be looking at. I am engrossed in the scene. I am not thinking

---

[11] Sartre (1943/1957), p. 347.

about myself, or about what I am doing, but am concerned only with the scene unfolding before me. In other words, I am not an object of my intentional consciousness ("there is no self in consciousness . . . my acts are in no way known"). The only object of my intentional consciousness is the scene on the other side of the door. However:

> [A]ll of a sudden I hear footsteps in the hall. Someone is looking at me! . . . I am suddenly affected in my being and . . . essential modifications appear in my structure . . . I now exist as *myself* for my unreflective consciousness . . . I see *myself* because *somebody* sees me. . . . So long as we considered the for-itself in its isolation, we were able to maintain that the unreflective consciousness cannot be inhabited by a self; the self was given in the form of an object and only for the reflective consciousness. But here the self comes to haunt the unreflective consciousness . . . this role which devolved only on the reflective consciousness—the making-present of the self—belongs now to the unreflective consciousness.[12]

Here, Sartre uses the expression "unreflective consciousness" (I refer you to the aforementioned bad habit). This is equivalent to—a notational variant on—non-positional self-consciousness, or pre-reflective consciousness. It is pre-intentional self-awareness in my preferred terminology.[13] The crucial point, for Sartre, is that:

> Only the reflective consciousness has the self directly for an object. The unreflective consciousness does not apprehend the *person* directly or as *its* object; the person is presented to consciousness *in so far as the person is an object for the Other* . . . I am conscious of myself as escaping myself, not in that I am the foundation of my own nothingness but in that I have my foundation outside myself. *I am for myself only as I am a pure reference to the Other.*[14]

---

[12] Sartre (1943/1957), p. 349.

[13] Sartre's claim that "this role [of] the making-present of the self—belongs now to the unreflective consciousness" seems, initially, puzzling. In such circumstances, it seems I would become reflectively—that is, intentionally—aware of myself. I would, presumably, be thinking thoughts such as: "Oh no, *I* have been seen! *I* must look like a total voyeur!" I am, thus, the object of my thoughts. This would be intentional self-consciousness. To solve this apparent puzzle, one should recall that, for Sartre, pre-reflective awareness makes reflective awareness possible. I can be intentionally aware of myself only because I am, first, pre-intentionally aware of myself. Pre-intentional self-awareness is the foundation that makes intentional self-awareness possible. Thus, Sartre's view seems to be that, in shame, I can be intentionally, but must be pre-intentionally, aware of myself.

[14] Sartre (1943/1957), p. 349. Italics in original.

In shame, I am (pre-intentionally) aware of myself only "as I am a pure reference to the other." I am (pre-intentionally) aware of myself as I must appear to the other. That is, I am aware of the other *through*, or *in virtue of*, being aware of myself in a certain way. What sort of awareness of the other is this? It is the awareness of the other as *subject*. Sartre writes:

> Nevertheless we must not conclude here that the object is the other and that the *Ego* present to my consciousness is a secondary structure or a meaning of the other-as-object; the other is not an object here and cannot be an object, as we have shown, unless by the same stroke *my* self ceases to be an object-for-the-other and vanishes. Thus, I do not aim at the other as an object nor at my *ego* as an object for myself.[15]

In shame, I am aware of the other, but aware of him as a subject rather than an object. To be aware of myself in a certain way is, therefore, to be aware of the other as a subject.

There is a way of developing this idea—perhaps Sartre would have liked it, perhaps not—that makes clear the parallels with the earlier case for pre-intentional self-awareness. In shame, I am aware of myself as being a certain way: I am aware of *me-as-I-appear-to-the-other*. *As-I-appear-to-the-other* is the *mode of presentation* of the intentional object of my awareness—namely, *me*. Thus, in shame, I am the *object* of my awareness, and the other is implicated in the *mode of presentation* of this object.

Once we frame this issue in terms of the idea of a mode of presentation, the parallels with pre-intentional self-awareness become very obvious. In seeing something *as* something—in, say, seeing an object *as* a book—I have various expectations about how appearances will change in the event of certain contingencies. These anticipations are responsible for my seeing the object as a book. However, I am implicated in many (perhaps all) of these anticipations. Therefore, pre-intentional awareness of self is implicated in seeing something *as* something. *I am aware of myself in virtue of being aware of something else in a certain way.* In shame, on the other hand, *I am aware of the other in virtue being aware of myself in a certain way.*

For those of you wondering what this has to do with animal minds in general— and the issue of other-awareness in particular—this is all I would like you to take away from this discussion of Sartre. Other-awareness is the ability to recognize the other as a person and treat her as such. Other-awareness has almost

---

[15] (1943/1957), p. 350.

always been conflated with mindreading—I recognize the other as a person when I can attribute a mind and mental states to her—but the two are not equivalent. Of course, mindreading is, certainly, one way in which other-awareness might be realized but, crucially, it is *only* one way in which other-awareness might be realized. Mindreading is an intentional form of other-awareness. The other is the object of my intentional acts of mental state attribution. But, we now see, there is another, pre-intentional, form that other-awareness can take. I recognize the other as a person *when I experience myself in a certain way because of her*—when I experience myself as appearing to her in a certain way. In experiencing myself in this way, I recognize the other as a subject to which I appear as an object. This is the pre-intentional recognition of the other as person. I recognize the other as the sort of thing to which I can appear. I recognize, pre-intentionally, the *mindedness* (as we might call it) of the other to the extent I experience myself as something that appears to her, for I can only appear to something that can experience me, and therefore has a mind.

In other words, the experience of shame is an experience that makes sense only if the other has a mind, and is therefore, in this sense, a person. In shame, I experience the other as *minded* by experiencing myself in a way that presupposes the other's mindedness. This presupposition is defeasible: the other might be a cleverly programmed robot. Nevertheless, a general skepticism about other minds has been discussed, and hopefully dealt with, in Chapter 2. If the other does, indeed have a mind, then in experiencing shame, I experience the other's mindedness, and I do so by experiencing myself in a way that makes sense only in the face of the other's mindedness. This is pre-intentional awareness of the other as a person.

## 5. THE REQUIREMENTS OF SHAME

Sartre's characterization of the awareness of the other as subject as *shame* might suggest the phenomenon is more restricted than it really is—and because of this only dubiously applicable to animals. Shame, as it is commonly understood, is a complex moral emotion, involving a belief that one has transgressed a moral or quasi-moral norm, and the undergoing of emotions with an unpleasant phenomenology as a result of this perceived transgression. The idea that animals can feel shame in this sense is questionable—evidenced by the old chestnut about whether the dog that has just chewed up your new shoes and now looks, to your eyes, distinctly guilty as a result, is really feeling shame or is just anxious because you are somewhat irked. Thankfully, we do not need to get involved in this debate, for this is not what Sartre means by shame. *Shame*, as Sartre uses it, is a technical term that covers far more than what we would, in ordinary parlance, call shame. Shame, for Sartre, is nothing more than the experience of oneself as an *object for the other*. Equivalently—for Sartre, the two are the same—it is the experience of the *other as a subject*. To experience yourself as an object for the other is precisely what it is to experience the other as subject, and vice versa. As such, shame comes in a wide variety of experiential forms, and many of these experiences, it is plausible to suppose, can be had by animals.

Consider, for example, the experience of *vulnerability*. One can experience vulnerability both with respect to the world and with respect to others. To experience vulnerability in the face of the world is, on Sartre's view, to experience oneself as an object (or, as Sartre puts it, a "destructible transcendent in a world of transcendents") and, as such, subject to all the usual principles and operations of the physical world.[16] More germane to our current concerns, however, is the experience of vulnerability in the face of others. We might imagine a *vulnerability spectrum*. The spectrum covers a range of experiences. At one end of the spectrum we have the experience of being completely defenseless in the face of the other. At the other end of the spectrum, there is the feeling of being completely invulnerable to the other, immune to whatever he or she may throw at us. All the experiences on this spectrum would qualify as shame on Sartre's view. I am pre-intentionally aware of myself in virtue of being aware of the other in a certain way—as dangerous, deadly, harmless, and so on. If animals can experience themselves in this way, then they are capable of shame in Sartre's sense. They will be, that is, pre-intentionally aware of the other as a subject.

To make this idea work, it is important that animals be able to differentiate vulnerability in the face of the world from vulnerability in the face of the other. An animal can also experience inanimate things as dangerous, deadly, and harmless. Think of a forest fire, for example. Thus, if they are to experience vulnerability in the face of the other, and not merely vulnerability in the face of the world, it seems that animals would require two things: (1) the ability to distinguish animate from inanimate objects and (2) the ability to respond experientially to the former in appropriate ways.

There are very good reasons for thinking that the ability to distinguish animate from inanimate things is a much more basic ability than mindreading. As we have seen, the ability to attribute mental states—including the propositional

---

[16] "Vertigo announces itself through fear. I am on a narrow path—without a guard rail—which goes along a precipice . . . I can slip on a stone and fall into the abyss; the crumbling earth of the path can give way under my steps. Through these various anticipations, I am given to myself as a thing . . . fear appears . . . [which is] the apprehension of myself as a destructible transcendent in the midst of transcendents, as an object." Sartre (1943/1957), p. 66.

attitudes—to others, and to explain their behavior on the basis of this attribution, is an ability that does not even begin to emerge until the second year of life, and takes several years to come to fruition—at least as judged by the ability to conclusively pass the false-belief test. However, prior to the emergence of mindreading abilities, there is strong evidence of a much more basic ability to distinguish *animate* from *inanimate* things.[17]

Infants as young as seven months of age appear to draw a basic distinction between things that can move themselves and things that require an external source of movement. To show the existence of this ability, Spelke et al. devised a series of experiments based on a violation of expectation protocol.[18] Infants watch a screen. In one scene, a large brightly colored object with a meaningless shape moves toward another similar object. In one scenario, the objects touch and the second object then moves. In the other, the second object moves before being touched. Children reliably stare longer at the second scenario, suggesting that the children are surprised by this violation of what is known as the *contact principle*—objects act on each other if and only if they touch. However, this is not the case when the objects on the screen are recognizably human, suggesting that children do not apply the contact principle to humans. In other words, at this stage, children—long before they acquire mindreading abilities—can distinguish between things that can move themselves and things that can only be moved by something else.

The animate/inanimate distinction in young children does not correspond to the human/nonhuman distinction. Gelman argues that, at an early age, children draw a *general* distinction between animate and inanimate things.[19] The distinction is based on two different principles—which she dubs the *innards principle* and the *external agent principle*. Children apply the innards principle to certain natural objects—animate objects—and treat them as if they have something inside them that explains their movement. The processing of an object by way of the external agent principle, in contrast, is driven by the expectation that movement in that object requires some sort of external force.

Gergely and Csibra usefully distinguish between an intentional—or mindreading—stance and what they call the "teleological stance."[20] Infants are habituated to a computer animation in which a small circle approaches, and then touches, a large circle by jumping over an intervening obstacle. In undergoing habituation, the children learn to adopt the teleological stance. To adopt this stance

---

[17] For an excellent discussion and exploration of some of the implications of this, see Steward (2009). The discussion of this section draws heavily on Steward's work.

[18] Spelke, Phillips, and Woodward (1995).

[19] Gelman (1990), Gelmna, Durgin, and Kaufman (1995).

[20] Gergely and Csibra (2003).

is to understand the relationships between three things: the action itself, a possible future state, and the relevant situational constraints. Given any two of these elements, mastery of the teleological stance allows the child to infer the third. This inference is based on what Gergely and Csibra call "the rationality principle": given situational constraints (as perceived by the child herself) agents will, in general, take the most efficient action for achieving a given goal. Thus, in a violation of expectation study, Gergely and Csibra observed the reaction of the removal of the intervening obstacle—the relevant situational constraint. Infants were shown two test displays: (1) the same jumping approach as they had seen during the habituation phase but this time without the obstacle and (2) a novel straight-line approach. Infants looked longer (indicating violation of expectation) at the old jumping action—arguably because they regard this as an inefficient means to the goal, in the absence of the obstacle. No attribution of intentional states is required for the adoption of the teleological stance. Rather, all that is required is the simple postulation of a goal, and an understanding of the most efficient way of achieving this goal. The ability to adopt this stance is, therefore, a much simpler ability than mindreading.

To sum up: there is a wealth of evidence that a basic distinction between animate and inanimate objects—between objects that move themselves[21] and objects that require something else to move them—emerges very early in the human developmental process: during infancy, and long before mindreading or theory of mind become possible. The ability to distinguish things that can move themselves from things that cannot is so basic to survival that it would be, frankly, incredible if it were not widely distributed through the animal realm. This does, indeed, appear to be so. Although most of the studies have been conducted on apes, there is also evidence that dogs distinguish between animate and inanimate things by attributing goals to the former but not the latter.[22]

## 6. FALSE SHAME?

This account may seem to suffer from a fatal flaw: the animate/inanimate distinction is not the same as the minded/non-minded distinction. This is so for the simple reason that while all minded things are animate, not all animate things

---

[21] The objects in the animated display appeared to move themselves. The function of habituation is to engender this appearance.

[22] Marshall-Pescini, Ceretta, and Prato-Previde (2014) argue that dogs actually attribute intentions to humans, as well as goals, but this is not a claim I need to defend here.

need have minds. This does put a little wrinkle in my account but, I think, no more than that.

We can all—whether we are humans or not—make mistakes about the mindedness of another. A human child might think her doll has feelings. A human adult might mistake a cleverly programmed, but insentient, robot for a minded individual. That an animal can sometimes make mistakes about what has a mind no more disqualifies it from having other-awareness than the corresponding mistakes would disqualify us. The question is not whether we are correct, in given cases, to (pre-intentionally) experience the other as minded, but whether we have the capacity to (pre-intentionally) experience the other in this way. We should apply the same standards to the question of other-awareness in animals.

Sartre considers the case of the experience of shame when there is nothing, in fact, to experience shame before:

> Nevertheless, someone will say, the fact remains that I can discover I have been mistaken. Here I am bent over the keyhole; suddenly I hear a footstep. I shudder as a wave of shame sweeps over me. Somebody has seen me. I straighten up. My eyes run over the deserted corridor. It was a false alarm. I breathe a sigh of relief.[23]

Sartre is emphatic that we should not think of this as a case of *false shame*.[24] His reasons are pertinent and, I think, correct:

> Is it actually my being-as-object for the Other which has been revealed as an error? By no means. The Other's existence is so far from being placed in doubt that this false alarm can very well result in making me give up my enterprise. If, on the other hand, I persevere in it, I shall feel my heart beat fast, and I shall detect the slightest noise, the slightest creaking of the stairs. Far from disappearing with my first alarm, the Other is present everywhere, below me, above me, in the neighboring rooms, and I continue to feel profoundly my being-for-others. . . . Thus, what is doubtful is not the Other himself. It is the Other's being-there; i.e. that concrete historical event which we can express by the words, "There is someone in this room."[25]

---

[23] Sartre (1943/1957), p. 369.

[24] "My shame was in fact shame before somebody. But nobody is there. Does it not thereby become shame before nobody? . . . does it not become a false shame?" (1943/1957), p. 368. His answer is no.

[25] Sartre (1943/1957), p. 370.

On the one hand, there is the question of whether an individual has the resources to represent the mindedness of the other. On the other hand, there is the question of whether those resources have been correctly deployed in any particular case. In experiencing themselves as vulnerable before the other, animals demonstrate that they have the resources to non-intentionally represent the other as minded. The fact that they can be mistaken—deploying these resources when they should not, in fact, be deployed—no more counts against their possession of these resources than our mistakes would count against our possession of them.

The animate/inanimate distinction is a way of homing in—loosely, not entirely accurately—on the distinction between minded and non-minded individuals. Some of these will not be minded. But many will, and when an animal experiences shame before an individual who is, in fact, minded, this shame is, indeed, the pre-intentional awareness of the other as a minded individual—a person.

## 7. OTHER-AWARENESS AND PERSONHOOD

Other-awareness is the fourth and final condition of personhood. Other-awareness is the ability to recognize other individuals as persons. This is not in some philosophically arcane, or conceptually sophisticated, way that involves identifying necessary and sufficient conditions for something to count as a person, but rather being able to identify, with a reasonable level of accuracy, which things have minds and which do not. Mindreading would be one way of doing this. There is a debate about whether other animals are capable of mindreading, and if so which ones have this ability. But, I have argued, mindreading is only one way in which the recognition of the mindedness of another might be implemented. Mindreading is a form or intentional other-awareness, and the principal goal of this chapter has been to argue for a pre-intentional form of other-awareness.

I am pre-intentionally other-aware when I experience myself in a certain way, and the mindedness of the other is implicated in the mode of presentation of myself. Pre-intentional other-awareness is, in this sense, the mirror image of pre-intentional self-awareness. In pre-intentional self-awareness, I am aware of myself in virtue of being aware of something else in a certain way. In pre-intentional other-awareness—in shame, broadly and technically construed—I am aware of the other in virtue of being aware of myself in a certain way. Intentional other-awareness requires considerable cognitive sophistication—which might or might not be beyond the abilities of nonhumans. But pre-intentional other-awareness is far simpler and, therefore, likely to be far more widely distributed through the animal kingdom. The requirements of intentional other-awareness include a metacognitive apparatus of some sort. But the requirements of pre-intentional other-awareness are much more basic. To be pre-intentionally other-aware, an animal need only be able to distinguish things that might have minds from things that can't have minds and to respond experientially to the former in ways in which they do not respond experientially to the latter. To the extent they are capable of pre-intentional other-awareness, animals will satisfy the other-awareness condition of personhood.

# 11

## ANIMALS AS PERSONS AND WHY IT MATTERS

### 1. ANIMALS AS PERSONS

When engaged in a philosophical dispute—assuming fisticuffs are not among the available options, although philosophy might be a lot more marketable if they were—one can, in general, proceed in one of two ways. One can question the premises of one's opponent. Or, one can accept the premises and show that one's opponent's conclusion does not follow. In this book, I have granted many questionable things to those who disagree with me. I do this on the altar of the *worst-case scenario* (an altar conveniently located in the temple of *for the sake of argument*).

I'm not sure I really am a *worst-case scenario* philosopher. But I've certainly played one in this book. It's not easy: all those claims you have to pretend you believe are true, even though you really doubt they are or believe they are not. It's difficult to keep track. Animals do not have first-person metacognitive abilities. I granted that for the sake of argument, but do I really believe it? In some of its forms, maybe. Can Shadow, my German shepherd, think? Of course. Can he think about his thinking? I don't know, but quite possibly not. Can he think thoughts about himself? It wouldn't surprise me at all if he could. But such variegation in response has no place in the world of the worst-case scenario philosopher. Is it true that no nonhuman animal, at any time, ever developed the concept of belief? Is it true that no nonhuman animal ever engaged in third-person metacognition? It's not at all clear that it is. Some recent evidence points to chimpanzees being able to pass the false-belief test, for example. But such evidence is, again, sacrificed at the altar of the worst-case scenario. I have made assumptions I don't believe, certainly not in the blanket form in which they are often presented, and I have tried to show that it does not matter one bit. Even in the face of unreasonably—and, given the way the empirical winds are blowing, I think unseasonably—hostile assumptions, animals can still qualify as persons. It should also be noted that on the altar of the worst-case scenario, I adopted a very unfavorable conception of personhood. If one's goal is to argue that animals are persons, some of them anyway, Locke's conception of personhood is about as hostile a conception as one can get. Other conceptions are far more favorable to the claim that animals are, or can be, persons. But once again, it does not matter: even on the least hospitable conception of a person imaginable—even on the most individualistic, rationalistic, Eurocentric, logocentric, and no doubt phallogocentric, conception of a person ever devised by a dead, white, privileged, cisgendered male—many animals still qualify as persons.

The reason for all this feigned magnanimity? Simple: from the perspective of the worst-case scenario philosopher, *non sequitur* is the worst of all possible intellectual crimes. Do your worst, assume your worst: animals still qualify as persons. The claim that they don't is a *non sequitur*. Thus have I argued.

To qualify as a person, in the eyes of this book at least, is to satisfy the four most commonly cited conditions of personhood: conditions that can be plausibly regarded as individually necessary and collectively sufficient for an individual to qualify as a person. Many animals qualify as persons in virtue of their being conscious, cognitive, self-aware, and other-aware individuals: they are individuals in which these four features coalesce. Because they are such individuals, there is no respectable reason to think of them as anything other than unified subjects of often quite complex mental lives—aka, persons.

To those who wish to resist—reject, ridicule—this conclusion, there is, as far as I can see, good news and bad news. The good news: when doing philosophy, it is always wise to bear in mind Wittgenstein's admonitions about the craving for generality. Animals are persons, I have argued, in that they are individuals in which consciousness, cognition, self-awareness, and other-awareness coalesce and, as a result, are the subjects of often quite complex, unified mental lives. That's *not* what a person is, you might reply. Or, even if that *is* what a person is, animals are not these things—conscious, cognitive, self-aware, and other-aware—in the right sort of way. I don't recommend that either of us go down this particular road. Years can be swallowed up arguing about things that, in the end, always fragment into lots of other, different, things, and everyone ends up talking past each other. I have been there, and I have done that, and I have no desire to rinse and repeat. If you want to reject the idea that animals are persons by rejecting the assumed concept of person, or by rejecting the assumed concepts of the constituents of persons, then that option is definitely available. If so, then you might think of this book as defending the claim that animals are conscious, cognitive, self-aware, and other-aware individuals—or, if you prefer, as identifying the sense in which animals are conscious, cognitive, self-aware, and other-aware individuals.

Such largesse, I have to admit, goes against the grain. And, after the better part of 100,000 words of worst-case scenario philosophizing, I'm going to allow myself a little off-leash time—a FRAP or zoomie.[1] Thus, I say, respectfully: You can't just make shit up! If you do, for example, want to reject the conception of personhood I have adopted, on the basis of extensive review and argument in Chapter 1, then you had better be prepared to say why it is deficient, and give some reasons in support of this judgment (and ideally, I suppose, offer some better alternative). And if you do, for example, want to add further conditions to the personhood list, ones that disqualify animals from acting as persons, you should bear in mind that such insertions must be both principled and plausible. A case must be made for why this additional condition—whatever it is—constitutes a *sine qua non* of personhood. One could always, for example, try to insist that intentional self-awareness is necessary for personhood. But, if one does wish to insist on this, one must also be willing to make a case for precisely why this is so—given that pre-intentional self-awareness is, for example, a far more plausible candidate for the supplier of unity to a mental life. That is, one must make a case based on what intentional self-awareness brings to personhood, and why there can't be personhood without it. I am not certain that such a case cannot be made—that goes without saying. But I am certain that I have not yet seen it.

Which animals thus qualify is, of course, ultimately an empirical question. I have surveyed, and where suitable employed, some of this empirical work. But my primary job, as a philosopher, is not an empirical one. Rather, my job is to remove some of the broadly logical and conceptual confusions that attend the question of whether animals can be persons: all self-awareness must take positional form, and so too must mindreading; to reason logically is to think thoughts about thoughts; a mental state is made conscious by a higher-order thought about it, and so on. If the arguments of this book are correct, these—and the many more we have looked at in the foregoing pages—are all confusions that should be excised from our understanding of animals. The project, then, has not been empirical but

---

[1] See: https://www.psychologytoday.com/blog/animal-emotions/201709/its-ok-dogs-engage-in-zoomies-and-enjoy-fraps.

rather one of laying the proper logical and conceptual foundations for thinking about the question of whether animals can be persons. The central contention of this book has been that when these foundations are properly poured, the claim that many animals are persons is not implausible at all. More than that: I think it is probably true.

## 2. WHY IT MATTERS

It is never a good idea to get too hung up on a word—or, for that matter, the concept expressed by a word. Some profess to find assigning what they call "human" concepts—applying human words—to animals is objectionable, either morally or conceptually. Of course, there is one sense in which the concept of a person is a human concept: humans first invented it, or grasped it—depending on your view of concepts. This is neither in doubt nor at issue. The question is not who first invented or understood the concept of a person but, rather, to which individuals the concept can be applied. To suppose that the concept of a person can't be applicable to animals because they cannot understand it is like supposing that the concept of an atom cannot be applied to atoms because they can't understand it.

Nevertheless, even when we dispense with this sophomoric confusion, there are further sources of resistance to the very idea that we can or should apply the concept of a person to animals. Some might see it as an objectionable form of biological *appropriation*. Why do we have to insist on assimilating animals to us, one might say? Can't we celebrate their differences? Can't they be important precisely *because* they are different from us? This sentiment, though currently fashionable, is, I suspect, nonsense. As I limp painfully toward my dotage, I have slowly become persuaded by a sentimentalist view of morality. Empathy, in my view, lies at the core of morality. And of this I am pretty sure: empathy is based on recognition of similarity, not difference. We can only empathize with something to the extent we recognize something of us in it. This point, however, does not depend on a sentimentalist view of morality. Most cases for the moral claims of animals have been grounded in the identification of something that we share with them: the capacity for happiness versus suffering, intrinsic value or worth, etc. The claim that animals are persons, in the form I have defended here, is the claim that animals share something with us: in many animals, as in us, consciousness, cognition, self-awareness, and other-awareness coalesce. These features converge both in us and in other animals. This is another, important, dimension of similarity between us. But it is a dimension of similarity that, I think, shifts the moral goalposts.

Bernard Williams once argued that, as far as our moral obligations to animals are concerned, "the only moral question for us is how we should *treat* them."[2] Of course, there is a broad way of understanding the notion of what it is to "treat" someone that makes this claim trivial. If, for example, allowing someone to live according to a rational plan for his life that he has himself drawn up is to "treat" him a certain way, then this claim would be obviously true. The assumed concept of treatment is so broad that even the most "hands-off" attitude with respect to another individual involves "treating" him in some way. However, Williams thinks the fact that the only question regarding our moral obligations to animals is how we should treat them decisively distinguishes the case of animals from the case of human beings. With respect to the latter there is not simply a question of how we should treat them. Respecting a person's autonomy, in this sense, does not consti- tute a form of treatment in the way Williams is using this term. The implication is, then, this: lacking autonomy, animals are simply moral patients. Questions arise about how we are to treat them, but these questions exhaust the moral debate with respect to animals. This is an assumption common to both foes and, I think, at least some friends of animal rights. Conceptualizing animals as persons, per- haps, entails refocusing the debate.

The idea that animals are moral patients is, of course, a huge improvement on the idea that they have no moral standing—and that we can, therefore, do what we want with and to them. Most of the good that can be done for animals in the world today requires only that we accept that animals are moral patients. This is because we currently treat them so poorly. Nevertheless, the idea that animals are merely moral patients embodies a residual prejudice and, thus, encourages ways of thinking about the moral issues that animals raise in ways that are, I think, less than ideal. For example, it might lead one to suppose that the fundamental— perhaps the only—moral question we face with respect to animals is how much suffering or enjoyment is present in their lives. This is an important question, to be sure. But imagine if we believed this of humans. Imagine if we thought the only moral issue involved, for example, in raising a child was the amount of suffering or enjoyment he or she experienced. A crucial consideration, it is true; but the life of a child raised on the basis of this consideration alone would be a sad waste of a life. The reason is that the child would not have the opportunity to develop the various abilities characteristic of the kind of being he or she is.

Still in the grip of Williams's idea that the only moral question vis-à-vis animals is how we treat them—that animals are merely moral patients—we might insist, for example, that an individual in whom consciousness, cognition, self-awareness,

---

[2] Williams (2009), p. 141.

and other-awareness converge is capable of suffering certain sorts of harms, of which an individual not defined by such convergence is incapable. A unified subject of a mental life can, for example, suffer the crushing boredom that stems from incarceration and the thwarting of its most natural impulses. It may be that this sort of harm cannot be experienced by an individual that is not the unified subject of a mental life. But to think of the significance of animals as persons only in this way yields too much to Williams's picture.

The significance of acknowledging the personhood of animals is to shift away from thinking of animals merely as the recipients of benefits and harms and, instead, regarding them as active shapers—*authors*—of their own lives. Exploring the moral implications of this is a project that lies far outside the scope of this book, of course. Thus, I shall conclude with some remarks that might, charitably, be called "suggestive," but might more accurately be called "hand-waving." First, there is the negative claim: if animals are persons, then our moral obligations to them are moral obligations of the sort one has to persons, and these obligations cannot be limned by asking ourselves how we should treat them, in Williams's narrow sense of "treat."

With an eye on something more positive, we might ask: what is the difference between the way we deal, or should deal, with a person and the way we deal with something that is a mere moral patient? The answer is reasonably clear: we don't merely *treat* persons, we *ask* them how they would like to be treated. Recognition of the other as a person shifts focus from a *treatment* paradigm to a *listening* paradigm. Sometimes, listening, is not easy. For some it is a skill that can only be achieved through protracted and meticulous practice. But the fundamental requirement for dealing with persons—a requirement that must be satisfied before one can even raise the question of what to do—is to listen. Instead of simply treating animals as we think best, we might try to *ask* them what they want.

It's never really advisable, when composing the closing stanza of an academic monograph, to go all Dr. Doolittle on one's readership. I realize that. But I don't have anything extravagant in mind when I talk of asking animals what they want. There was a time in the evening, after had he been fed and after my sons had gone to bed, when Hugo would sit in front of me—obstructing my view of all the high-quality offerings Direct TV was beaming into my living room—staring at my face. In these moments, I knew—and when I say I knew, I mean would have bet my house on it—that he wanted one of two things. He either wanted to be let out to the garden for his nightly constitutional. Or he wanted to climb up on the settee next to me. He was a very polite dog, and always asked for permission first. So, I would ask him: what do you want? And he would reply: either by trotting toward the back door, or by climbing up on the settee.

Much of the time, to meaningfully ask an animal what it wants is simply to see what it does, for this is often the most straightforward answer it can give to the question of what it wants. But this will work only when one has acquired enough theoretical knowledge and practical expertise required to understand which questions to ask and how, specifically, the animal answers these questions. Acquiring these things is neither easy nor quick, but it is do-able. So, I reiterate, non-extravagantly: we should try asking them what they want. Some of their answers might be entirely expected. Others might surprise us.

# Bibliography

Aaltola, Elisa (2008) "Personhood and animals," *Environmental Ethics* 30, 2, 175–93

Allen, Colin (2013) "The geometry of partial understanding," *American Philosophical Quarterly* 50, 3, 249–62

Allen, Colin and Bekoff, Mark (1997) *Species of Mind: The Philosophy and Biology of Cognitive Ethology* (Cambridge, MA: MIT Press)

Andrews, Kristin (2011) "Beyond anthropomorphism: attributing psychological properties to animals," in T. Beauchamp and R. Frey eds., *The Oxford Handbook of Animal Ethics* (New York: Oxford University Press), pp. 469–94

Andrews, Kristin (2014) *The Animal Mind: An Introduction to the Philosophy of Animal Cognition* (New York: Routledge)

Ari, C. and D'Agostino, D. (2016) "Contingency checking and self-directed behaviors in giant manta rays: do elasmobranchs have self-awareness?" *Journal of Ethology* 34, 2, 167–74

Aristotle (1999) *Nichomachean Ethics*, trans. T. Irwin (New York: Hackett)

Aune, Bruce (1986) "Other minds after twenty years," *Midwest Studies in Philosophy* 110, 559–74

Baars, B. (2005) "Subjective experience is probably not limited to humans: the evidence from neurobiology and behavior," *Consciousness and Cognition* 14, 7–21

Baars, B., Banks, W., and Newman, J. eds. (2003) *Essential Sources in the Scientific Study of Consciousness* (Cambridge, MA: MIT Press)

Babb, S. and Crystal, J. (2005) "Discrimination of what, when and where: implications for episodic-like memory in the rat," *Learning and Motivation* 36, 177–89

Babb, S. and Crystal, J. (2006) "Discrimination of what, when and where is not based on the time of the day," *Learning & Behavior* 34, 124–30

Bachelard, Gaston (1958/2014) *The Poetics of Space* (New York: Penguin)

Baron-Cohen, S., Leslie, A., and Frith, U. (1985) "Does the autistic child have a theory of mind?" *Cognition* 21, 1, 37–46

Beauchamp, Tom (1999) "The failure of theories of personhood," *Kennedy Institute of Ethics Journal* 9, 4, 309–24

Beck, Jacob (2017) "Do nonhuman animals have a language of thought?" in K. Andrews and J. Beck eds., *Routledge Handbook of the Philosophy of Animal Minds* (New York: Routledge), pp. 46–55

Bekoff, Marc (2001) "Observations of scent marking and discriminating self from others by a domestic dog (*Canis familiaris*)," *Behavioral Processes* 55, 75–79

Bekoff, Marc (2003) "Considering animals—not 'higher' primates: consciousness and self in animals: some reflections," *Zygon*, 38, 2, 229–45

Bekoff, Marc and Sherman, Paul (2004) "Reflections on animal selves," *Trends in Ecology and Evolution* 19, 4, 176–80

Bermudez, Jose Luis (2003) *Thinking Without Words* (Oxford: Oxford University Press)

Bermudez, Jose Luis (2007) "Thinking without words: an overview for animal ethics," *Journal of Ethics* 11, 319–35

Blackburn, Simon (1984) *Spreading the Word* (Oxford: Oxford University Press)

Block, Ned (1995) "On a confusion about a function of consciousness," *Behavioral and Brain Sciences* 18, 2, 227–87

Brewer, A., Press, W., Logothetis, N., and Wandell, B. (2002) "Visual areas in macaque cortex measured using functional magnetic resonance imaging," *Journal of Neuroscience*, 22, 10416–26

Brook, Andrew (2001) "Kant, self-awareness and self-reference," in A. Brook and R. DeVidi eds., *Self-Reference and Self-Awareness* (Amsterdam: John Benjamins), pp. 9–30

Burge, Tyler (1979) "Individualism and the mental," *Midwest Studies in Philosophy* 4, 1, 73–122

Call, J. (2004) "Inferences about the location of food in the great apes (*Pan paniscus, Pan troglodytes, Gorilla gorilla*, and *Pongo pygmaeus*)," *Journal of Comparative Psychology* 118, 232–41

Call, J. and Carpenter, M. (2001) "Do apes and children know what they have seen?" *Animal Cognition* 3, 207–20

Call, J. and Tomasello, M. (2008) "Do chimpanzees have a theory of mind? Thirty years on," *Trends in Cognitive Sciences* 12, 5, 187–92

Camp, Elizabeth (2007) "Thinking with maps," *Philosophical Perspectives* 21, 145–82

Carruthers, Peter (1989) "Brute experience," *Journal of Philosophy* 86, 258–69

Carruthers, Peter (1992) *The Animals Issue* (Cambridge: Cambridge University Press)

Carruthers, Peter (2004) "On being simple minded," *American Philosophical Quarterly*, 41, 205–20

Castañeda, Hector-Neri (1966) "'He': a study in the logic of self-consciousness," *Ratio* 8, 130–57.

Chalmers, David (1995) "Facing up to the hard problem of consciousness," *Journal of Consciousness Studies* 2, 3, 200–19

Cheney, D. and Seyfarth, R. (1998) *Why Animals Don't Have Language; The Tanner Lectures on Human Values* (https://tannerlectures.utah.edu/_documents/a-to-z/c/Cheney98.pdf)

Churchland, Paul (1981) "Eliminative materialism and the propositional attitudes," *Journal of Philosophy* 78, 67–90

Clark, Andy (1997) *Being There: Putting Brain, Body and World Back Together Again* (Cambridge, MA: MIT Press)

Clark, Andy (2016) *Surfing Uncertainty: Prediction, Action and the Embodied Mind* (New York: Oxford University Press)

Clayton, N. and Dickinson, A. (1998) "Episodic-like memory during cache recovery by scrub jays," *Nature* 395, 272–274

Clayton, N. and Dickinson, A. (1999a) "Memory for the contents of caches by scrub jays (*Aphelocoma coerulescens*)," *Journal of Experimental Psychology Animal Behavior Processes* 25, 82–91

Clayton, N. and Dickinson, A. (1999b) "Motivational control of caching behavior in the scrub jay, *Aphelocoma coerulescens*," *Animal Behaviour* 57, 435–44

Clayton, N. and Dickinson, A. (1999c) "Scrub jays (*Aphelocoma coerulescens*) remember the relative time of caching as well as the location and content of their caches," *Journal of Comparative Psychology* 113, 403–16

Clayton, N., Yu, K., and Dickinson, A. (2001) "Scrub-jays (*Aphelocoma coerulescens*) form integrated memories of the multiple features of caching episodes," *Journal of Experimental Psychology Animal Behavior Processes* 27, 17–29

Coke, Sir Edward (1628) "The institute of the lawes of England, or commentary on Littleton," in S. Sheppard ed., *The Selected Writings and Speeches of Sir Edward Coke* (Indianapolis: Liberty Fund), pp. 573–1185

Cowey, A. and Stoerig, P. (1995) "Blindsight in monkeys," *Nature*, 373, 247–49

Cristol, Daniel, Switzer, Paul, Johnson, Kara, and Walke, Leah (1997) "Crows do not use automobiles as nutcrackers: putting an anecdote to the test" *The Auk* 114, 2, 296–98

Davidson, Donald (1982) "Rational animals," *Dialectica* 36, 317–27

DeGrazia, David (1997) *Taking Animals Seriously* (New York: Cambridge University Press)

DeGrazia, David (2009) "Self-awareness in animals," in R. Lurz ed., *The Philosophy of Animal Minds* (New York: Cambridge University Press), pp. 201–17

de Kort, S., Dickinson, A., and Clayton, N. S. (2005) "Retrospective cognition by food-caching western scrub-jays," *Learning and Motivation* 36, 159–76

Dennett, Daniel (1971) "Intentional systems," *Journal of Philosophy* 68, 87–106

Dennett, Daniel (1973) "Mechanism and responsibility," in Ted Honderich ed., *Essays on Freedom of Action* (London: Routledge), pp. 157–84

Dennett, Daniel (1987a) "Conditions of personhood," in *Brainstorms* (Cambridge, MA: MIT Press), pp. 176–96

Dennett, Daniel (1987b) *The Intentional Stance* (Cambridge, MA: MIT Press)

Dere, E., Huston, J. P., and De Souza Silva, M. A. (2005) "Integrated memory for objects, places and temporal order: evidence for episodic-like memory in mice," *Neurobiology of Learning and Memory* 84, 214–21

Dinets, V., Brueggen, J. C., and Brueggen, J. D. (2015) "Crocodilians use tools for hunting," *Ethology, Ecology and Evolution* 27, 74–78

Dretske, Fred (1982) *Explaining Behavior* (Cambridge, MA: MIT Press)

Erdőhegyi, Á., Topál, J., Virányi, Z., and Miklósi, Á. (2007) "Dog-logic: inferential reasoning in a two-way choice task and its restricted use," *Animal Behaviour* 74, 725–37

Ergorul, C. and Eichenbaum, H. (2004) "The hippocampus and memory for 'what,' 'where,' and 'when.'" *Learning and Memory* 11, 397–405

Evans, Gareth (1982) *The Varieties of Reference*, ed. J. McDowell (Oxford: Oxford University Press)

Evans, Natalie (2016) *Animal Ethics and the Autonomous Animal Self* (Basingstoke, UK: Palgrave Macmillan)

Ferkin, M., Combs, A., del Barco-Trillo, J., Pierce, A., and Franklin, S. (2008) "Meadow voles, *Microtus pennsylvanicus*, have the capacity to recall the 'what,' 'where' and 'when' of a single past event," *Animal Cognition* 11, 147–59

Finn, Julian, Tregenza, Tom, and Norman, Mark (2009) "Defensive tool use in a coconut-carrying octopus," *Current Biology*, 19, 23, R1069–70

Fodor, Jerry (1975) *The Language of Thought* (New York: Thomas Crowell)

Fodor, Jerry (1986) *Psychosemantics* (Cambridge, MA: MIT Press)

Fodor, Jerry (2008) *LOT 2: The Language of Thought Revisited* (New York: Oxford University Press)

Fodor, Jerry and Pylyshyn, Zenon (1988) "Connectionism and cognitive architecture," *Cognition* 28, 1–2, 3–71

Fortin, N. J., Wright, S. P., and Eichenbaum, H. (2004) "Recollection-like memory retrieval in rats is dependent on the hippocampus," *Nature* 431, 188–91

Frankfurt, Harry (1971) "Freedom of the will and the concept of a person," *Journal of Philosophy* 68, 1, 5–20

Gaita, Raymond (2003) *The Philosopher's Dog* (London: Routledge)

Gallagher, Shaun (2005) *How the Body Shapes the Mind* (Oxford: Oxford University Press)

Gallup, Gordon (1970) "Chimpanzees: self-recognition," *Science* 167, 86–87

Gallup, Gordon (1982) "Self-awareness and the emergence of mind in primates," *American Journal of Primatology* 2, 3, 237–48

Gatti, Roberto (2016) "Self-consciousness: beyond the looking glass and what dogs found there," *Ethology, Ecology and Evolution* 28, 232–40

Gelman, R. (1990) "First principles organize attention to and learning about relevant data: number and the animate-inanimate distinction as examples," *Cognitive Science* 14, 79–106

Gelman, R., Durgin, F., and Kaufman, L. (1995) "Distinguishing between animates and inanimates: not by motion alone," in D. Sperber, D. Premack, and A. Premack eds., *Causal Cognition: A Multidisciplinary Debate* (Oxford: Oxford University Press), pp. 150–84

Gergely, G. and Csibra, G. (2003) "Teleological reasoning in infancy: the naïve theory of rational action," *Trends in Cognitive Sciences* 7, 287–92

Gibson, James (1979) *The Ecological Approach to Visual Perception* (Boston: Houghton-Mifflin)

Goodall, Jane (1986) *The Chimpanzees of Gombe: Patterns of Behavior* (Cambridge, MA: Harvard University Press)

Grahame, Kenneth (1908) *The Wind in the Willows* (London: Methuen)

Grether, W. F. and Maslow, A. H. (1937) "An experimental study of insight in monkeys," *Journal of Comparative Psychology* 24, 127–34

Griffin, D. and Speck, G. (2004) "New evidence of animal consciousness," *Animal and Cognition* 7, 5–18

Hare, B., Call, J., and Tomasello, M. (2001) "Do chimpanzees know what conspecifics know?" *Animal Behaviour* 61, 139–51

Harnad, Stevan (2016) "Animal sentience: the other minds problem," *Animal Sentience* 1, 1–11

Heidegger, Martin (1927/1962) *Being and Time*, trans. J. Macquarie (Oxford: Blackwell)

Henderson, J., Hurly, T., Bateson, M., and Healy, S. (2006) "Timing in free living rufus humming birds *Selasphorus rufus*," *Current Biology* 16, 512–15

Herman, L., Morrel-Samuels, P., and Pack, A. (1990) "Bottlenosed dolphin and human recognition of veridical and degraded video displays of an artificial gestural language," *Journal of Experimental Psychology* 119, 215–30

Hohwy, Jakob (2015) *The Predictive Mind* (New York: Oxford University Press)

Holmes, Oliver Wendell, Jr. (1881) *The Common Law* (Boston: Little Brown)

Horowitz, Alexandra (2017) "Smelling themselves: dogs investigate their own odours longer when modified in an 'olfactory mirror' test," *Behavioural Processes*, 143, 17–24

Hume, David (1739/1975) *A Treatise of Human Nature*, ed. L. A. Selby-Bigge, 2nd ed., revised by P. H. Nidditch (Oxford: Oxford University Press)

Hunt, G. and Gray, R. (2004) "The crafting of hook tools by wild New Caledonian crows," *Proceedings of the Royal Society B* 271, Suppl. 3, S88–90

Hurley, Susan (1998) *Consciousness in Action* (Cambridge, MA: Harvard University Press)

Husserl, Edmund (1912/1980) *Ideas Pertaining to a Pure Phenomenology and to a Phenomenological Philosophy*, Vol. 3, *Phenomenology and the Foundations of the Sciences*, trans. T. Klein and W. Pohl (The Hague: Martinus Nijhoff)

Jamieson, D. and Bekoff, M. (1992) "Carruthers on nonconscious experience," *Analysis* 52, 23–28

Jelbert, Sarah, Taylor, Alex, Cheke, Lucy, Clayton, Nicola, and Gray, Russell (2014) "Using the Aesop's fable paradigm to investigate causal understanding of water displacement by New Caledonian crows," *PLoS One* 9, 3, e92895, DOI: 10.1371/journal.pone.009289

Kaminski, J., Brauer, J., Call, J., and Tomasello, M. (2009) "Domestic dogs are sensitive to a human's perspective," *Behaviour* 146, 7, 979–98

Kant, Immanuel (1781/1787) *Critique of Pure Reason*, trans. N. Kemp-Smith (Basingstoke, UK: Palgrave Macmillan 2007)

Kant, Immanuel (1974) *Anthropology from a Pragmatic Point of View*, trans. M. McGregor (The Hague: Martinus Nijhoff)

Kaplan, David (1989) "Demonstratives," in J. Almog, J. Perry, and H. Wettstein eds., *Themes from Kaplan* (New York: Oxford University Press), pp. 481–563

Kart-Teke, E., De Souza Silva, M. A., Huston, J. P., and Dere E. (2006) "Wistar rats show episodic-like memory for unique experiences," *Neurobiology of Learning and Memory* 85, 173–82

Keijzer, Fred (2013) "The *Sphex* story: how the cognitive sciences kept repeating an old and questionable anecdote," *Philosophical Psychology* 26, 4, 502–19

Kirsh, D. and Maglio, P. (1994) "On distinguishing epistemic from pragmatic action," *Cognitive Science* 18, 4, 513–49

Klein, Stanley (2013) *The Two Selves: Their Metaphysical Commitments and Functional Independence* (New York: Oxford University Press)

Klein, Stanley (2015) "What memory is," *WIREs Cognitive Science* 6, 1–38

Kriegel, Uriah (2011) *Consciousness: A Self-Representational Theory* (New York: Oxford University Press)

Krueger, Joel (2012) "Seeing mind in action," *Phenomenology and the Cognitive Sciences* 11, 149–73

Locke, John (1689/1979) *An Essay Concerning Human Understanding*, ed. P. Nidditch (Oxford: Oxford University Press)

Lycan, William (2001) "A simple argument for a higher-order representation theory of consciousness," *Analysis* 61, 1, 3–4

Mackay, D. (1967) "Ways of looking at perception," in W. Watthen-Dunn ed., *Models for the Perception of Speech and Visual Form* (Cambridge, MA: MIT Press), pp. 25–43

Malcolm, Norman (1972) "Thoughtless brutes," *Proceedings and Addresses of the American Philosophical Association* 46, 5–20

Marino, L. (2002) "Convergence of complex cognitive abilities in cetaceans and primates," *Brain, Behaviour and Evolution*, 59, 21–32

Marsh, H., Vining, A., Levendoski, E., and Judge, P. (2015) "Inference by exclusion in lion-tailed macaques (*Macaca silenus*), a hamadryas baboon (*Papio hamadryas*), capuchins (*Sapajus apella*), and squirrel monkeys (*Saimiri sciureus*)," *Journal of Comparative Psychology* 129, 256–67

Marshall-Pescini, Sarah, Ceretta, Maria, and Prato-Previde, Emanuela (2014) "Do domestic dogs understand human actions as goal-directed?" *PLoS One* 9, 9, e106530, https://doi.org/10.1371/journal.pone.0106530

Martín-Ordás, G., Haun, D., Colmenares, F., and Call, J. (2010) "Keeping track of time: evidence of episodic-like memory in great apes," *Animal Cognition* 13, 331–40

McBeath, M. K., Shaffer, D. M., and Kaiser, M. K. (1995) "How baseball outfielders determine where to run to catch fly balls," *Science* 268, 5210, 569–73

Menary, Richard (2007) *Cognitive Integration: Mind and Cognition Unbounded* (Basingstoke, UK: Macmillan)

Menary, Richard ed. (2010) *The Extended Mind* (Cambridge, MA: MIT Press)

Millikan, R. (1984) *Language, Thought and Other Biological Categories* (Cambridge, MA: MIT Press)

Millikan, R. (1993) *White Queen Psychology and Other Essays for Alice* (Cambridge, MA: MIT Press)

Mody, S. and Carey, S. (2016) "The emergence of reasoning by the disjunctive syllogism in early childhood," *Cognition* 154, 40–48

Nader, Karim (2003) "Memory traces unbound," *Trends in Neurosciences* 26, 2, 65–72

Nagel, Thomas (1979) "What is it like to be a bat?" *Philosophical Review* 83, 1974, 435–50. Reprinted in *Mortal Questions* (Cambridge: Cambridge University Press, 1979), pp. 165–80

Nishida, T. (1990) *Chimpanzees of the Mahale Mountains: Sexual and Life History Strategies* (Tokyo: University of Tokyo Press)

Noë, Alva (2004) *Action in Perception* (Cambridge, MA: MIT Press)

Olson, Eric (1997) *The Human Animal: Personal Identity Without Psychology* (New York: Oxford University Press)

Owren, M., Rendall, D., and Ryan, M. (2010) "Redefining animal signaling: influence versus information in communication," *Biology and Philosophy* 25, 755–80

Parfit, Derek (1984) *Reasons and Persons* (Oxford: Oxford University Press)

Penn, D. and Povinelli, D. (2007) "On the lack of evidence that non-human animals possess anything remotely resembling a 'theory of mind,'" *Philosophical Transactions of the Royal Society B* 362, 1480, 731–44

Pepperberg, I. and Shive, H. (2001) "Simultaneous development of vocal and physical object combinations by a grey parrot (*Psittacus erithacus*): bottle caps, lids, and labels," *Journal of Comparative Psychology* 115, 376–84

Pepperberg, I. and Wilcox, S. (2000) "Evidence for a form of mutual exclusivity during label acquisition by grey parrots (*Psittacus erithacus*)?" *Journal of Comparative Psychology* 114, 219–31

Petit, O., Dufour, V., Herrenschmidt, M., De Marco, A., Sterck, E., and Call, J. (2015) "Inferences about food location in three cercopithecine species: an insight into the socioecological cognition of primates," *Animal Cognition* 18, 821–30

Povinelli, D. J. and Eddy, T. J. (1996) "What young chimpanzees know about seeing," *Monographs of the Society for Research in Child Development* 61, 1–152

Povinelli, D. and Vonk, J. (2003) "Chimpanzee minds: suspiciously human?" *Trends in Cognitive Science* 7, 4, 157–60

Premack, D. and Woodruff, G. (1978) "Does the chimpanzee have a theory of mind?" *Behavioral and Brain Sciences* 1, 515–26

Preutz, J. D. and Bertolani, P. (2007) "Savanna chimpanzees, *Pan troglodytes verus*, hunt with tools," *Current Biology* 17, 5, 412–17

Prinz, Jesse (2004) *Gut Reactions: A Perceptual Theory of Emotion* (New York: Oxford University Press)

Putnam, Hilary (1964) "Robots: machines or artificially created life?" *Journal of Philosophy* 61, 21, 668–91

Putnam, Hilary (1975) "The meaning of 'meaning,'" *Minnesota Studies in the Philosophy of Science* 7, 1975, 131–93

Rawls, John (1971) *A Theory of Justice* (Cambridge, MA: Harvard University Press)

Rendall, D. and Owren, M. (2002) "Animal vocal communication: say what?" in M. Bekoff, C. Allen, and G. M. Burghardt eds., *The Cognitive Animal: Empirical and Theoretical Perspectives on Animal Cognition* (Cambridge, MA: MIT Press), pp. 307–14

Rescorla, M. (2009) "'Chrysippus' dog as a case study in non-linguistic cognition," in R. Lurz ed., *The Philosophy of Animal Minds* (New York: Cambridge University Press), 52–71

Roberts, W. A., Feeney, M. C., MacPherson, K., Petter, M., McMillan, N., and Musolino, E. (2008) "Episodic-like memory in rats: is it based on when or how long ago?" *Science* 320, 113–15

Rowlands, Mark (1999) *The Body in Mind: Understanding Cognitive Processes* (Cambridge: Cambridge University Press)

Rowlands, Mark (2001) *The Nature of Consciousness* (Cambridge: Cambridge University Press)

Rowlands, Mark (2003) *Externalism: Putting Mind and World Back Together Again* (London: Acumen)

Rowlands, Mark (2006) *Body Language: Representation in Action* (Cambridge, MA: MIT Press)

Rowlands, Mark (2010) *The New Science of the Mind: From Extended Mind to Embodied Phenomenology* (Cambridge, MA: MIT Press)

Rowlands, Mark (2012a) *Can Animals Be Moral?* (New York: Oxford University Press)

Rowlands, Mark (2012b) "Representing without representations," *Avant* 1, 1, 133–44

Rowlands, Mark (2015a) "Arguing about representation," *Synthese* 1, 18, DOI: 10.1007/s11229-014-0646-4

Rowlands, Mark (2015b) "Consciousness unbound," *Journal of Consciousness Studies* 22, 3–4, 34–51, special edition, *Consciousness Unbound*, ed. M. Silberstein and T. Chemero

Rowlands, Mark (2015c) "Bringing philosophy back: 4e cognition and the argument from phenomenology," in D. Dahlstrom, A. Elpidorou, and W. Hopp eds., *Philosophy of Mind and Phenomenology* (New York: Routledge), pp. 310–26

Rowlands, Mark (2016) *Memory and the Self: Phenomenology, Science, and Autobiography* (New York: Oxford University Press)

Sanz, C. and Morgan, D. (2007) "Chimpanzee tool technology in the Goualougo Triangle, Republic of Congo," *Journal of Human Evolution* 52, 4, 420–33

Sartre, Jean-Paul (1943/1957) *Being and Nothingness*, trans. H. Barnes (London: Methuen). Originally published as *L'être et le néant* (Paris: Gallimard, 1943)

Schloegl, C., Dierks, A., Gajdon, G., Huber, L., Kotrschal, K., and Bugnyar, T. (2009) "What you see is what you get? Exclusion performances in ravens and keas," *PLoS One* 4, e6368

Sellars, Wilfred (1966) "Fatalism and determinism," in K. Lehrer ed., *Freedom and Determinism* (New York: Random House), pp. 141–74

Sellars, Wilfred (1997) *Empiricism and the Philosophy of Mind* (Cambridge, MA: Harvard University Press)

Seth, A., Baars, B., and Edelman, D. (2005) "Criteria for consciousness in humans and other animals," *Consciousness and Cognition* 14, 119–39

Seyfarth, R., Cheney, D., and Marler, P. (1980) "Monkey responses to three different alarm calls: evidence of predator classification and semantic communication," *Science* 210, 4471, 801–3.

Seyfarth, R., Cheney, D., Bergman, T., Fischer, J., Zuberbuhler, K., and Hammerschmidt, K. (2010) "The central importance of information in studies of animal communication," *Animal Behaviour* 80, 3–8

Shaffer, D. M., Krauchunas, S. M., Eddy, M., and McBeath, M. K. (2004) "How dogs navigate to catch Frisbees," *Psychological Science* 15, 437–41

Shoemaker, Sydney (1968) "Self-reference and self-awareness," *Journal of Philosophy* 65, 555–67

Rumelhart, David E., McClelland, James L., and the PDP Research Group (1986) *Parallel Distributed Processing: Explorations in the Microstructures of Cognition*, Vol. 1, *Foundations* (Cambridge, MA: MIT Press)

Snowdon, Paul (2014) *Persons, Animals, Ourselves* (Oxford: Oxford University Press)

Solomon, Robert (1984) *The Passions: The Myth and Nature of Human Emotions* (New York: Doubleday)

Solomon, Robert (2004) *In Defense of Sentimentality* (New York: Oxford University Press)

Spelke, E., Phillips, A., and Woodward, A. (1995) "Infants' knowledge of object motion and human action," in D. Sperber, D. Premack, and A. J. Premack eds., *Causal Cognition: A Multidisciplinary Debate* (Oxford: Oxford University Press), pp. 44–78

Srinivasan, R., Russell, D., Edelman, G., and Tononi, G. (1999) "Increased synchronization of magnetic responses during conscious perception," *Journal of Neuroscience* 19, 5435–48

Steward, Helen (2009) "Animal agency," *Inquiry* 52, 3, 217–31

Stich, Stephen (1979) "Do animals have beliefs?" *Australasian Journal of Philosophy* 57, 15–28

Stich, Stephen (1983) *From Folk Psychology to Cognitive Science: The Case Against Belief* (Cambridge, MA: MIT Press)

Stoerig, P. and Cowey, A. (1997) "Blindsight in man and monkey," *Brain* 120, 535–59

Strawson, Peter (1959) *Individuals* (London: Methuen)

Strawson, Peter (1962) "Freedom and resentment," in *Proceedings of the British Academy*, Vol. 48 (Oxford: Oxford University Press), 1–25

Suddendorf, T. and Busby, J. (2003) "Like it or not? The mental time travel debate," *Trends in Cognitive Science* 7, 437–38

Suzuki, T., Wheatcroft, D., and Griesser, M. (2017) "Wild birds use an ordering rule to decode novel call sequences," *Current Biology* 27, 15, 2331–36, DOI: 10.1016/j.cub.2017.06.31

Tooley, Michael (1972) "Abortion and infanticide," *Philosophy and Public Affairs* 2, 1972, 37–65

Tooley, Michael (1983) *Abortion and Infanticide* (Oxford: Oxford University Press)

Tulving, Endel (1983) *Elements of Episodic Memory* (Oxford: Oxford University Press)

Tulving, Endel (2002) "Episodic memory: from mind to brain," *Annual Review of Psychology* 53, 1–25, DOI: 10.1146/annurev.psych.53.100901.135114

Vygotsky, L. (1986) *Thought and Language*, ed. A. Kozulin (Cambridge, MA: MIT Press)

Vygotsky, L. and Luria, A. (1993) *Studies in the History of Behavior: Ape, Primitive Man, and Child* (New York: Psychology Press)

Weir, A. and Kacelnik, A. (2006) "A New Caledonian crow (*Corvus moneduloides*) creatively re-designs tools by bending or unbending aluminium strips," *Animal Cognition* 9, 317–34

Weiskrantz, L. (1998) *Blindsight: A Case Study and Implications* (Oxford: Oxford University Press)

White, Thomas (2007) *In Defense of Dolphins: The New Moral Frontier* (Malden, MA: Wiley-Blackwell)

Whitehead, Alfred North (1911) *An Introduction to Mathematics* (London: Williams and Norgate)

Williams, Bernard (2009) "The human prejudice," in his *Philosophy as a Humanistic Discipline* (Princeton, NJ: Princeton University Press)

Wittgenstein, Ludwig (1953) *Philosophical Investigations*, trans. E. Anscombe (Oxford: Blackwell)

Wittgenstein, Ludwig (1958) *The Blue and Brown Books* (New York: Harper and Row)

Yamakoshi, Gen and Sugiyama, Yukimaru (1995) "Pestle-pounding behavior of wild chimpanzees at Bossou, Guinea: a newly observed tool-using behavior," *Primates* 36, 4, 489–500

Zahavi, Dan (2005) *Subjectivity and Selfhood: Investigating the First-Person Perspective* (Cambridge, MA: MIT Press)

Zhou, W. and Crystal, J. (2009) "Evidence for remembering when events occurred in a rodent model of episodic memory," *Proceedings of the National Academy of Sciences USA* 106, 9525–29

Zinkivskay, A., Nazir, F., and Smulders, T. (2009) "What–where–when memory in magpies (*Pica pica*)," *Animal Cognition* 12, 1, 119–25

# Index